In some

ordinary minutes become

extraordinary moments to remember,

and personal treasures of the heart.

For today, yesterday, and

once-upon-a-time,

I hope you enjoy reading the

"menu" selections

from

the Mind Cafeteria.

Also by Albert R. Koch

**Help Mom with the Dishes: Lessons
from Life's Classroom**

Koch's Choice

MEMORIES AND MUSINGS FROM THE MIND CAFETERIA, A TO Z

ALBERT R. KOCH

iUniverse®

KOCH'S CHOICE
MEMORIES AND MUSINGS FROM THE MIND CAFETERIA, A TO Z

Some of the essays in this book were originally published in slightly different form. They have been edited here for additional clarity and accuracy.

iUniverse books may be ordered through booksellers or by contacting:

iUniverse
1663 Liberty Drive
Bloomington, IN 47403
www.iuniverse.com
1-800-Authors (1-800-288-4677)

ISBN: 978-1-5320-6428-9 (sc)
ISBN: 978-1-5320-6429-6 (e)

Library of Congress Control Number: 2019901407

Print information available on the last page.

iUniverse rev. date: 08/23/2019

To Suzanne.

You were 17,
I was 19.
At the close of our first date,
I looked into your eyes and saw the rest of my life.
58 years on,
The magic continues!

So many moments,
So many memories.
Treasure the moments,
Savor the memories!

Contents

G

H

I

J

K

L

M

N

O

P

Q

Preface

Koch's Choice: Memories and Musings from the Mind Cafeteria, A to Z is a companion to my first book, *Help Mom with the Dishes: Lessons from Life's Classroom.* Like that previous compendium, many of the essays collected here first appeared in various local publications and encompass a wide variety of subject matter, including my observations as a public school teacher for more than 40 years as well as my experiences growing up in my hometown of Whiting, Indiana.

In these essays, I also honor the ordinary men and women who've had an extraordinary impact on my life. We're told that the journey should be as enjoyable as the destination, and those who shared these times with me—family, friends, teachers, classmates, clergy, coworkers, merchants, and townspeople—helped fulfill that goal. I extend my heartfelt thanks to those who were part of the experiences recounted in the pages that follow. Some have passed on, and to them I offer prayerful words and petition. (See Appendices A, B, and C for extended acknowledgments.)

Thanks for visiting the Mind Cafeteria. Being able to share my thoughts and stories with readers is a great pleasure and privilege. "I'll Be Seeing You," the Whiting High School Class of 1958's song, perfectly captures my promise and commitment to continue along the path that lies past these pages.

Finally, a note about the way this book is organized: Instead of grouping essays thematically as I did for *Help Mom with the Dishes*, this time I opted to do so alphabetically by title. *Koch's Choice* serves up comfort food for the soul as well as more adventurous offerings, and it's my hope that this A to Z arrangement encourages sampling that both suits your particular tastes and surprises your appetite along the way.

The Mind Cafeteria is open. Grab a seat and peruse the menu. Whether you're in the mood for a quick nibble or a full banquet of gray-matter gastronomy, I hope you enjoy our time together.

Albert R. Koch
May 2019
Dyer, Indiana

Acknowledgments

Appreciation and thanks to Gayle Faulkner-Kosalko for providing the opportunity to contribute to *The WRite Stuff*, the monthly newspaper published by the Whiting-Robertsdale Chamber of Commerce, since the inaugural edition in July 1999. Her encouragement and support were the catalysts for my monthly column, "Koch's Choice." Thanks also to the Whiting-Robertsdale Chamber of Commerce for its continued support and to Sue Baxter of Baxter Design & Advertising for making it all possible.

A substantial quantity of gratitude goes to Christine Koch-Brenner and John Koch for their counsel, insight, and literary advice while reviewing and editing drafts over the years. They've kept their dad's words concise, focused, and in harmony with grammatical standards, usage, and mechanics. Additional thanks to John for his creative direction and extra efforts to prepare this book for publication, and to David Lennie for his patience and understanding. I must also recognize Mary Elisa Calvano for lending her expert artistic eye to the process.

Special acknowledgment is extended to Kevin Koch, Daniel Koch, and Andrew Brenner for their creativity, problem-solving skills, and logistical efficiency.

Appreciated beyond words, their contributions are evident from A to Z.

Introduction

One of the most treasured words in the English language is home. More than a location or a point on a map, home can also mean a place of the heart. Whiting, Indiana, located on the southern shore of Lake Michigan in the state's Calumet Region, is both to me.

Comprised of 3.23 square miles (1.8 square miles of land, 1.43 square miles of water), Whiting was founded in 1898 when J.D. Rockefeller selected "Pop Whiting's railroad siding" to expand his growing Standard Oil Company. Whiting grew into a municipality rich in history, tradition, and accomplishments. Family, church, and school formed a societal triad that nurtured, strengthened, and transformed the city's character.

Generation after generation found employment at the Standard Oil refinery, which provided economic stability to Whiting and instilled pride in its residents. With "The Little City by the Lake" at its core, subsequent industrial development in the Calumet Region enabled thousands to put down roots in the area, raising families and securing future opportunities for their children.

An industrial Mayberry, Whiting was the world's best place to be a kid in the 1940s, 1950s, and 1960s, a sentiment that encompasses the adjacent neighborhood of Robertsdale, located directly west. Though technically part of the city of Hammond, Robertsdale enjoys a uniquely symbiotic relationship with Whiting: They share a zip code (46394), a telephone prefix (659), schools, businesses, places of worship, parks, recreational facilities, and the lakefront. Residents regularly travel throughout both communities as part of their daily routines, and the combined name of the Whiting-Robertsdale Chamber of Commerce recognizes these interdependent civic, cultural, and commercial ties. (Appendix D offers further detail.)

Whiting is the city where I was born, grew up, and then, as an adult, raised my own family. For all of those same 65 years through today, I've maintained a Whiting, Indiana, state of mind. This full spectrum of meaning—both the tangible and intangible places we call home—is what I celebrate in this collection.

It's likely that many who read this book will have a connection to Whiting-Robertsdale or the Calumet Region, so they'll have some familiarity with the geography and inhabitants of the home I cherish. To these readers, I hope these essays engender smiles and fond remembrance.

For those who have otherwise stumbled upon this volume, a special word: While much of what's on these pages took place in a particular corner of the world and timeframe, by sharing my personal recollections I aim to reveal the universal themes we all experience as humans. My hope is that you might picture yourself in similar circumstances, leading you to recall memories of the places you consider home.

Wherever home is or once was, remember that it's always accessible inside your heart whenever your mind's in the mood to do a bit of traveling.

GUEST CHECK

TABLE	PERSONS	46394	SERVER
A	6		S-9

After-School Lesson
Alleys: Childhood Boulevards and Wall Street
Always a Warm Winter
Animal Speak
At 65
At 70

TAX

After-School Lesson

In the fall of 1956, I was a 15-year-old junior at Whiting High School in Whiting, Indiana, struggling to make passing grades. Poor overall performance during my sophomore year resulted in a scheduled academic course being replaced by machine shop. The high school principal—there were no guidance counselors at that time—wished to direct my focus from university campus to factory floor. Though I remained enrolled in college prep courses, I no longer entertained the possibility of going to college. I selected those classes solely because several friends were in them.

Suffice it to say, I wouldn't be posing a threat for scholarships or challenging valedictorian candidates. A running joke was that I should join the navy because all my grades were below C level.

Mr. James Ulrich, a new faculty member, became my English teacher. A no-nonsense, work-oriented classroom general reliably attired in jacket, shirt, and tie, Mr. Ulrich created a suitably business-like atmosphere for learning. I, alternatively, did my immature best to sidetrack his lessons by playing the comic.

One afternoon, after a particularly woeful demonstration of my unpreparedness (I didn't know the difference between an adverb and a noun, and also had defined a semicolon as half an intestine), Mr. Ulrich wrote my name at the top of the chalkboard, adding "Dummkopf #1!"

He then both startled and rattled me with this exclamation: "You know, Al, you're going to be the first member of your family not to graduate high school on time!"

Later, after my fourth consecutive failing grade on his weekly vocabulary test, Mr. Ulrich ordered me to report back to his classroom after school. When school was dismissed at 3:38 pm, while students headed to athletic practice, extracurricular meetings, the drugstore counter for a cherry Coke, or Nick's Pool Room for a game of snooker, I dutifully reported to Mr. Ulrich's classroom and took a seat.

Stern-faced and firm, Mr. Ulrich told me my current average in class was 46 percent. He explained in no uncertain terms that in order for me to pass English I'd need to complete all forthcoming assignments, papers, and quizzes with a score of 80 percent or higher.

I sat in stunned silence.

Mr. Ulrich's mood and words softened. He inquired as to what I wanted to do after high school—my plans, hopes, and dreams.

At 15, I didn't have a clue.

"Al, would you like to be successful, regardless of whatever you decide to do?"

I nodded yes.

From the center drawer of his desk, Mr. Ulrich took out a small stack of 3-by-5 index cards and placed them on my desk, blank side up.

"Turn the cards over, Al, one at a time, and line them up on the desk."

Carefully, I turned over each card. I was puzzled. What was this all about?

"What do you see, Al?" Mr. Ulrich asked.

"These are the letters of the alphabet," I answered.

"Exactly," he replied. "What you have in front of you are the 26 most powerful symbols known to humankind. Think about this. If you learn how to arrange these alphabetical letters in the right way, at the right time, for the right reason, the world is yours! The words they form have the power to describe, convey, and liberate emotions, feelings, and thoughts. Written or spoken, the potential of these words is unlimited. They allow us to convert intangible, invisible thoughts to crystal-clear information. We can communicate love or hate, cause joy or sadness, help or hurt, build or destroy, and elicit laughter or tears simply by selecting and arranging letters in proper order."

Mr. Ulrich closed by saying, "Al, take these cards with you. Every time you write or speak words, think about the potential and power you have at your command."

For the remainder of the term, with less comedic behavior and considerably more focus and effort, my performance improved. Quiz scores, written assignments, and in-class participation elevated my grade to passing by the end of the semester.

Mr. Ulrich continued to mentor and help me until his death many years later. He was a gifted teacher and treasured friend who taught me, in an after-school lesson, a love for English and the magic of words.

(2016)

Alleys: Childhood Boulevards and Wall Street

Many modern suburbs don't have alleys. Property lines blend with adjoining landscape and front-facing garages have street-connected driveways that allow for convenient access. Curbside trash pickup and in-ground utilities negate the need for such rear roadways.

Whiting-Robertsdale, Indiana, always had alleys, however, and for a kid growing up in this community in the 1940s and 1950s with limited financial means, these routes afforded opportunities unknown to today's young suburban residents.

Early on, kids learned the value of alleys. On a daily basis, they served as shortcuts to and from destinations. Using such less-traveled thoroughfares, we cut through neighborhood backyards on our way to school or uptown shopping and services. These byways also became a place to play and hang out, provided easy transit to vacant lots, and most importantly, displayed a daily inventory of trash and collectibles.

Thanks to residents who discarded their deposit pop bottles and the kindness of local grocers, it was possible for an enterprising 11-year-old to attend the Saturday matinee at the Capitol Theater. The return of seven pop bottles brought in 14 cents, enough for admission. Any additional alley-sourced bottles meant a box of popcorn (10 cents) and soda pop (5 cents). As soon as I saw the Coming Attractions, I'd set my procurement goal for the next week. Then I'd check garbage cans and trash barrels every day for empties.

It was essential, of course, to know city trash pickup schedules for my "territory," and thus I planned my route accordingly. With my trusty red Radio Flyer wagon in tow, I transported empty Nehi, Kayo, Pepsi, and

Coca-Cola bottles home for cleaning before returning them to stores willing to refund the deposit. Dutifully I presented my glass bounty, pestering local merchants to pay the 2-cent deposit per bottle even though they knew the beverages might have been purchased elsewhere.

More than six decades later, recalling their generosity brings back fond memories of my visits to Condes' Grocery, IGA, Park View Foods, National Tea, A&P, and Kroger. Together these merchants served as my "capital investment group." Occasionally I'd be lucky enough to find a large Canfield's pop bottle. Highly coveted, it carried a return deposit of 5 cents!

Along with deposit bottles, I was also on the lookout for cereal box tops and other packaging necessary for the countless premiums offered by sponsors of my favorite radio programs. Procuring badges, decoders, secret-signal rings, and official memberships all required proof of purchase and a few coins. Besides checking trash containers for empty Ovaltine jars, I was expertly scanning for cereal boxes from Wheaties, Ralston, Shredded Wheat, Pep, Quaker Puffed Wheat, and Quaker Puffed Rice. Faithful to *The Lone Ranger*'s sponsor, Cheerios, I kept a ready supply of those box tops on hand for the masked-man's next offer.

My scavenging prowess in these familiar neighborhood alleys also paved the way for the acquisition of my first bicycle. One day I noticed that a discarded bicycle frame—front fork and handlebars—had been set out with the trash. I scanned the vicinity for the other parts (seat, handlebar grips, fenders, chain, pedals, wheels, tires, and tubes) to no avail, but the frame was solid.

Cutting short my bottle search, I placed the frame on my wagon over the bottles and headed home. From that point on, the additional bicycle parts I needed were added to my alley searches, though some would ultimately prove elusive.

Disappointed but undaunted, I decided to find a steady source of income. I became a paperboy, delivering afternoon editions of *The Hammond Times*, *Chicago Daily News*, and *Chicago Herald American* to subscribers on Cleveland Avenue, Route 6B. And having learned that a local scrap dealer paid a penny per pound for used newsprint, I also began collecting old newspapers and magazines (some previously delivered on my route).

When school resumed in September, I gave up Route 6B, but I continued to gather scrap paper. Regardless of the season, I made my scheduled rounds, hauling wagonload after wagonload from neighborhood basements and garages. Back at home, I'd weigh and tie the papers in 25-pound bundles and stack them in our old coal bin until ready for the scrap dealer.

By March, total profits from the paper route and collecting old newsprint not only paid for the parts I needed to complete my alley bike (a seat and fenders), but also my baseball glove and spiked shoes from Neal Price's Firestone Store.

This diversified portfolio—scouring alleys for deposit bottles, delivering newspapers for a time and collecting old ones, as well as cutting lawns, pulling weeds, cleaning garages, and shoveling snow—is how I earned spending money until I turned 16. Then I transitioned from neighborhood alleys to the bowling alley at the Whiting Community Center, working as a pinboy. Earning actual folding money by setting pins paid for teenage expenses, while also strengthening my resourcefulness, enhancing my independence, and enriching my self-reliance.

Looking back on these formative experiences, the alleys in Whiting-Robertsdale were both my childhood boulevards and my Wall Street. Trash and timber were turned into treasure, imparting important life lessons. Whether the alleys I traveled were outdoors or indoors, gravel or varnished hardwood, they certainly served me well.

One last thing: Does anyone need a Cheerios box top?

(2012)

Always a Warm Winter

With the winter season well underway, we must fortify ourselves from the onslaught of inclement weather in order to maintain desired levels of health, stamina, and strength. Of constant concern is warding off the winter chill. During the day, residents of northern latitudes supplement their raised thermostats with warm beverages: coffee, tea, and hot chocolate, plus broth too. They're a quick way to keep internal temperatures comfortable. As an added precaution, vitamins and over-the-counter remedies are consumed to soothe sore throats, stop runny noses, stifle sniffles, and quiet pesky coughs.

Of course, everyone tries to keep their resistance to germs in tip-top shape. Long before winter's arrival, pneumonia and flu shots are available for those who are more susceptible to these maladies. Whatever the form or shape they take, winter ills are not welcome.

When venturing outdoors, layers of warm clothing are the foundation to down-filled jackets, car coats, and parkas. Hats, scarves, and mittens or gloves complete the ensemble for defense against blustery, uncomfortable conditions—protection for both warmth and wellness.

Even so, regardless of precautions and preventive measures, not everyone stays warm. We forget that generating warmth is a team effort involving mind, body, and spirit. Although we keep our bodies well fed and wrapped in heat-retaining fabrics, we need a core supply of energy. Whether this is called attitude, outlook, or personal sunshine, the desired outcome is cozy, comfortable warmth.

More important than blankets, quilts, flannel, and fleece is the inner warmth we create. So many people glide through the winter months with joyful exuberance, gleeful hearts, and sparkling eyes. They seem not to notice the extended hours of darkness, frigid temperatures, and limited sunshine. Even those with limited economic resources or troubled by ailments often glow with a tranquil and unflustered composure.

What's the source of such satisfaction? I suspect it's the understanding of the important things in life. We're all on a similar journey, and though the roads traveled and rest stops along the way might be different, each of us decides what's important and what's not. As one accumulates years spent on earth, our inventory of experiences allows for the choice of treasure or trash. Which memories should be savored? What moments to remember should be embraced?

Winters must be cold for people who don't have warm memories. No article of clothing can warm a vacancy of the heart. No thermostat can fill the emptiness of the spirit with comforting warmth. No meal can satisfy the pangs of loneliness. Only the inner source of our personal sunshine can warm, comfort, and dispel unwanted feelings of emotional isolation.

So many times during life, we must draw strength from our faith and beliefs. Admittedly, there are circumstances when core values don't seem all that important, but in difficult, stressful, and troublesome moments, they can be all we have to hold on to. Of all living things on the earth, only humans pray, or need to. And it's our prayerful words that fuel our inner sunshine, providing warmth to the mind, comfort to the spirit, and nourishment to the body. When our personal sunshine is willingly shared with others, darkness gives way to light, coldness no longer has dominion, and we can fully enjoy the seasonal offerings of winter.

Those who keep in close contact with family and friends and make the effort to focus on doing for others are healthier, happier, and more vibrant. Winter doldrums are inevitable as short days and long nights challenge peace of mind. Cabin fever and Seasonal Affective Disorder can also take a toll on our energy and enthusiasm. But those who understand the importance of tending to and adapting to the seasonal changes within us are rewarded with an abundance of peaceful easy feelings, cherished memories, and a warm winter, always.

(2012)

Animal Speak

Whether domesticated or wild, animals have become an integral part of human life and communication as we convey our feelings, opinions, and perceptions. We evoke names of animals to clarify and expound upon thoughts about numerous human conditions, behaviors, and deeds. With apologies to all living creatures for our labeling, here's a representative sample of human "animal speak."

Busy as a *bee* ... at a *snail*'s pace ... You can't teach an old *dog* new tricks ... That'll open a can of *worms* ... Go on a wild *goose* chase ... Happy as a *clam* ... The world is your *oyster* ... Watching like a *hawk* ... Raining *cats* and *dogs* ... He sold him a *pig* in a poke ... Don't count your *chickens* before they hatch ... Mad as a *hornet* ... *Eagle* eye ... Get your *ducks* in a row ... The early *bird* gets the *worm* ... Be a *guinea pig* ... Hold your *horses* ... Strong as a *bull* ... I'll be a *monkey*'s uncle ... Let sleeping *dogs* lie ... *Puppy* love ... Like shooting *fish* in a barrel.

A little *bird* told me ... Quiet as a church *mouse* ... Having *butterflies* in the stomach ... A *wolf* in *sheep*'s clothing ... She's a one-trick *pony* ... The *lion*'s share ... That really gets my *goat* ... He's so *pig*-headed ... Try and *weasel* out of something ... Let the *cat* out of the bag ... Quit cold *turkey* ... That's a red *herring* ... She's got *ants* in her pants ... Even a blind *squirrel* finds a nut now and then ... Wouldn't hurt a *fly* ... Tell the kids about the *birds* and the *bees* ... Take a *cat* nap ... Dropping like *flies* ... Eager *beaver* ... Don't have a *cow*! ... Kill two *birds* with one stone.

He's in the *dog* house ... *Monkey* see, *monkey* do ... Act like a *jackass* ... *Pig* out ... Running the *rat* race ... Take the *bull* by the horns ... Straight from the *horse*'s mouth ... Don't *badger* me ... *bird*'s eye view ... Full as a *tick* ... Top *dog* ... Fat *cat* ... Like water off a *duck*'s back ... The *elephant* in the room ... She's got bigger *fish* to fry ... He's sly as a *fox* ... I'd like to be a *fly* on the wall ... Don't look a gift *horse* in the mouth ... Scared as a *rabbit* ... Have a *tiger* by the tail ... Let's talk *turkey* ... The *worm* has turned ... She has *bats* in her belfry ... That's for the *birds*.

That's the *bee*'s knees ... That's the *cat*'s pajamas ... Snug as a *bug* in a rug ... Let the grease *monkey* fix it ... Smell a *rat* ... Like a beached *whale* ... He's *cuckoo* in the head ... She's got a memory like an *elephant* ... He's as mad as a March *hare* ... He's proud as a *peacock* ... That's like trying to put lipstick on a *pig* ... Scarce as *hen*'s teeth ... That's finer than *frog* hair ... You're a sitting *duck* ... Don't be a *snake* in the grass ... There's a *fly* in the ointment ... That's the straw that broke the *camel*'s back ... He's as drunk as a *skunk* ... She's sick as a *dog* ... He's stubborn as a *mule* ... A dumb *bunny*.

A fraidy-*cat* ... Go *ape* at a party ... *Clam* up ... Get off your high *horse* ... More fun than a barrel of *monkeys* ... Enjoy a white *elephant* sale ... Look like a *deer* in the headlights ... It's a *dog*-eat-*dog* world ... Something sounds (or smells) *fishy* ... Work like a *dog* ... Looks like an old *buzzard* ... Don't act like a *baboon* ... He's an old *goat* ... She's as graceful as a *swan* ... Don't give them anything to *crow* about ... He's a dead *duck* ... Give a *bear* hug ... He's a card *shark* ... Like a *moth* to a flame ... That's a fine kettle of *fish* ... He's a night *owl* ... *Pony* up ... A paper *tiger* ... A sacred *cow*.

Stool *pigeon* ... *Swan* song ... Happy as a *lark* ... That's the tail wagging the *dog* ... When the *cat*'s away, the *mice* will play ... Knee high to a *grasshopper* ... Packed liked *sardines* ... Slippery as an *eel* ... Curiosity killed the *cat* ... Like a *fish* out of water ... Beating a dead *horse* ... Playing *possum* ... Ugly *duckling* ... A *bird* in the hand is worth two in the bush ... That's a *mite* too small ... A *leopard* can't change its spots ... A woman needs a man like a *fish* needs a bicycle ... Playing *cat* and *mouse* ... As the *crow* flies ... That's the *albatross* around his neck.

She's got a *bee* in her bonnet ... He's *pigeon*-toed ... She has *crow*'s feet ... He's the black *sheep* of the family ... Bundle up, it's brass *monkey* weather ... *Birds* of a feather flock together ... *Cat* got your tongue? ... Like a frightened *turtle* ... The *chickens* came home to roost ... She shed *crocodile* tears ... Can't sleep? Count *sheep* ... He drinks like a *fish* ... In a *pig*'s eye ... *Horse* feathers! ... Like leading a *lamb* to slaughter ... His argument is so offbeat, it's like putting legs on a *snake* ... He's a lame *duck* ... Running around like a *chicken* with its head cut off ... Graceful as a *bull* in a china shop ... Having staged so many comebacks, she's like a *cat* with nine lives ... Naked as a *jaybird* ... I double-*dog* dare you ... She'll *parrot* everything back to you!

I bet you can add a few more. Isn't it interesting how humans love to illustrate their thoughts by referencing animals? Such sayings cover a wide range of feelings and emotions. Bestowing these tidbits of zoological prowess upon others can elicit affection, appreciation, scorn, disgust, or mere indifference.

How do animals feel about such verbal elevation? Well, some keep quiet as a mouse, while others laugh loudly like hyenas. When sheep laugh they go, "BAA-HA, BAA-HA, BAA-HA!"

That's all for now. See you later, alligator. After a while, crocodile!

(2017)

At 65

The letter from the Social Security Administration was straightforward and to the point: *Sign up for Medicare!* Medicare? Me? And then reality set in. The notice *was* for me.

On January 21, 2006, I turned 65 years of age. A milestone both celebrated and dreaded, it's the one birthday that demands taking inventory of our life. As Charles Dickens wrote long ago, "It was the best of times. It was the worst of times." So it is with most of us. I arrived from the kid factory eleven months before the start of World War II. But in spite of the war, family financial difficulties, and a number of health issues, I not only survived but thrived in Whiting, Indiana, "The Little City by the Lake."

I grew up in the 1940s and 1950s in what certainly felt like a less complicated time. There were three major keystones to society then: family, church, and school. Attached to this societal triad were supporting values of respect, honesty, trust, hard work, and responsibility. These characteristics were essential in strengthening and reinforcing the bond to the keystones.

As life unfolds, internal and external forces beget change, presenting questions to answer, problems to solve, and consideration of our purpose in life. Some time ago I came to realize that the most important things in life are not material things but those that are more contemplative in nature. They have a much more profound effect on our quality of life.

Using headings from a long since forgotten source, I've compiled a list of items for reflective thought as I turn 65 and gingerly approach my not-quite-ready-for-the rocking-chair phase of life.

Things I Wish I Could Remember

Not to get upset when things don't turn out as I'd hoped
To write things down so I won't forget
All of the names of my students from the past 38 years
All the minutes of all the days of my life

Things I Wish I Could Forget

All people are not kind, honest, or trustworthy
All the dumb things I've done
The meanness, selfishness, and cruelty by humans to
humans and animals
The unkind remarks made about others

Things I Hope I Never Forget

The sight, sound, and touch of my family
The sound of children laughing
Family, friends, classmates, and teachers who have
passed on
The meaning and purpose my wife and children bring
to my life

Things I Have Trouble Remembering

We all don't see things the same way
How important it is to listen
Others have pain and sorrow, too
Telephone numbers

Things I Wish I'd Never Found Out

Most of my heroes are flawed
In spite of my best efforts, I may still fail
Growing old is scary
Things in life don't always have a happy ending

Things I Still Need to Learn

Listen more effectively
Be more tolerant
Be kind to those who have been hurtful
Be more understanding and patient

Things I'm Certain Of

God's love
All living things die
The uncertainty of life
Friendship is one of life's treasures

Things I Used to Believe

Parents have all the answers
I could accomplish everything and get everything done
Everyone wants to be kind, decent, and honest
Dreams come true just because they're supposed to

Things I Don't Want to Believe

That I can't
Some parents hate their children
Some children hate their parents
Some people just don't care

Things I'd Like to Believe But Can't

All elected officials are honorable
Our government always has our best interests in mind
We can trust our well-being to others
Every eligible voter will vote intelligently

Things I Wish I'd Discovered Sooner

Not to be afraid to try, risk, or fail
The only way to have what you want is to give it away
How to set priorities
How to be unselfish

Things I Still Don't Understand

Why blameless children have to suffer
Why some people who are able to help others don't
Why the United States doesn't have a good healthcare
program for all citizens
Why some of my friends died so young

Things I Wish Were True But Aren't

Everyone believes in God's goodness and love
All students come to school prepared to learn
All parents are good, loving parents
Prejudice, corruption, and self-importance have become extinct

Things I Can't Accept

Life without love
Life without laughter
Life without family and friends
Doing less than your best

Things I Should Do More Often for People I Care About

Tell them that I love them
Help them at every opportunity
Share their laughter, tears, and joy
Remember them in my prayers

Now, if you're so inclined—and whatever age you happen to be—why not make your own list of items that impact or otherwise guide your life.

(2006)

At 70

When I was a kid, I eagerly shared my age or grade level in school. A particular age or grade level was a badge of honor or position of celebrity. Grade school gave way to high school and each one of those four years increased prominence. Age became a marker along the way to measure independence and self-reliance.

We learn early that reaching a specific age brings certain privileges: later bedtimes, watching particular television shows, or going to the movies at night. We also became aware that as we accumulated years, gratuity increased on birthdays, holidays, and special occasions. During adolescence, coins were replaced with denominations of folding money. As our personal list of wants and needs increased, items were prioritized according to available funds and social pressure. Spending conflicted with saving, a matter of satisfying immediate desires versus delayed or deferred gratification.

Various milestones validated our accomplishments or achievements: work permit, Social Security card, driver's license, bank account, part-time job, tax return, and sundry associated responsibilities. Shopping for clothes transitioned from going with Mom to shopping solo or with friends. Decisions went from parental mandate to personal choice. Constant adult supervision eased into that of relaxed overseers, ebbing until individual sovereignty was finally bestowed.

Growing up, we knew that someone would be there to set boundaries and borders. Someone was always available to keep us safe, guide and counsel us, and support our endeavors. They were mostly family members at first, but with each orbit around the sun, others would assume roles to help with life's journey—teachers, clergy, classmates, peers, coworkers, friends, acquaintances, and on occasion, complete strangers. Bits and pieces of human interaction and pearls of wisdom about life-learned lessons were dispensed at random for our acceptance or rejection.

We crossed thresholds, met challenges, succeeded, failed, stumbled, struggled, achieved, and continually added to the depth and expansion of our experience, intelligence, and intellect. Somehow we survived the hurdle of turning 16, arguing for grown-up privileges. With high school graduation came choices regarding work (military service, college, factory, or office) and residence (remain with our families or make a home of our own). Stark evidence of this newly granted independence for 18-year-old males included the Selective Service Draft Card. By 19, often there was also a driver's license in our wallet, plus car payments and auto insurance. Then as quickly as it had arrived, adolescence abdicated its rule when we became legal at the magic age of 21. Relationships began to solidify, and lifelong friends and new acquaintances joined the journey and shared adventures as the future unfolded before us.

A number of childhood friends disconnected and moved on with their lives. Reconnection would be limited to high school reunions, correspondence, and occasional random meetings here and there. Affairs of the heart captured and consumed our emotions causing the pronouns "I," "me," and "mine" to be replaced with "we," "us," and "ours." At the speed of life, our twenties flew by. Our thirties seemed to rocket along, and though we were once solitary travelers, now many of us had families and responsibilities that grew exponentially.

In the midst of the prime of our lives, hours and days are consumed with work, family, obligations, duties, commitments, and promises that must be kept. There's struggle to enjoy Heaven's sunshine, stars, moonlight, and rainbows. Even though we're now in the driver's seat, many things remain out of our hands. Countless hours are spent worrying about things we cannot control. The accompanying anxiety, stress, and emotional turmoil take a toll on mind, body, and spirit. Health and well-being are added to existing primary concerns.

Shortly upon turning 40, medical abbreviations, maladies, and terms unexpectedly assume significance. Blood pressure, cholesterol, lipid profile, and all enzymes in between are now topics for discussion during scheduled checkups. Favorite foods become diet restricted. Salt, sugar, carbohydrates, and calories are viewed as adversaries. Fats and sugars are closely scrutinized as a precaution against obesity and diabetes. Bifocals are recommended after an annual eye exam. We become aware of limitations and other changes that impact our lifestyles. During youthful years, the candle burns at both ends. After 40, nightlights are necessary to illuminate the way.

At 50, we're accustomed to annual diagnostic tests. At home, we become more comfortable watching others do what we used to do. Couches, recliners, TV remotes, and an ample supply of comfort food become favorite companions. We enjoy more completely those simple pleasures heretofore discounted as unimportant or wimpy.

At 60, we gear down obligation and gear up relaxation. Occasional naps and an early bedtime are welcomed like dear friends. When retirement is offered, it's accepted with a smile bright enough to ripen bananas.

At 70, we're content with ourselves. Competition takes a backseat to enjoyment, reverie, remembrance, and a do-as-you-please mindset of peaceful, easy feelings. Flexible scheduling is readily adopted. Every day is a welcomed gift. The challenge is to stay well and enjoy Heaven's blessings. So many moments, so many memories. Treasure the moments, savor the memories.

The adventure continues. The best is yet to come!

(2011)

GUEST CHECK

TABLE	PERSONS	46394	SERVER
B	8		S-9

Before the Chalk Dust Settles
Beginnings
The Best Part of the Day
Be Thankful
The Biography of Maia Bona Dea
Birthday
The Blizzard of '67
By the Numbers

TAX

Before the Chalk Dust Settles

At the close of the 2009-2010 school year, I will retire from the Lake Central School Corporation in St. John, Indiana, and close out my teaching career. For the past 12 years, it's been my privilege and good fortune to teach Lake Central High School students, both as a general education instructor and serving those with special needs.

With prior teaching experience in Illinois and southern Indiana, my tenure as a classroom teacher totals 44 years. Forty-four years?! It seems like 44 minutes! So before the lights are turned off, and the classroom door is closed for the last time, I want to take a few moments and share some thoughts about teaching and the process of education.

We've all been around long enough to realize that life is a series of beginnings and goodbyes, and no matter the number of our years, we never quite get used to it. Most of us enjoy beginnings. Goodbyes are a different matter. But change is part of the parade of seasons and we must face it and any accompanying challenges. Still, before the goodbye part, a return to the beginning.

When I walked into a classroom for the first time as a teacher in late August 1967, I was unseasoned, minimally skilled, and uncertain as to my effectiveness. But it didn't take long for me to develop a personal methodology, coping mechanisms, and survival skills.

Now, after 44 years in the trenches, I'm a fully seasoned, reality-based, capable, effective, adaptable, even-tempered, well-educated, and confident pedagogical unit. Over the past four-plus decades, I've witnessed events, innovations, happenings, fads, policies, catchphrases, procedures, institutes, workshops, and sundry educational instructional approaches—all designed to improve the process of education. Even so, I firmly believe that a good teacher remains essential to effective learning.

Over the years, students have arrived in my classroom prepared and unprepared, properly parented and woefully neglected, nurtured and ignored, well nourished and underfed, behaved and disruptive, respectful and disrespectful, joyful and sad, happy and angry, eager and ambivalent, active and passive, energetic and tired, outgoing and shy, courageous and fearful, and confident and timid. Many times I witnessed a weed become a rose when the spark of understanding took flame. Those truly magical moments have become treasures of the heart.

There were times that challenged every ounce of my resolve, energy, and commitment in order to get through the day. But most of my 7,200-plus school days have been flooded with sunshine. When shadows would threaten that brightness, I drew upon faith and prayerful intercession for help through difficult times. I thank my coworkers and colleagues for being there to share this mixture of moments with me.

Thanks, too, for their support, assistance, and help. I'm a technological novice (only recently have I acquired the skill to change my stereo receiver from AM to FM), and my lack of computer proficiency is legendary. For all of their individual and collective help, allowing me to interrupt their day asking for assistance to unravel my electronic knots, I am eternally grateful.

I have often been asked why I decided to become a teacher. During my senior year of high school in 1958, after much academic mediocrity, struggle, and setback, there was a glimmer of understanding. That's why I wrote in a classmate's scrapbook, "All I want is a chance to do better." I promised that if such a chance was presented to me, I would do what I could to help others learn.

All through my formative years, in addition to my family, there were teachers, mentors, classmates, and friends who helped me along the way. At Whiting Primary for summer school in 1948, Miss Evelyn Stewart accepted a parochial school second-grader with learning deficiencies. She helped me control my stuttering so I could read aloud without embarrassment.

As a teenager, the teachers at Whiting High School never gave up on me: Mr. Allen, Mr. Burkholtz, Mr. Faulkner, Mr. McClure, Mr. Taylor, and Mr. Ulrich. Each of these pedagogical apostles encouraged, guided, and helped me to understand the subject matter, teaching lessons of life that have served me well. By their word, example, and kindness, they gave me the confidence to risk and reach for unreachable dreams and the courage to achieve them.

Classmates, who became like family to me, offered their support and encouragement, and most importantly, the gift of friendship. Special thanks to my fellow graduates of the Whiting High School Class of 1958—in my estimation, the finest class ever, anywhere.

Whenever I enter a classroom, I remember the goodness of those special folks and all who have touched my life and provided me with the chance to do better. Having been around long enough to know that the journey should be as enjoyable as the destination, I've had many opportunities to think about the purpose of teaching: To make a positive, constructive difference in the lives we touch.

In those moments, I recall my favorite poem by Robert Frost, "Stopping by Woods on a Snowy Evening," which ends with words of commitment, duty, and responsibility that continue to have personal resonance. Whatever adventures lie beyond the classroom door will unfold as destined by the stars and will be welcomed and pursued with energy, enthusiasm, and excitement. Without question, I've had a great time!

Some parting thoughts: Over the years, schools have become society's fix-it shops. So many ancillary responsibilities have been added to teachers' traditional duties that it's a credit to their ability, talent, and commitment that students continue to prosper academically, socially, and morally. To my fellow teachers, please keep up your good work. So many students want a chance to do better.

Finally, as a former altar boy, I would be remiss if I didn't leave you with just a smidgen of a benediction, so let it be this:

May each day be filled with laughter, love,
good health, and good fortune.
May Heaven's angels guide you every step of the way.

May the Good Lord keep you close to Him forever.
May you always take time to help Mom with the dishes.
And may you always remember to convey appreciation
to all the good people who touch your life.

(2010)

Beginnings

Life is a series of beginnings and goodbyes. No matter the number of our years, we never quite get used to it. This is the story of a beginning.

If I had a dime for every time I heard the retort "Grow up!" I'd have a tidy sum today. From the time I was a little kid, whenever things went awry or mistakes were made, someone in authority would direct their focus to me and say: "Grow up!" Attending parochial school in the 1940s and 1950s, nuns were more than willing to dispense that phrase to anyone whose immaturity caused them consternation. For the greater portion of my grade school years, I could've been the poster child for immaturity with "Grow up!" tattooed on my forehead.

In high school, immaturity is magnified due to adolescence's rapid infusion of cognitive and physical growth, developmental hormones, and growing social responsibilities. We enter secondary school as an old child and leave four years later as a young adult. Within those 48 months, we're expected to acquire the appropriate academic, social, and personal skills to function in the world of grown-ups—a formidable assignment for anyone. For me, it was an embarrassing struggle that challenged my self-esteem, had me questioning my self-worth, and tested my personal discipline and resolve.

The full impact of these feelings of inadequacy became evident a few days after graduation as I warily pondered my future. My four years in the comfort zone of high school classrooms and supportive classmates was over, and now a single question demanded my full attention: What do I do now? The choices are nearly the same today as they were back then: college, military service, or employment. But due to low academic achievement and class rank, college was out of the question. Military enlistment required a level of confidence and maturity I didn't possess. Therefore, finding a job was my only viable option.

Now, up until that moment, every male in my family had worked at the Standard Oil refinery in Whiting, Indiana, including my grandfather, uncle, father, and eldest brother. Standard Oil was the financial engine that kept food on our table. When my second-oldest brother returned from the navy, he, too, added his name to this employment legacy.

My decision, however, was to forego the refinery altogether. Machine shop was an academic highlight of my time at Whiting High School, so with three years of machine tool training as a foundation, I decided to apply for the machinist apprenticeship program at Inland Steel's Indiana Harbor Works in East Chicago.

One of the major drawbacks of being told to grow up is the lack of information. No one ever told me how to grow up. Progress was hindered by confusion, awkwardness, anxiety, insecurity, immaturity, and ignorance. Most prominent was a fear of rejection. I realized I was now on my own. No one ever told me how to apply for a job, how to get to the Inland Steel employment office in Indiana Harbor, what materials I needed, or what to say. Still full of uncertainty, I managed to muster up my courage and put growing up on the fast track.

On Tuesday, June 17, 1958—not knowing bus routes or schedules, and too embarrassed to ask—I set out on foot to Inland Steel's employment office.

Leaving home on that summer morning at 7:45 am, wearing a dark suit, white shirt, and tie, I walked from Cleveland Avenue and followed 119th Street down to Front Street and Dickey Road. Then I crossed the railroad tracks from the Union Carbide side of Dickey Road to the Standard Oil side. Reaching the intersection of 129th Street at Markstown, I jogged across it to Youngstown Sheet and Tube Company.

I continued past the Mill Gate Inn, crossing the East Chicago Ship Canal Bridge. Passing by the entrance to Inland Steel Coke Plant 3, I reached the Standard Forge Company on the corner of Dickey Road and Watling Street and turned left, walking the remaining five blocks to the Inland Steel employment office at 3210 Watling Street. Total distance traveled on foot: 4 miles.

Arriving around 9:00 am, I took my place in line with dozens of fellow job seekers. Entirely male, the largest group of applicants was under 30, with a sizeable number of recent high school graduates like me. A few older men stood hopeful in search of a new beginning. While I wore a suit and tie, aiming to make a good first impression, my wardrobe choice was in stark contrast to the majority who opted for a more casual approach: T-shirts, walking shorts, shoes of varying styles, and many sans socks.

Forty-five minutes later, it was my turn at the front. A personnel representative handed me an application and a well-used pencil (I didn't think to bring one along), and directed me to fill in the required information. After submitting the completed form, he noticed I was not yet 18 and informed me I needed a work permit with a parent's signature before proceeding further. Little did I know!

I left the employment office immediately and walked back to Whiting, going directly to Mr. Kosalko's office at Whiting High School to procure the permit. From there, I walked over to Standard Oil's personnel office on Front Street where my dad worked and secured his signature. Permit in hand, and with my watch reading 11:15 am, I began the trek back to Inland Steel.

Arriving at half-past noon, the waiting room in the employment office was now empty. Most of the staff appeared to be on lunch break. I walked up to one of the service windows and a gentleman who was eating lunch at his desk came to the window. After I explained the situation to him, he went through the stack of new applications, located mine, and attached the signed permit.

Shortly after 1:00 pm, I was ushered to a conference room. After a brief interview, I had to take two pre-apprenticeship tests: Mechanical Reasoning and Spatial Recognition. Finishing up around 3:00 pm, I was told that should I be hired, I'd be contacted to schedule the pre-employment physical exam. (Thank goodness it wasn't that day!)

Tired, hungry, and both mentally and physically exhausted, I began the journey back to Whiting. Walking during rush hour only added to the day's cumulative discomfort of having skipped lunch and my perspiration-soaked clothing. I arrived back home just after 4:15 pm.

The process of becoming a grown-up left much to be desired.

My efforts (along with a helping of Heaven's kindness) did bear fruit, as I was hired a few weeks later and began my machinist apprenticeship on August 11, 1958. That day I said a final farewell to youthful innocence and dependence. Childhood was over.

Crossing the threshold to adulthood was difficult. Countless life lessons, struggles, challenges, and unanswered questions would be confronted. I'd be tested in ways never envisioned. Without any rehearsal, adult responsibilities arrived, demanding attention and problem solving at the speed of life.

Growing up, we learn to draw upon experience, emotional strength, spiritual faith, loved ones, and all avenues of information. But cut me some slack—the process continues!

(2011)

The Best Part of the Day

Now that I'm enrolled in the Geriatric Adventure, there's time to think about things I never paid much attention to when I was young. Youthful times are filled with so many different experiences, distractions, and day-to-day happenings that the idea to dwell on any specific thought with a depth of analysis is too time-consuming and uninteresting.

By the time awareness sets in when we're young, we've already been conscripted to school, studies, homework and after-school chores. When free time is available to us, personal contemplation is way down the list of preferred activities. With adulthood comes a myriad of additional responsibilities and the pace of daily living is at times a blur. Often exhausted at the end of the day, we seek restful sleep rather than a cognitive review. As tired as we are, however, we automatically savor certain moments from the day just ending. Doing so begets the question: What's the best part of the day? What number from the allotted 1,440 minutes serves to ease the mind, comfort the soul, and energize the spirit?

Regardless of age, gender, status, or circumstance, each of us has moments that define our days. Take your own personal inventory and enjoy the review of those special segments that bring satisfaction, comfort, accomplishment, peace of mind, and prayerful thanks. For me, each second is the best part of the day. I view each day as a gift with the intention to enjoy and savor every part thereof.

Near the top of my list are the moments in the wee small hours of the morning, when the night is wrapped around us like a warm comforter. Familiar sounds of home appliances tease the silence, providing a soundtrack for those of us sleep less soundly and share starry moonlit skies.

Numerous times during the year, the sound of rain against windowpanes and roofs elicits a feeling of tranquility that encourages reflection.

When skies are clear, there are pristine moments of sunrise and sunset, dawn and dusk. Beginning a day with hot coffee at the kitchen table or sharing evening togetherness on the porch swing with a cup of freshly-brewed tea is a gift within a gift.

For parents, the most cherished moment of the day arrives at night, saying prayers with their children or reading bedtime stories together, a ritual that ends with a hug and a goodnight kiss. For others, the standout part of the day is spent with friends, interacting with coworkers and colleagues, or savoring aloneness. Sometimes there can be several best parts of the day—moments when we're solo and others when we're in the company of others. During the week, the choice part of the day can come at different times—prayerful contemplation, boisterous gatherings, family activities, romantic interludes—public, private, and all occasions in between.

The best part of the day can be watching a favorite TV show or sporting event, relaxing in a favorite chair or couch-potato sofa. It can also be listening to a ballgame while working in the yard on a delicious summer afternoon or enjoying the symphony of spring nights, swaying restfully on the screened porch glider.

What is the best part of your day? The answer is largely dependent on your personal attitude, philosophy, and perspective. How vigorously do you pursue the potential of each day? To what degree do you dispense thoughtfulness, effort, goodness, and kindness in order to harvest the bounty provided?

Each day arrives like a banquet brimming with promise, opportunity, and a chance to do better. But the best part of the day—the dessert for our efforts—is achieved through individual and collective offerings of faith, hope, and charity.

The best part of the day can be whatever you want it to be. The way you use the gift of each day's 86,400 seconds, 1,440 minutes, or 24 hours will determine the quality of your life.

(2010)

Be Thankful

During our annual Thanksgiving celebration, amid the clamor of family, food, football, and fun, we'll hopefully find a few quiet moments and review our personal inventory of things to be thankful for.

Ideally, thankfulness should be part of every day, spontaneously expressed in whatever manner we choose—informally, as we go about other tasks throughout the day, or given thoughtful deliberation at day's end as we tally the plusses and minuses of the past 24 hours. It's of little consequence whether our thankfulness is great or small, tangible or intangible, profound or sublime, public or private. What matters is the degree of gratitude, appreciation, and acknowledgment we hold in our heart.

Helping to tidy up insufficiencies in our thankfulness account, we set aside the fourth Thursday in November as Thanksgiving Day. We're truly blessed to live in the United States of America, enjoying the exceptional bounty of sovereignty, democracy, and opportunity this country offers. There are so many ordinary, taken-for-granted day-gifts we readily accept without any forethought much less a thank-you.

Be thankful for well-stocked service stations, supermarkets, department stores, and malls. Be thankful for other businesses providing sundry services, whether banking, insurance, automotive, entertainment, transportation, or recreation. Be thankful for public servants on watch 24/7 who protect, defend, and assist in time of emergency or need. Be thankful for medical personnel and caregivers that attend to our well-being, often working long, intense shifts.

Be thankful for the men and women of America's armed forces here and overseas, many serving in harm's way. Be thankful for public officials who represent our viewpoints and give voice to our concerns at all levels of government. Be thankful for public workers who maintain our cities, communities, and neighborhoods. Be thankful for parents, clergy, teachers, administrators, and staff who help young and old alike keep their moral compass pointed in the proper direction.

At home, be thankful for faithful utilities that light, heat, and cool us for comfort. Be thankful for clean water for drinking, taking baths and showers, washing dishes, and laundering clothes. Be thankful for free-flowing drains that carry away wastewater from basins, showers, tubs, and porcelain lifesavers—ordinary conveniences that are so necessary to maintain healthy hygiene and a tranquil mindset. Be thankful for electronic devices that allow access to information, news, events, entertainment, and personal communication.

Be thankful for prescription medications, over-the-counter remedies, vitamins, and health aids that combat infirmities, reduce pain, keep maladies at bay, and support overall wellness. Be thankful for emergency rooms, clinics, hospitals, and specialized healthcare facilities available in time of trauma and crisis.

Be thankful for the bed in which you sleep, with clean comfortable sheets and blankets to keep us cozy and warm through cold winter nights. Be thankful for Heaven's gift of another day and the blessings that foster peace, goodness, kindness, thoughtfulness, and love.

Be thankful for the important people in your life: family, friends, loved ones, classmates, coworkers, and neighbors. Treasure the moments you share together. Appreciate their individual and collective contributions to your life. Give prayerful thanks for those who have passed. Remember, too, how they touched your life and the positive, constructive difference they made. Be thankful for all creatures, great and small—wildlife that enriches the outdoor landscape and pets that provide companionship, comfort, and unconditional love.

A note of personal thanks from this writer to all who read these words. It's a privilege to be able to share my stories, experiences, and perspectives on topics from today, yesterday, and once-upon-a-time. May the meaning of Thanksgiving Day nourish our hearts, nurture our minds, and sustain our spirits with goodness, kindness, thoughtfulness, and love.

(2012)

The Biography of Maia Bona Dea

May, named for the Greek goddess Maia and the Roman goddess of fertility, Bona Dea, is the fifth month of the Gregorian calendar. May is also permission, possibility, and wish month: "May I?" "It may rain." "May all good things come your way."

May is awash in emerald color, symbolizing love and success and showcasing spring's artistic greening. During the 31 days of May, landscape vegetation receives permission to bud and bloom. Birds seek sanction to build nests on deciduous and conifer branches where young nestlings will soon add their vocals to the aviary chorus. Sun-drenched blue skies partner with rain clouds to ensure all living things are nourished and sustained. Led by lily of the valley, bulbs and seeds eagerly germinate and send their botanical poetry sunward in order to show off their growing skills and individuality while fending off pesky, wind-chilled temperatures.

The first breath of a May morning causes our spirits to soar to heights usually reserved for angels. Senses savor addictive springtime perfume that complements the sweet nectar of newness as heartfelt thoughts encourage memories of earlier times and treasured emotions. Playgrounds and schoolyards kept vacant by winter's unfriendliness now resound with the joyful voices of children's frolic. A tsunami of exuberant energy floods every location where children and adolescents gather, and countless pairs of sneakers eagerly dance the dance of carefree moments.

As May delivers radiant sunshine, senior residents welcome the soothing warmth for aches and pains earned from years of activity, work, and other responsibilities. Compared to younger persons, their pace is slower, more deliberate, and limited in duration, but their appreciation and enjoyment of May's weather is unrivaled.

May is spring's showcase. Baseball diamonds sparkle as athletes of all ages vie for success with bat, ball, and glove. Other diamonds adorn ring fingers as a symbol of love, passion, engagement, and promise of marriage. Novice romantics nervously begin their quest for happily-ever-after, holding hands and enjoying each other's company, drenched with May's pre-summer sunshine. After sunset, the same couples share quiet, once-upon-a-time moments under a star-filled night sky awash in soft, saffron moonlight. Seasoned sweethearts share a special togetherness of love strengthened over a lifetime of understanding, give-and-take, change, challenge, and Heaven's blessings. Families and spouses separated by loss find comfort and solace in the promise of another spring.

Parochial schools' May Crowning ceremonies celebrate Roman Catholic devotion to the Blessed Virgin Mary with prayers and pageantry. May is high school prom, when adolescents mark another milestone toward maturity and formalwear finery is captured in family videos and photographs. May is delivery time for class rings and preparation for commencement. Compiled in yearbooks and stored in hearts, these moments will be nostalgically remembered at future class reunions.

May signals the fast-approaching end of the school year. For students, it's a time of mixed feelings. Summer school for some, but most grammar students and underclassmen know they'll begin again in a few months and rejoin classmates for additional lessons, activities, and coursework. Some will return to familiar surroundings, while others will transition from elementary school to middle school or from middle school to high school. For soon-to-graduate seniors, the end of school marks a major life change as they approach the threshold of adulthood, deciding to pursue college, employment, or military service. Commencement for college seniors will lead to job interviews or graduate school. Familiar routines, new pathways, and uncharted experiences await travelers of life's journey.

May is soon-to-be brides attending to sundry arrangements for upcoming June nuptials—final dress fittings, invitations, and balancing emotional issues of friends, family, and future in-laws. May is open-minded to all suggestions: Maybe yes, maybe no.

May is Mother's Day—cards, corsages, and calls. On this special Sunday, Mom rules and receives heartfelt affection and appreciation for all she is and does. May is zodiac birthdays for Taurus and Gemini. May is Memorial Day, when our nation gives pause to remember citizen soldier heroes who made the ultimate sacrifice defending America's liberty, freedom, and ideals. May is the Indy 500—"Ladies and gentlemen, start your engines!" These words also serve as a klaxon call for everyone to gear up for summer.

Finally, a wish: May each day be filled with laughter, love, good health, and good fortune. May Heaven's angels guide you every step of the way. May the Good Lord keep you close to Him forever. May you always take time to help Mom with the dishes. And may you always remember to convey appreciation to all the good people who touch your life.

(2014)

Birthday

I've marked more than six dozen birthdays, but just a few are particularly memorable. The earliest one I remember was my fourth birthday. Our family was visiting my grandma and aunts at their home on Oliver Street. They had a dog, a Boston terrier named Buzzy. Maybe he simply didn't like chubby little boys wheezing with asthma, but as I ate a piece of my chocolate birthday cake, Buzzy jumped up and bit me in the left ear.

Karma arrived a few months later when someone came to Grandma's house and rang the doorbell, one of those mechanical hand-cranked bells that sounded like a fire station alarm. Buzzy went into a barking frenzy, charging down the hallway toward the front porch. But the terrorizing terrier's momentum caused the rug to slide on the waxed wood floor, folding up like an accordion. Unable to stop, Buzzy launched himself airborne head first toward the figure on the porch and crashed through the door's beveled glass. Contrary to the popular idiom, Buzzy was not saved by the bell.

Fast-forward to Thursday, January 21, 1954. Now an eighth-grader at Sacred Heart School, my thirteenth birthday was like most other school days: Work on assigned lessons and try not to incur the wrath of Sister Marian Loretto (aka Sister Bruiser), a tall, overpowering figure in a flowing habit and what seemed like yards of black robe. From a braided sash fastened to her waist hung a huge rosary, a heavenly anchor of salvation that jingled and jangled against her skirt with every step. (Even after all these years, just thinking about the sound of those celestial chimes is enough to bring on the cold sweats.)

After school there were household chores to do and supper to help get started before Mom and Dad came home from work. Growing up, birthdays were basically workdays and not much of a big deal. But it still felt good to be an official teenager!

I remember my eighteenth birthday in 1959 because I had to register for the military draft. In the second year of my machinist apprenticeship at Inland Steel's Indiana Harbor Works in East Chicago, and therefore draft-deferred until I completed the program, I nevertheless had to register and procure my draft card. A week after my birthday, I got off the Shoreline bus by the Whiting Post Office, picked up the form, and walked home to Cleveland Avenue. Early the next week, I mailed the completed form to Uncle Sam's Selective Service. Upon earning my Machinist Journeyman card, I received my draft notice for the army in June 1963.

My 21st birthday was particularly memorable, but not for the typical reasons one might expect. (Apropos, I turned 21 on January 21, 1962.) Nearing the end of my machinist apprenticeship training, I had incurred the wrath of the apprentice coordinator who found out I was taking night classes for radio and television repair. As punishment, he scheduled me to work the midnight shift for six weeks from early January to late February. So on a frosty Saturday, January 20, I reported for work shortly before midnight at Inland Steel's Plant 1 to begin my Sunday to Thursday workweek.

Having the lowest seniority on the midnight crew, I was assigned the coffee run. Around 2:00 am, I securely tied my shirt cuffs and the legs of my jeans with twine, put on a heavy coat, and headed to the canteen about 50 yards from the machine shop. In one hand, I carried a cardboard tray for the coffee. In the other hand, a long wooden broom handle with a metal scraper attached to it. On the way back from the canteen with eight cups of aromatic hot coffee, the tightly tied twine and metal scraper were my only defenses against emboldened rats jumping up around me, trying to get warm under my clothes or hoping to reach the heavily creamed and sugared coffee.

Vapors from the coffee mingled with my breath and crystalized in the frigid night air. Overhead, a procession of bare bulbs illuminated the way back to the shop. Amid the scurrying rats, the frost-covered buildings, the foreboding darkness, and emotionally depressing environment of a steel mill in midwinter, I wished myself a happy birthday. Voicing out loud my resolve to the giant, aggressive rats, I proclaimed, "Someday I'll laugh about this!"

Every year on my birthday, I reflect upon the past and remember life-changing moments. And true to those words spoken during the midnight shift on my 21st birthday, I have laughed every day, celebrating Heaven's blessings of family, friends, and all who have touched my life with their goodness, thoughtfulness, and kindness.

(2017)

The Blizzard of '67

Fifty years ago, on January 26, 1967, we experienced the fiercest blizzard in the history of the Chicago area. Everyone remembers where they were at the time, with personal experiences readily recalled.

I'd recently turned 26 and was in between semesters at Indiana State University, on track to complete course requirements for graduation in June. To help defray expenses, I was working as a laborer at Inland Steel's Indiana Harbor Works in East Chicago, Indiana, on weekends and during college breaks. On this particular day, I was doing routine plant cleanup when it started to snow. Just a few days earlier, it had been unseasonably warm on campus, offering short-sleeve, spring-like weather.

At about 9:30 am, the foreman instructed us to begin shoveling the walkways that served Inland Steel's employment office and the West Annex addition on Watling Street. As we shoveled, the snow continued to accumulate—first lightly, then more heavily. After an hour, it was snowing so hard we couldn't keep the pathways clear.

Payloaders, trucks, and extra laborers were added, but around noon the foreman told us to put up our equipment. It was snowing so heavily that vehicular movement was hazardous and safe operating conditions were no longer possible. As a final attempt to provide traction against the snow and ice, two tons of rock salt were spread on walkways and the adjacent parking lots.

When my shift ended at 3:00 pm, roads had become nearly impassable. I made it to the parking lot in Plant 3, where I fired up my 1960 Oldsmobile two-door sedan, navigated out of snow-rutted drifts to Dickey Road, and headed north for home. As I turned west on 129th Street, city workers were now closing Dickey Road to all traffic. I was worried that my wife would be stranded at her job at GATX in East Chicago. However, when I neared the garage apartment in Whiting that we were renting, her car sat parked by the curb. Her office had been sent home at noon due to the adverse weather.

By the time it finally stopped snowing, 26 inches of snow had fallen. Drifts over five feet high were common, and mobility was limited to walking—plodding, really—through the hip-deep snow. For four days throughout the Chicago area, nothing moved. Expressways, highways, major thoroughfares, and city streets were devoid of traffic. Abandoned cars and buses at every imagined angle filled right-of-ways. Schools, businesses, and factories were closed, with a few sustained by stranded workers who'd been unable to go home.

As difficult as things were, something marvelous occurred. Kindness, goodness, and charitable acts filled communities and neighborhoods. Strangers helped strangers and neighbors helped neighbors. Without pretense or prior conditions, people went out of their way to be helpful and kind.

However, as soon as the snow blockage was removed, everyone returned to their normal routines, resuming life as it had been before the blizzard. Some routines did soon change though, because nine months later several thousand babies were born. After all, television wasn't all that interesting, and propinquity has a power all its own.

Newspapers published stories and printed photographs of the "Great Blizzard of '67!" Articles related in vivid detail the what, where, when, why, and how. Follow-up pieces about the storm's aftermath filled daily editions for some time. The *Chicago Tribune* published a special keepsake edition of its magazine all about the blizzard. I still have my copy, tucked away.

Today, when people comment about a particular day of adverse weather and get anxious about icy roads and difficult travel, those of us who survived the Blizzard of '67 just smile, knowing that once upon a time, we had a whopper of a snowstorm and lived to tell about it.

Where were you during the Blizzard of '67? What do you remember? How did you spend that time? I'll close with the line I used during the blizzard as I went from neighbor to neighbor, clearing their sidewalks: "I have to be shoveling off!"

(2007)

By the Numbers

Our lives are governed by numbers. We use calendars and clocks to keep things orderly and in sequence. Our calendar has 12 months consisting of 365 and ¼ days. Each month has a set number of days: January, March, May, July, August, October, and December all have 31 days, while April, June, September, and November tally 30 days apiece, and February, the runt of the litter, counts a comparatively scant 28 days (though every four years, February leaps ahead and gains an additional day).

Each day contains 24 hours. Each hour, 60 minutes. And each minute, 60 seconds. Running the numbers, it goes like this: 24 x 60 = 1,440 minutes each day. 1,440 x 60 seconds equals 86,400 seconds per day. That comes out to 525,600 minutes or 31,536,000 seconds per year!

We use whole numbers, fractions, decimals, and numerical variations thereof to manage our lives. Even our bodies are number machines. A normal heart rate of 72 beats per minute results in 103,680 beats per day. Some numbers are set, while other numbers fluctuate as we go about our daily routines. Some we can control, others we cannot (blood pressure, pulse, height, weight, waist, age, IQ, cholesterol, etc.). And depending on circumstances, we blink our eyes 15 to 20 times a minute. We also take between 17,000 and 30,000 breaths per day, governed by age, health, and activity.

Now consider how much time is spent in school, a near-daily habit that fills the better part of our younger years. From Grade 1 through Grade 12, we spend approximately 15,120 hours in the classroom. Hours for preschool, kindergarten, and extracurricular activities add to this total. This 12 plus year apprenticeship—not counting more time in the pursuit of any secondary education—merely provides the basics for what lies ahead as an adult. Each age offers new responsibilities, challenges, and expectations, plus more monitoring by numbers. From millimeters to trillions, numbers run rampant in all aspects of daily life.

Our human brain processes, inventories, remembers, and accesses numbers for all sorts of purposes. Think of the numbers involved in daily activities like making phone calls, sending emails, driving a car, or even using the ATM. There's an agreed-upon necessity of having such an abundance of numbers attached to day-to-day living. We rarely leave home without numbered credentials like ID cards, driver's licenses, and credit cards, with other important numbers (address, home and cell phones, zip codes, and Social Security) committed to memory.

From cradle to grave, womb to tomb, we face scores of numbers. It's the way of modern life that we've come to accept in order to function successfully. Our computer-like brains keep track of birthdays, anniversaries, ages, number of children, grandchildren, and important events. Some numbers are also committed to hard copies or electronic files so that acknowledgment and celebration of certain milestones aren't overlooked. We share important numbers with the IRS and other government entities. Every transaction with a business or service company involves numbers on invoices, orders, accounts, and associated paperwork. We keep track of personal tasks and family needs by numbering their priority on lists or other means of scheduling.

As we mature, some numbers are retired because they served their purpose and no longer warrant priority: old addresses, telephone numbers, license plates, paid bills, closed accounts, inactive credit cards, filed tax returns, etc. Some numbers continue to serve a purpose for what seems like a lifetime: car payments, mortgage payments, bank accounts, insurance policies, health records, tuition and fees, credit cards, and current contact information. A review of our personal directory is a plethora of numbers utilized for communication, connection, and accurate accounting.

But not all numbers are dull and uninteresting. Some can be fun and playful. Numbers can generate smiles and joyfulness that enrich our day: "You're 21!" "Happy 50th Anniversary!" "Here's your DD 214, thank you for your military service!"

We can also enjoy uses of numbers that go unnoticed: The number of holes in a White Castle slider? Five. The number of holes in a Nabisco Premium saltine cracker? 13. The standard size of an automobile license plate? Six inches by twelve inches. The total of the numbers on opposite sides of a dice? Seven. The number of rows of horizontal stars on the American flag? Nine. The number of ridges on the edge of a dime? 118. And my favorite: The number of sides of a circle? Two. The inside and the outside!

That's life by the numbers, and each of ours is worth celebrating. May you enjoy more than 32,000 sunrises!

(2016)

GUEST CHECK

TABLE	PERSONS	46394	SERVER
C	8		S-9

Camelot Moments
A Chance to Do Better
Change
Choices
Christmas 1952: A Remembrance
Christmas Thoughts
A Container for Dreams
Cultural Awakening

TAX

THANKS FOR VISITING THE MIND CAFETERIA

Camelot Moments

Camelot, the Broadway musical based on the legend of King Arthur and adapted from T. H. White's tetralogy novel, *The Once and Future King*, tells a story of courage, insecurity, wisdom, weakness, betrayal, and love. First staged in 1960, the epic tale's main theme is the power of striving for ideals ("Might for right") even when challenged by conflict or setbacks, proving the strength and resiliency of the human spirit.

Listening to the words and melodies of *Camelot*'s Alan Jay Lerner and Frederick Lowe, it's not hard to romanticize the legend of chivalry, brave knights, and royal intrigue the pair so beautifully captured. It's very much part of the human condition to focus on matters of the heart and emotional relationships.

President John F. Kennedy was a noted fan of the musical, and shortly after his assassination in November 1963, the word "Camelot" began to be associated with his time in the White House, especially his picture-perfect family. In the decades since, Camelot has come to signify idyllic happiness, beauty, peacefulness, and enlightenment. Some of these Camelot moments are fleeting, while others span much longer lengths of time.

So many of life's treasured moments center on feelings of self-worth, success, and love. As seasons accumulate, we review experiences, episodes, and events—from the mundane to the exquisite. Without any means of explanation, these moments become signposts of life's journey. Some are sun-drenched, while others are flooded with moonlight. A few life-changing moments are gifts written in Heaven's stars, interspersed among gloomy clouds of uncertainty. Regardless of origin, however, these moments cozily wrap our heart, emotions, and mind in an addictive comfort we never want to end.

What Camelot moments fill your life? What milestones or achievements identify your kingdom of the mind? Success in school, being accepted in a particular group, or sharing moments with a special loved one? For some, a Camelot moment is often a first-time experience, a newness that leaves an indelible, idealistic impression upon emotions and memory. Perhaps it was landing your first job or winning an award. Maybe it was passing your driving test or graduating from high school, college, or military boot camp.

Camelot moments can be wrapped in solitude, like lying in bed in the quiet early morning hours before dawn, coasting beneath a warm blanket with peaceful thoughts. Camelot moments can also come at the end of a hectic day, thanks to a soothing bath or shower that washes away stress as droplets of warm water refresh body and spirit. Camelot moments can be reading bedtime stories to pajama-clad children, listening to their night prayers, or silently wishing them sweet dreams as you watch them sleep.

Camelot moments are the reward for facing daily challenges, meeting obligations, accomplishing goals, and dispensing human kindness, consideration, and love. Amid our struggles, sorrows, sadness, and tears, Camelot moments await their turn to renew the spirit, validate efforts, and encourage us to pursue our destiny with courage and resolve.

When your years become measured in decades and the speed of life has been reduced to school-zone standards, an unstructured schedule offers additional opportunities to reflect upon previous choices, intentions, promises, regrets, plusses, minuses, plans, and projects. Elevating any of these to Camelot moments is a personal choice. Contributing factors may be subtle or profound, selected and nominated by a committee of one—you.

As past days are remembered, memories guide you through the most treasured times of your life. Truly, these are very private places of the heart. At times these moments arrive completely unannounced, causing the spirit to soar, heart to sing, and eyes to glow with a smile of joy at the unexpected recollection.

These moments are the precious gemstones of living. Be willing to share their brilliant poignancy with family, friends, and colleagues. Recall that at the end of Lerner and Lowe's musical, King Arthur knights a young boy, telling him to pass on the story of Camelot so that future generations never forget what once was. By having a Camelot moment exchange with the ones you love, you fulfill that promise.

(2012)

A Chance to Do Better

A few days before graduating from Whiting High School in June 1958, a girl in my senior class passed around a scrapbook and asked each of us to write something in it. Quickly reviewing the last four years, I was fully aware of my lack of achievement, woeful academic standing, inept social skills, misuse of time, and wasted opportunities. When it came time to record my entry, I wrote these words: "All I want is a chance to do better."

At 17, I didn't have a clue how life would unfold, but trusted that Heaven would be kind. Such trust was well placed because opportunities for a chance to do better arrived frequently. In December 1960, the editors of *McCall's* magazine printed their annual holiday message, asking readers to spare five minutes of their day and give that time as a gift. "This allotment of time is at once the most precious and most common. It is bestowed on all—young and old, high and low, just and unjust, wise and foolish, ill and well—and the use we make of it may enrich us beyond dreams of avarice or render us very poor indeed."

We don't think about it often, but each day arrives as a gift of 1,440 minutes. I promised myself then that if I ever became a teacher—a dream then in the most embryonic of stages—I'd challenge my students to share a portion of their day-gift with others. Fast-forward over a decade later, when as a full-fledged teacher instructing high school students, I was ready to put my earlier thoughts into action.

Now I didn't want to sound preachy or lofty and risk turning my students off. My goal was to create a bumper sticker-length phrase that was easy to understand but also carried a deeper meaning. Thus in September 1972, just prior to dismissing my class, I said: "Remember to help Mom with the dishes!"

I explained that "Help Mom with the dishes" is a personal commitment to promote and demonstrate kindness, thoughtfulness, and love. "Help Mom with the dishes" means we make our own sunshine and willingly share it with others to brighten, enrich, and enhance the lives we touch. With busy schedules and preoccupation with daily activities, seldom do we pause long enough to give thanks or acknowledge appreciation for life's good moments. While we do identify a few special occasions to celebrate loved ones and friends, we can do better.

Everyone ought to stand for something. Our character should be so well defined that at the mention of our name, specific images appear in others' minds. This is true for celebrities, political figures, and other renowned (or infamous) individuals. What about us? What image comes to mind at the mention of our name?

Our image—validation of who and what we are—reflects the sum total of our character. Words and deeds over a lifetime demonstrate the values we hold most dear. Hopefully trust, honor, respect, and responsibility are top-most, seasoned with thoughtfulness, kindness, and love to form the essence of our humanness.

Regardless of gender, age, station in life, color, or creed, we're all the same. We want to be successful, feel necessary, and belong. We want to be accepted, valued, and loved, and we want to find someone we can love in return. Most importantly, we are all teachers, as we learn so much from each other.

Some might question the value of five minutes. How can 300 seconds from a daily supply of 86,400 give meaning to this chance to do better? Ask yourself: Could you spare five minutes to turn the other cheek, be tolerant, and do unto others as you would have done unto you? Could you spare five minutes to protect the weak, defend the persecuted, comfort those who mourn, and love your neighbor as yourself? Could you spare five minutes to feed the hungry, assist a stranger, or cherish a child? Could you spare five minutes to offer mercy, give without expectation of receiving, and forgive those who have been unkind? Could you spare five minutes to lessen anxiety, choose between good and evil, and share your sunshine?

How could five minutes make a difference or have an impact? Because we share a common journey and understand that the journey should be as enjoyable as the destination. Even though we favor an occasional respite—time to kick back, relax, and put things on hold—we should be acutely aware of our duties, commitments, and responsibilities, remaining faithful to the promise for a chance to do better.

(2012)

Change

This is about change. Not the stamped metal coins we carry in a pocket or purse, but the change that affects the way we live our lives.

One of life's most important lessons is how long to hold on and when to let go. We learn, too, that this lesson is continuous throughout our days and affects the seasons within ourselves. Change is caused by time, technology, knowledge, and people. The majority of change is automatic, gradual in nature, and usually unnoticed. However, there are occasions when unexpected circumstances and events result in anxiety, uncertainty, and concern. Preparing for these passages affords us the time to make necessary mindset adjustments. Even so, we have a reluctance to embrace uncharted pathways, and emotional discomfort isn't always easy to accept.

Change is inevitable. Often when it occurs, change pushes aside values and traditions, causing stress and unsettled feelings. Some change is welcomed and accepted, particularly when longstanding, cherished traditions are retained, honored, and celebrated. But other changes are more difficult to reconcile and endorse. The challenge is finding and sustaining the proper balance between what is new and what is old, what to save and what to discard, and what to hold on to and what to let fade away.

Not too many years ago, traditional values were well defined, acknowledged, and readily accepted. Basic codes of family, self-reliance, independence, faith, and responsibility served as the foundation for a productive life. Youngsters, for the most part, followed examples taught by their elders as they matured to adulthood. Maintaining the status quo in society was rewarded with support, approval, positive self-image, and elevated self-esteem. In schools throughout America, Judeo-Christian principles and common sense were at the core of the curriculum. Good judgment was the product of effective parental nurturing, family upbringing, religious instruction, structured schooling, and personal interaction. Communities were anchored and strengthened by the societal triad: family, church, and school.

Today, accelerated by technology, we're living in an age where change has affected many traditional values. A number of these values have been ridiculed and presented as outdated remnants of past times and unsophisticated human behavior. In vogue are viewpoints that promote political correctness, challenge gender roles, devalue religious beliefs, propagate secular tenets, deride parental and educational authority, and sanction crude and rude behavior.

Treasured values of work ethic, initiative, honor, trust, and responsibility are too often degraded, denigrated, and marginalized. They're being replaced with phony praise, bogus achievements, and gratuitous handouts. Adding further negative influence to change is the misuse of electronic technology. Hurtful comments, damaging allegations, and gossip—often posted anonymously—are inescapable in online forums and social media.

Often change is instituted and promoted by elected officials through policies and agencies that serve political agendas. Legislative consent, executive orders, and court decisions override and replace longstanding values with both subtle and drastic change. Founded in political ideology and supported by special interests, biased media, pundits and agenda-driven activists, perspectives of traditional values are often skewed and distorted. In recent years we've witnessed an erosion of social, personal, and virtuous behavior and values.

But all is not dark clouds and gloom—there's some good news! The majority of change comes from the actions of honorable, well-intentioned citizens. At conferences, summits, committees, and dinner tables throughout America, decisions are made after careful consideration of facts, insightful analysis, mathematical certainty, public opinion, social behavior, and study and review of circumstance. Executive, legislative, and judicial accord, coupled with voter consensus, is also a catalyst for change. Not everyone always agrees, of course. Compromise always comes at some cost to all sides of an issue. And there's always discourse to refine, amend, or repeal unfavorable aspects of change.

We often forget that we change every day. We're certainly not the person today that we were as a child. We've experienced internal and external change. Each day we adapt to current circumstances. We develop strategies to compensate for physical maladies, limitations, decreased energy, and declining vitality. We fully understand if there is no struggle, there is no progress.

We live in a rapidly changing world. Every one of the day's 1,440 minutes is filled with adventure, challenge, promise, and potential. As seasoned citizens, we understand the sometimes unexpected and unsettling feelings caused by change. But we must remember that change is an integral part of life, tangible evidence of our participation in the parade of seasons and confirmation of progress along life's journey.

(2014)

Choices

Every day we make choices. Choices that determine what we eat, how we shop, the way we work, and overall, the way we live. For example: pencil or pen, save or spend, cash or charge, paper or plastic, credit or debit, savings or checking, fixed or ARM, cell or landline, cable or dish.

Or consider all of the choices we make when eating: McDonald's or Burger King, White Castle or Wendy's, tacos or burgers, coffee or tea, regular or decaf, sweetened or unsweetened, sugar or artificial sweetener, fat or nonfat, whole or skim, Coke or Pepsi, regular or diet, red or white, meat or fish, chicken or turkey, regular or crispy, fried or broiled, soup or salad, french fries or hash browns, salted or unsalted, fried or scrambled, white or wheat, butter or margarine, "For here" or "To go."

How did we come to the point in life where it's this or that, here or there? Solids or stripes, Cubs or White Sox, Bears or Colts, hurry or wait, smoking or non-smoking, black and white or color, fresh or frozen, Republican or Democrat, oil or latex, laptop or desktop, PC or Mac, Blackberry or iPhone, online or in person, Google or Yahoo, public or private, shower or bath, hot or cold, combed or messy, clean-shaven or bearded, shorts or slacks, button-down or pullover, heels or flats, glasses or contacts, parallel or angle.

Choice is everywhere and for everything: *Times* or *Tribune*, AM or FM, radio or television, avenue or street, highway or byway, car or train, fly or drive, Ford or GM, sedan or SUV, V6 or V8, automatic or stick, tinted or clear, Shell or BP, walk or don't walk, stop or go, enter or leave, brand name or generic, Nike or Reebok, Target or Walmart, Carson's or Kohl's, Jewel or Strack's, Menards or Home Depot, single or married, marriage or divorce, faithful or unfaithful, press 1 or press 2.

Some choices are made without our input: male or female, young or old, brother or sister, uncle or aunt, right-handed or left-handed, tall or short. But so many others are ours alone to make: open or closed, locked or unlocked, digital or analog, cold or hot, oven or microwave, clean or dirty, neat or sloppy, washed or unwashed, classy or tacky, honest or corrupt, trustworthy or false-hearted, truthful or deceitful, responsible or reckless, loving or hateful, generous or selfish, help or hinder, praise or punish, give or take, contribute or withhold, add or subtract, unite or separate, agree or disagree, laugh or cry, smile or frown, hug or hurt.

We have so many choices to make, so many opportunities to enrich lives, touch hearts, lift spirits, and celebrate one another and ourselves. Some choices can be life changing, while others are more mundane and so seemingly insignificant that they slip by unnoticed. But some choices made in ordinary moments, meant to simply to embellish our day, help transform those moments into extraordinary opportunities.

Everywhere and always there are choices. Choices beget options, options beget decisions, and decisions beget character. The sum total of our choices defines the quality of our character: optimist or pessimist, positive or negative, joyful or unhappy, pleased or displeased, cherished or unloved, prayerful or arrogant, together or alone, at peace or in turmoil, connected or isolated, welcomed or shunned, part of the problem or part of the solution, forgiving or unforgiving, even-tempered or rigid, open-minded or closed-minded, willing or unwilling, bitter or sweet, fulfilled or unfulfilled, regretful or satisfied.

Each of us every day, from dawn to dark, employs thoughts and other mechanisms to navigate through the maze of choices that confront and challenge our wants and needs. How effectively we make these choices and the manner in which our decisions are rendered will enrich and enhance or detract and diminish the quality of our lives. Some choices become habits while others are just one-time necessities, but regardless of frequency or circumstance, the choices we make leave indelible marks on us—mind, spirit, and heart.

What's your next selection? The choice is yours.

(2010)

Christmas 1952:
A Remembrance

One of the things I love about Christmas is thinking about that time of year when I was a youngster. In 1952, I was a seventh-grader at Sacred Heart School under the watchful eyes of Sister Bernard Marie. Early in the semester, we'd tested her patience by stringing an extension cord from the cloakroom outlet to a small radio stashed behind some volumes in a classroom bookcase so we could clandestinely listen to the New York Yankees defeat the Brooklyn Dodgers in the World Series. Discovered only when we forgot to turn down the volume during a Gillette Blue Blades commercial, we learned Sister was a Yankees fan and enjoyed listening too.

Returning to school after Thanksgiving, we began preparing for Christmas. For years, Sacred Heart Church featured a boys' choir prior to the start of Midnight Mass, and I'd been a choirboy since fifth grade. I was now also an altar boy, but serving at Midnight Mass was an exclusive privilege for high school students, so the boys' choir it was for me.

On Christmas Eve, Wednesday, December 24, 1952, at 10:30 pm, with Sacred Heart Church filled to capacity, we filed out of the sacristy on either side of the sanctuary, holding booklets with the carols and hymns we would be singing. With single blue votive candles marking each choirboy's place behind the communion rail, we faced the congregation. Melvin Schaffer accompanied us on the small pedal organ in the sanctuary, and as was tradition, we began the evening's program with "O Little Town of Bethlehem." Ending just before 11:00 pm with an acappella "Silent Night," many in the congregation joined in with us, singing about heavenly peace through tear-filled eyes.

As Midnight Mass formally began, we turned toward the altar. Celebrants included the pastor, Father Herman J. Miller, the assistant pastor, Father John Daniels, and two deacons who were sons of the parish, twin brothers John and Stephen Vrabel. Folding chairs provided choirboys seating for the homily, but we knelt on the floor during the Mass of the Faithful. We also served as candle bearers during the Offertory and Consecration. Standing, kneeling, or walking in procession required extra focus to keep the candle ramrod straight, preventing hot, melting wax from dripping on tender fingers.

Years before Vatican II, liturgical prayers were in Latin. Congregational responses resounded throughout the church like ecclesiastical poetry. The atmosphere within Sacred Heart was solemn and reverent, but also festive. Colorful lights and tinsel decorated fir trees in the sanctuary and served as background to the Nativity scene displayed in an alcove by the confessional on the church's east side.

Mass ended around 12:30 am with the whole congregation singing "Joy to the World." Then, amid blessings and exchanging earnest wishes of "Merry Christmas," parishioners, servers, and choirboys headed into the 23-degree darkness of early Christmas morning. Walking the three blocks back to our house on Cleveland Avenue with my dad, I quick-stepped in and out of frozen footprints left by neighbors during an earlier snowfall.

Returning home, we immediately felt the warm embrace of the radiators' steam heat as we entered through the front door. The aroma of the fresh bread and nut roll my mom had baked earlier on Christmas Eve still hung in the air. Mom hadn't gone to bed yet, and was tidying up the kitchen.

Sleepy as I was, I found enough energy for a glass of milk and a thick slice of homemade bread, buttered and jellied. Enjoying this ultimate late-night snack in our darkened parlor, I sat near the unlit Christmas tree, its strands of tinsel shimmering like crystals of ice. A few moments later, now upstairs in my bed—warm, well fed, and snuggled cozily under a down-filled comforter—I drifted off to sleep.

The most popular Christmas song of 1952 was a new one. "I Saw Mommy Kissing Santa Claus" was recorded by 13-year-old Jimmy Boyd, just two years my senior. Played alongside seasonal standards "White Christmas," "Jingle Bells," "Frosty the Snowman," and "It's Beginning to Look a Lot Like Christmas," there was music galore coming from the Montgomery Ward Airline radio/phono console in our parlor that December.

As I recall, 1952 had been an event-filled year: the Korean War raged, Dwight D. Eisenhower had been elected president for the first of what would be two terms, the Yankees had won the World Series, and Sears catalogs continued to dazzle and entice consumers of all ages. As a seventh-grader, a maturing awareness of world events vied with personal interests for my pre-adolescent attention. Movies, music, sports, radio, and a new gadget called television were becoming ever more important to my own social well-being.

While a multitude of memories have been formed in the many years since, Christmas 1952 always engenders heartfelt remembrance and appreciation of faith, family, and friends. As I approach my seventy-fifth orbit around the sun, there remains a childlike wonder and joy for this very special day of days. Merry Christmas, everyone!

(2015)

Christmas Thoughts

As daylight hours diminish and temperatures recede to adolescent numbers, northern latitudes gear up for the seasonal change from autumn to winter. Weather conditions are erratic. One day might be balmy enough for a light jacket, but the next brings blustery, bone-chilling cold with precipitation in both liquid and frozen forms. As darkness encroaches further into late afternoon, both pedestrian and vehicular travel require additional concentration. Shoppers negotiate hectic parking lots and maneuver in store aisles in an effort to fill lists of treasures believed essential for a merry Christmas.

Malls, stores, and shops of all stripes are in full holiday mode in their attempt to attract, court, and convince consumers to spend, charge, lay-away, or special order gifts in time for them to be wrapped and under the tree on Christmas Eve. Festive music, holiday lights, evergreens festooned with ornaments, and other decorations of ribbons, baubles, and bells stimulate the senses to capture the spirit of the season.

Last month, we were focused on Thanksgiving. It was nice to remember the Pilgrims and enjoy the bounty presented on the dinner table, but now we're focused on Christmas. So long Pilgrims, hello Santa! Holiday advertising is everywhere, from television and radio to print and online. There are door-buster bargains, slashed prices, big sales, special coupons, gift-card bonuses, and early-bird offers. We're in a dizzying blizzard of cost-saving opportunities that won't let up until stores close on Christmas Eve.

Hopefully, the true message of Christmas will be at the forefront and not obscured by excessive commercialism, thing-driven mindsets, and materialistic secular symbols. Christmas is a time for celebrating the most important birth the world has ever known.

Ages before slick advertising, electronic messaging, and contrived holiday spin, the gift of gifts was presented without pretense or fanfare to all humankind. The birth of Jesus Christ signaled the manifestation of the Word. God sent His only son, the Savior, to teach, suffer, redeem, and defeat the corruption of sinfulness. He provided salvation and the pathway to Heaven's endless happiness and love. The Prince of Peace was born in humble surroundings, and the tidings were clear: "Peace on earth, good will to men." Although Jesus Christ never wrote a single word on His own behalf, His message has endured, thrived, and remains powerful after more than 2000 years.

Amid all modern seasonal trappings, galas, parties, and other social gatherings, may your heart, mind, and spirit be filled with all that is kind, thoughtful, good, and blessed. May agreement be reached whereby the true meaning of Christmas takes priority over all manufactured holiday ploys. And may human actions worldwide reflect heartfelt sharing and giving of time, love, kindness, thoughtfulness, caring, and compassion.

As a child, Christmas was a time of anticipation, wonder, mystery, and magic. Tempered by economic realities, there were questions about a family in Bethlehem and a fellow from the North Pole. Christmas traditions of Midnight Mass, decorated conifers, and brightly wrapped presents were complemented with seasonal radio programs, music, carols, and hymns.

Beginning with the wonder years of adolescence and continuing throughout adulthood, we discover and understand how emotions and matters-of-the-heart enrich the spirit of Christmas. There's a realization that God's gift of love is ours to convey, bestow, share, and live each day. The gift of Christmas is humankind's ultimate present: unlimited quantity, one size fits all, no assembly or batteries required, no expiration date, and recipients are encouraged to exchange this present with everyone!

Today, as a seasoned citizen, with the accumulation of calendars well documented and a once carefree mind now mature and experienced, my celebration of Christmas is more subdued than in years past. There's less emphasis on gift-wrapped things and more focus on family get-togethers and holyday commemoration of Christ's birth.

Due to favoring an early bedtime hour, Midnight Mass has given way to the Christmas Vigil or Morning Mass. Thanks to adult children, our home's landscape and interior continue to be fully decorated in yuletide splendor. The tree is trimmed with keepsake ornaments, as gaily-wrapped presents bask underneath artificial pine branches with colorful lights. A homemade Nativity is prominently displayed for all to see. Currier and Ives would be pleased.

May Santa fill your stocking with all good things. May it be a Merry and Most Blessed Christmas for you and your loved ones. May the gift of the first Christmas be received, accepted, cherished, and shared. And may God bless us all.

(2012)

A Container for Dreams

As soon as we reach the age of awareness, dreams become part of life. Sparked by events and imagination, each of us begins a wish list. Special events during the year, like our birthday and Christmas, increase the urgency, but our dreams, wishes, hopes, and wants are usually an outgrowth of personal and private experiences.

In ways not completely understood, we store our dreams in containers within ourselves. As kids, we guard these dreams in very private ways. We don't enjoy being teased or chided about our far-fetched, pie-in-the-sky desires that might seem even more impossible to others, so we often keep these wishes to ourselves.

But as we gain self-confidence and self-assurance, we begin to talk about our hopes and dreams, albeit only with trusted family members or friends. We still remain guarded, proceeding cautiously about when and where we give voice to our innermost fantasies. During adolescence, this approach-avoidance conflict is further tested with considerable anxiety, apprehension, and uncertainty. On occasion, our trust in others is misplaced, and we suffer embarrassment and personal distress when promises are broken, confidence is violated, and our private feelings are laid bare for all to know.

As we mature, we become more protective of our secret dreams and hopes, wary of thrusting ourselves into the spotlight. We subconsciously build protective walls around emotions and feelings in order to prevent or reduce discomfort, pain, and negative reactions to our most sensitive thoughts. Unfortunately, such safeguards can have an adverse impact because without external encouragement and support, many dreams die.

But maturity also provides the ability to reconsider earlier hopes and dreams. As a kid, I dreamed of having a horse like 12-year-old Bobby

Benson did on the *B-Bar-B Ranch* radio program. And for a time, I thought it would be cool to have a cave like Batman. Thankfully, there are unseen monitors who prevent such dreams from becoming reality.

As a youngster, I was promised a bicycle but family financial problems prevented that dream from coming to fruition. Instead I scavenged neighborhood alleys for essential parts and ultimately only had to purchase a seat and fenders. My alley bike served me well for several years, and a valuable lesson was learned: Most of the time we have to make our own dreams come true.

Even so, there are numerous occasions when the Dream Maker takes control and guides events just enough for dreams to take hold, to keep hope alive, and to grant wishes unexpectedly and at opportune moments. The Dream Maker employs strangers, acquaintances, friends, family and a multitude of circumstances—some planned, some happenstance—in order to set into motion the actions necessary for dream elements to blossom. The dream may involve relationships, employment, life lessons, success, recognition, or acquisition of personal property. Some call such opportune moments luck, good fortune, blessings, or fate.

Most of us accept life's benevolence without much reflective thought. But analysis would reveal our personal contributions—hard work, preparation, faith, dedication, and resolve—in partnership with the Dream Maker. Without personal involvement, dreams wither. Dreams don't come true because they're supposed to. They bear fruit because of commitment and investment of time, energy, and effort.

Over a lifetime, we accumulate dreams, wishes, hopes, and wants that never come to be. Some are discarded as ill-conceived, unrealistic, or impractical, and are tossed away. Others are set aside due to unforeseen circumstances like new obligations, health issues, financial limitations, or simply waiting for the right time. A few, just on the verge of accomplishment, are consciously ended because the price is too high. These all fill our container for dreams.

How many of our dreams have been set aside and left unrealized? How often have our hopes been dashed or wishes silenced due to fear of criticism, ridicule, and rejection from others? How many times has the Dream Maker been shunned because of our timidity? How many opportunities were bypassed due to insufficient emotional strength? Why were there times we remained silent about our dreams, wishes, hopes, and wants because of apprehension, suspicion, or doubt?

Now is the time to open your container for dreams. Give them a fresh look and consider how much richer life would be if these personal desires came to be. Most dreams, hopes, wishes, and wants don't have an expiration date. Like honey, they never spoil and are always ready to nourish the heart, energize the spirit, and bring a special peace of mind.

What treasures are in your container for dreams?

(2011)

Cultural Awakening

America recently celebrated the 50th anniversary of the Beatles' first television appearance in February 1964 on *The Ed Sullivan Show* and the Fab Four's subsequent impact on American culture. On TV, retrospective programs focused on the Beatles' talent and how they changed popular music in the 1960s, while on the radio, hosts used the occasion to ask listeners to call in and share significant events that affected their youth, altered the status quo, and brought about a cultural awakening.

My teenage years, comprising the period from January 1954 to January 1961, were spent in Whiting, Indiana, my hometown. With a population of just over 10,000, this municipal square mile and a half of neighborhoods, schools, churches, businesses, and factories served as the ideal locale for families to work, learn, worship, shop, and relax. Whiting residents (and those in the neighboring Robertsdale community) had access to the best amenities and enjoyed the time of their lives in "The Little City by the Lake."

Traditional family values, appropriate personal and social behavior, solid moral reputation, and respect for adult authority were hallmarks of this industrial Mayberry. Even so, emerging youthful independence, growing self-confidence, teenage freedom, and adolescent rebellion— represented by fads, fashion, and music, and emboldened by spending money from part-time jobs—challenged the status quo and tested adults' understanding and tolerance.

In concert with biological maturation, my cultural awakening involved a transition from parochial grade school to Whiting High School, and was further shaped by radio, television, music, movies, books, and regular visits to the Community Center as both patron and pinboy. Many of these teenage chronicles were interrelated and interconnected. Invisible threads of friendship, education, faith, and mentoring provided the support and courage necessary to take risks and pursue personal ambitions and dreams. Though fraught with anxiety and apprehension, as well as fear of rejection and failure, these years were filled with exciting, impulsive, passionate, and wonderful moments of youthful invincibility. Fortunately, the majority of these youthful escapades resulted in pleasant consequences.

With apologies to the Fab Four, who arrived a few years too late to impact my adolescent awakening, here's a partial record of the people, places, and events that did:

AM radio begins airplay of Rhythm & Blues ... Eddie Fisher, Doris Day, et al, give way to The Crew-Cuts, The Chordettes, and The Penguins ... Freshman year begins at majestic Whiting High School—tradition, quality, and excellence ... The Oilers win the 1954 State Football Championship! ... Drugstores and street corners become teen hangouts ... Whiting Park ... Local radio picks up on R&B and Doo-Wop ... WWCA (Gerry Gerard), WJJD, WJOB, WIND (Howard Miller) ... *Blackboard Jungle* is the top movie at the Hoosier Theatre in April 1955 ... "Rock Around the Clock" reaches #1 on the charts ... Hollywood movies with an anti-authority theme (*Rebel Without a Cause, The Wild One*) resonate with teens, and James Dean and Marlon Brando become the newest heartthrobs of the silver screen.

RCA introduces the 45 rpm record ... Television in glorious black & white! ... Elvis Presley's first TV appearance in January 1956 ... His popularity skyrockets and "Heartbreak Hotel" becomes a #1 hit ... Billboard's Hot 100: The Platters, Bill Haley & His Comets, Pat Boone, Fats Domino, Ricky Nelson and others ... Street dances ... Neal Price's selection (listening booths, records, radios, phonographs, and TVs!) and the best staff (Mr. Price, Jim Grass, Lulu Kammer) ... Rock 'n' roll becomes the anthem of teenagers ... Dick Clark's *American Bandstand* debuts in August 1957 ... Local teens in Philadelphia become national celebrities (Justine Carrelli, Bob Clayton, Kenny Rossi, Arlene Sullivan) and the show becomes teen central for top hits, recording artists, and new dances.

The Mickey Mouse Club introduces America to *Spin and Marty* and Annette Funicello ... Every home has ears—rabbit ears for TVs and mouse ears for Mouseketeers ... ABC launches *The Dick Clark Saturday Night Beech-Nut Show* in February 1958 ... IFIC buttons ... WWCA disc jockeys become celebrity personalities, including Vivian Carter's "Livin' with Vivian" ("How are all you powder puffs and sponges out there?") and Dizzy Dixon ("Spinning 45s back-to-back without much yakety-yak!") ... Pocket transistor radios ... Sunday night dances at St. John's Panel Room ... Condes Restaurant ... The payphone booths at the Illiana Hotel and the Whiting Community Center for privacy ... Nick's Pool Room ... Hot Dog Louie's "gourmet" dining ... Portable 45 rpm record players ... Jukeboxes offering three plays for 25 cents ("Moonlight Gambler," "Love Is Strange," "The Green Door").

Chandik's adolescent oasis, The Oil Can ... Shoreline buses ... Friday-night sock hops after the game ... Work permit ... Whiting Community Center (WCC) and its general, Andy Yanas ... WCC pinboy ... Whiting High School Senior Prom at Madura's Danceland ... Graduation 6-4-58 ... Inland Steel apprenticeship ... April 1959: First wheels, a 1954 Oldsmobile Rocket 88 ... Driver's license ... Drive-in restaurants and carhops (Art's, Blue Top, Fat Boy, Kelly's, Patio, Pow-Wow, Serenade, and Son's) ... Cruisin' with friends ... Gas for 25 cents a gallon ... Sandra Dee and Troy Donahue in *A Summer Place* ... Movies and soundtracks capture teen hearts ... Teen idols become recording stars (Frankie Avalon, Annette Funicello, Fabian, Ricky Nelson, and the Everly Brothers).

WLS switches over to rock 'n' roll on June 1, 1960 ... "Alley-Oop!" ... Dick Biondi, Mort Crowley, Jim Dunbar, Art Roberts, Clark Weber, and the rest of the Silver Dollar Survey gang rule the airwaves ... Top 40 radio is king! ... The 41 Outdoor Drive-In ... a 1960 Oldsmobile 98 convertible with custom-made bug-proof screens ... One-hit wonders add to the soundtrack of our life ... Movies with favorite teen stars capture adolescent hearts ... White Castle, Ande's Pizza, and drugstore soda fountains, where fun and food fueled youthful exuberance.

All too quickly, such moments pass, and life continues on. But wasn't that a time!

(2014)

GUEST CHECK

TABLE	PERSONS	46394	SERVER
0	8		S-9

Dandelion, O Dandelion
A Day in the Life: Parochial School, May 1948
Delegating Blame
Diamond Cutters
Diamond Masters
Difference
DIY Driving Lesson
Drive-In Vespers

TAX

Dandelion, O Dandelion

Every spring, as the sun's daily delivery warms both earth and sky, the greenery of a new season takes the cue to display its remarkable diversity across the landscape. One plant makes its yearly appearance like an unwanted relative, however, popping up in lawns, sidewalk cracks, and other crevices. With the boldness of brass, this perennial interloper takes deep-rooted residence wherever it can, arrogantly defying humans, machines, and chemistry intent on eradication. Welcome to the annual invasion of the dandelion.

For the botanically inclined—or any future *Jeopardy!* contestants—the scientific name of this turf trespasser is Taraxacum officinale. The dandelion got its start in Eurasia millions of years ago, and while there are now a number of varieties worldwide, Taraxacum officinale is the most common.

Now before any culinary connoisseurs come after me in protest with salad forks and tongs dripping with dressing, yes, I'm fully aware of dandelions being a delicious addition to plates. But let's first focus on the plant's potential pharmacological benefits, which might make this otherwise unwanted intruder an attractive addition to our diet. Dandelions are purported to provide relief from liver disorders, jaundice, diabetes, anemia, urinary tract infections, and acne.

Dandelions are an excellent source of vitamins A, C, and K and flavonoids like luteolin that support liver function, help maintain the proper flow of bile, and encourage efficient digestion. They're diuretic in nature, and along with encouraging the production of insulin via the pancreas, can help remove excess sugar from the renal system. The bitter taste of dandelion juice further encourages lower blood sugars.

Rich in calcium, the dandelion plant can help maintain healthy skin and bones and also promote weight loss. Additionally, an enzyme is said to inhibit unwanted microbial growth and help cleanse the intestinal tract. This generous plant offers an additional therapeutic bonus: Its sap can be useful for treating certain skin conditions. In addition to incorporating raw or cooked dandelion greens at the table, some folks ingest Taraxacum officinale's botanical benefits by brewing dandelion tea or drinking dandelion wine.

Suffice it to say, this golden flower-topped plant appears to possess some surprising positives. And yet these less-heralded attributes make little difference to me. When spring arrives and dandelions sprout up again, my main objective is twofold: keeping the saffron floral seed pods from defiling my landscape and preventing the spread of seeds for the next generation.

Despite being an annual nuisance to gardens, golf courses, and other green spaces, the dandelion is a symbol of adventure. Capricious winds launch the cottony seedpods airborne, providing random dispersion far and wide—where they land and take root offers little rhyme or reason. Dandelions are an equal opportunity vegetal aggravator, readily taking up residence on neighborhood lawns and open pastures, along fairways, beside parkways, and in asphalt fissures. Sporting jagged-edged leaves that betray its tenacious grasp, dandelions send roots deep down into the soil. Stubbornly staking claim with this territorial approach, the plant challenges eviction by herbicides, weed-whackers, lawnmowers, and garden tools of every type.

The yearly battle against the takeover of Taraxacum officinale leaves me to wax poetic in both plea and protest:

O Dandelion, O Dandelion, why do you sprout?
To aggravate homeowners who must dig you out?
Why so many seeds, is that a malfunction?
Is there no such thing as dandelion dysfunction?

Your golden flower erupts through the green,
Sporting scalloped-edged leaves looking sinister and mean.
You bully your way on a stalk firm and tough,
Crowding out grass and all the good stuff.

You eagerly invade pastures and prairies,
Lawns, parkways, and golf course fairways.
Every crack in the sidewalk, crevice, or cranny,
Your procreation is unashamedly canny.

Without forethought of lust or botanical regret,
You multiply and flourish, making homeowners upset.
You produce little flowers and seeds that soar,
Knowing full well next spring there'll be more.

A smug little plant with benefits to many,
You think that'll save your flowered antennae?
After my weed-whacker has felled and feasted,
You'll be reduced to *dandy* little pieces!

Some brew and blend you into a tea,
Others make wine so potent they cannot see.
I, too, will rearrange you from plant to mulch,
And gleefully add you to my compost gulch.

I do not discount or diminish your worth,
Without question your qualities are salt of the earth.
So don't misunderstand or think that I'm crass,
But, Dandelion, O Dandelion, you're a royal pain in the grass.

(2019)

A Day in the Life: Parochial School, May 1948

He was now in the second grade in the same room as last year, a combined class of first- and second-graders that totaled 52 students, equally divided between boys and girls. Other than being chubby for his age, having a mild case of asthma, and a left ear that caught more than its share of wind, he was like any other second-grade pupil. At the Catholic school he attended, 254 students were enrolled in Grades 1 through 8, but with only six classrooms, first and second grades were combined, as were fourth and fifth grades. Taught by the Sisters of Providence, their lessons were supplemented by the weekly instructions of the parish monsignor.

The school was built, if cornerstones are to be believed, in AD 1909. Since then, the interior walls had tasted more than a score of coats of paint, while untold gallons of disinfectants had been sloshed across the floors and through the snaked plumbing of the latrines.

Every classroom featured seven rows with seven seat-desks, save for Room 1, which had a shortened eighth row near the door with four desks. All of the desks had been screwed to the floor since the school opened, with numerous applications of varnished determination glazing the desktops. Inkwell holes were left empty to thwart prankster boys from dipping the pigtails of unsuspecting girls. Desktop markings in primary grades were of simple letters, a few scratches, and an occasional heart and arrow—no profanity or real creativity. Strictly small time yet charming.

The desktops were fixed so a book and pen slid into a front opening. These seat-desks had a hinged bench that folded up when not in use and a desk attached directly to the back of the seat. With a steel frame strengthened with lattice work that spelled "school" by the time the metal met the dark-stained wood-plank floor to which it was permanently screwed, these wooden monuments to learning couldn't generate enough charm to entice a chainsaw.

Four 5-foot double-sash windows peered into an alley. Each window was fitted with a dark green shade, which usually remained at half-mast. A few struggling plants sat on the sill, pleading their case for morning sun.

The chalkboards were slate slabs. A display of machine-made ABCs printed in script on light green paper was bannered atop the one at the front of the classroom. Religious sayings decorated bulletin boards and cabinets, while a picture of a 12-year-old Jesus smiled down from its position on the wall. A statue of the Virgin Mary was majestically placed on a doily-covered mahogany pedestal in the corner.

In the front of the room, placed kitty-corner on the far left side, was the oaken throne and desk of the classroom monarch. The Good Sister, in addition to serving as their teacher, was policeman, judge, jury, and executioner. When she vented her anger with full wrath, the Good Sister gushed with all the kindness of Attila the Hun.

She was an overpowering figure dressed in a flowing habit and yards of black cloth, an outfit that only amplified the massiveness of her authority. Hanging from her waist by a braided sash of black nylon was a huge rosary, a heavenly anchor of salvation that jingled and jangled with her every step. These celestial chimes signaled an approaching alarm for misbehaving little boys who would scatter and shout, "The penguin is coming, the penguin is coming!"

As commander of the class, she was thorough and effective. Her forte was discipline through fear. A good class was one where every occurrence was planned and controlled: No one talked without first raising their hand, being acknowledged, and granted permission. Only then did a student rise from their desk, stand erect, and speak. Everything was regimented—everything! Once school began, pupils were expected to control their activities to meet the established rules.

Lavatory time came at 10:00 am and 2:00 pm—no other time. At precisely those times, the class paraded out of the room in single file, girls ahead of the boys—silently! Once in the hall, the girls would march to the far end of the hall, descend the stairs, and wait at the entrance of the washroom. The boys did the same, except their washroom was on the opposite end downstairs, adjacent to the lobby by the school's front entrance. An eighth-grade monitor (monitors were always girls) led the girls. The Good Sister led the boys.

Arranged alphabetically in three groups, the boys lined up in the lobby and stood facing the threshold of relief. Beyond the washroom's door, eight upright wall-length urinals and eight stalls of porcelain lifesavers awaited the challenges of 26 young boys.

Sister would intone, "Restroom Group 1, proceed." Nine boys hurriedly went into the restroom and relieved themselves. Within a minute, Group 1 was back in line. Group 2 proceeded with an added degree of urgency. As soon as Group 2 returned, Sister called for Group 3 to utilize the facilities. There was always a chance of accidents with Group 3. No matter how forcefully the Good Sister and monitors preached self-control, arrogant kidneys and bladders filled to capacity had their way. (Six years later, graduating from eighth grade, how much of an education they'd acquired at Sacred Heart School was uncertain but their bladder control was remarkable!)

It was in this climate of strict rules and regulations that the young second-grader prepared to meet the challenges of a new day, with all the hope and expectation that's genuinely part of a child his age.

His school day began with attendance at Holy Mass. The arrangement in church was the same as in school—girls first, then boys, with a monitor assigned to the girls and the Good Sister keeping watch over the boys. In church, however, an additional monitor was assigned to help Sister detect infractions of the rules because of the larger group assembled. There was a list of no-nos, cardinal rules that could not be broken. It was mandated that during Mass every pupil must:

1. *Look straight ahead at all times.*
2. *Kneel up perfectly straight.*
3. *Follow the Mass, pray the Rosary, and keep your hands piously folded.*
4. *Pay no attention to your neighbor next to you.*
5. *Keep your elbows off the top of the pew.*
6. *March slowly in and out of the church.*

7. *Practice self-control at all times.*
8. *Absolutely NO talking.*

Students disobeying these rules were poked, prodded, and punished. A violation, unless caused by some obvious physical illness, demanded prompt remedial action. Sister, too busy praying for the collective salvation of her pupils, left the watchdogging to the monitors. They would write down the student's name, along with the infraction, and pass it along to Sister after Mass while marching their charges back to school.

To receive Holy Communion during Mass, students were to have fasted since midnight (no food, no water). Therefore, they were allowed to bring breakfast with them to school.

Now in the classroom after church, the boy spread a protective oilcloth on his desk and unwrapped the peanut butter and jelly sandwich his mom had prepared. A half-pint bottle of milk (purchased for 6 cents) stood like a perspiring soldier, awaiting the insertion of a straw. On days when he received Communion, he wore his Sunday clothes—a white shirt and tie— as Sister encouraged this display of additional respect for the Sacrament. He'd have to be careful not to spill anything while he ate.

The class was in order. First-graders recited their numbers, while second-graders silently read a grammar lesson. Even those eating at their desks were expected to read along, too. In fifteen minutes, recitation would begin, and the first-graders would silently practice printing numbers. With a mouthful of sandwich and milk, he was enjoying his breakfast, occasionally glancing at his text to see what kind of words made nouns.

Now, in a momentary lapse of concentration during Mass, he had spread his elbows along the edge of the pew. Unbeknownst to him, the monitor had observed the infraction and reported the violation to the Good Sister: A rule had been broken, a sin committed. Exhibition of such weakness had to be corrected. Without hesitation, the Good Sister decided he must suffer the consequences.

With a single motion of her right arm, the Good Sister clamped her fingers on his right ear and pulled. At once he was airborne, leaving a spray of partially chewed sandwich and swallowed milk. The milk bottle fell to the floor and broke but went unnoticed—all eyes were on them.

Yanked across row eight, he landed semi-erect and found himself pinned against the cold slate by the strength of righteousness. Towering over him with her robe whirling and celestial chimes violently rattling, she pushed, pulled, yanked, and jerked the very devil from him.

All but hidden from view, he was an image of terror as he struggled for release. Necktie askew, food on his lips, her voice thundering in his ear: "No self-control, no self-control!" Fingers once on his ear now gripped his shoulders as both aggressive arms came into play. He was getting it, but good.

Throttled with such force, his head bounced and re-bounced against the slate. It was a kaleidoscope of disorder. The punisher and the punished. *CRACK*. A bone? The blackboard. It had fractured top to bottom.

At once the cranial dribbling stopped. The devil was gone. The boy was banished to sit on the floor for the remainder of the day, the vacant front corner of the classroom now filled. There he worked on his lessons, each stroke of the pencil adding soil to his paper. Total castigation. The price had been paid.

Early religious lessons taught him not to condemn but forgive, not to harbor hate but offer kindness. He remembered the words about God's goodness, and that God sees goodness in everyone. To himself, he thought, that might be true, but God's eyesight was so much better than his.

He returned to school the next day, of course—and the day after that, month after month—but it was never quite the same. Even so, aside from an occasional pitfall here and there, his progress throughout school was commendable. Notwithstanding a brief suspension in seventh grade, his overall record was something to be proud of. Early in June 1954, he graduated. The beginning was over. He would comment later that after eight years of grade school, his cup of kindness was not quite half full.

EPILOGUE

Secondary school was a place of exuberance, an unbelievable place where no one stayed in the same classroom all day. A place where each student had a locker—their own locker, with a lock! A place where a kid could go to the restroom as needed. High school encouraged responsibility, self-reliance, independence, and self-discipline.

High school students were offered a variety of choices: English, mathematics, social sciences, foreign languages, physical education, and various electives. He found he enjoyed academics, but machine shop soon became his favorite and the focus of his available time. Though some kids and a few teachers distanced themselves from students taking non-college prep courses, he didn't mind. The sight of metal cutting metal, perfumed by heated oil, was worth the price of their prattle. He liked this class, and he belonged. Time and again he sought counsel from his teacher, a master of machines and pedagogics, and his respect for this apostle of basement scholars paralleled that of his parents.

On the fourth day in June 1958, after four seemingly short years, he graduated from high school. He followed this with an apprenticeship in machine trades that bore fruit of accomplishment five years later—a Machinist Journeyman card. But with steel-mill monotony and sleep-robbing shift work, his feeling of satisfaction diminished. What should he do? What could he do?

Once more, he turned to his former machine shop teacher for advice. And like so many times before, the reply came back seasoned with wisdom and kindness: "Why, you must become a teacher, of course." And so he did—I did.

Over the years, I've looked back on these experiences with mixed emotions. From classroom to factory, factory to campus, and campus to classroom, there was a continual search for satisfaction—a desire to grow, improve, and learn. The most important thing I learned is that the triumph over sadness isn't easy. Such personal victory requires that we pardon ourselves and forgive all others. In addition, we need an unflinching belief in the goodness of people, a positive sense of humor, and a degree of faith and reverence for things that cannot be seen.

Even though as a second-grader I played a role that resulted in a cracked blackboard, my spirit remained resilient, whole, and intact. I believe everything that ever happened to me was a lesson I needed to learn. Regardless of method or means of instruction, those events and experiences helped me acquire essential insight, problem-solving skills, and coping strategies. Most importantly, I discovered the healing power of laughter and how to enjoy and celebrate life's blessings.

(2018 - Previously unpublished)

Delegating Blame

Delegating blame is fast becoming our new national pastime. At all levels of American life, we're quick to identify bad guys and point fingers.

In the good ol' days of the Cold War we could shake a collective fist at Communism and the Soviet Union. Along the way, we've had problems with Iran, Grenada, Nicaragua, Libya, Panama, and Iraq. These trouble spots helped keep attention away from us, focusing our resentment and displeasure on any and all of these villains. Today, there's a new supply of global targets as well as a few recycled foes. This time, however, America's in the spotlight, and judging from the outcry heard near and far, people don't like what they're seeing

While it's easy for some to jump on the villain-bashing bandwagon, that's not the problem. And without question, our country must sometimes employ measures to reduce the threat of ill-minded individuals, adjust foreign policy, and employ diplomatic expertise to resolve any number of inequities. But the truth is that we did much of this to ourselves. Americans have been complacent for too long—content to rest on our laurels and not exercise our civic duties.

Today, too many of us act as if dreams come true because they're supposed to, rather than through hard work, dedication, and perseverance. This country's work ethic, coupled with inventiveness, ingenuity, and imagination, has always been the hallmark of the American spirit. Lately, we seem to have set aside the very values that made this country the crown jewel of planet Earth. In their place, we now assign blame.

With the economy erratic and struggling for positive consistency, outcries to question all things foreign gain favor. With rising social problems, the government is urged to do more. Elected officials are challenged to find solutions, and organizations of every persuasion are asked to provide more to those in need. Many of these requests are well founded and deserve attention. Some, however, are misguided and warrant careful review.

Our litany of concerns reads like a Who's Who of what's wrong with the country. Our nation is hurting, and as Americans we must heal the wounds within. Somehow we have to find effective, equitable solutions to problems. Consider healthcare, energy dependence, budget deficits, abortion, dysfunctional families, child abuse, racism, drug addiction, joblessness, alcoholism, discrimination, HIV/AIDS, cancer, other diseases, an overburdened criminal justice system, inept public officials, illiteracy, overcrowded and inferior schools, environmental desecration and destruction, corporate and political corruption, street crime, the across-the-board erosion of social, moral, and spiritual values, and... well, the list seems endless.

Studying this list carefully and honestly, it's difficult to blame anyone but us. We have allowed the fabric of our country's character to fray along the edges and tear at critical boundaries. In many ways, we have unwittingly sanctioned this erosion of responsibility. As citizens, we must reaffirm this country's ideals. We have to decide just how much we value our nation—and each other—and get the USA back on track. As a proud and honorable people, we have to work harder and more efficiently, think creatively, and increase the level of quality in all that we do.

At home and in classrooms, churches, factories, boardrooms, and government offices, Americans must renew their dedication and commitment to excellence. Parents must be accountable for their children and not expect schools or social agencies to raise them. Schools shouldn't serve as society's fix-it shops. School officials and teachers should be able to focus on their primary task of educating children.

The United States needs all of its citizens to contribute, roll up their sleeves, and do something positive and constructive each and every day. What we need is a renewal of will, a positive epidemic of responsibility and accountability. America is a generous country that welcomes all races, religions, colors, and creeds. But we need to reaffirm that the United States is also a nation of laws.

As a nation, we need to capture, cultivate, and celebrate difference. Difference is what gives democracy its strength. And the strength of America is measured in faith, goodness, and opportunity.

Americans were once demonstrably proud of their country. We had an insatiable desire to improve and welcomed the challenge to do better. Our official motto, "In God We Trust," was ingrained in every citizen. Not too many years ago, the United States was the envy of nations worldwide. Today in some areas of the world, our country is either despised as an evil empire or mocked as a laughing stock, a joke.

How can such a great nation explain and justify the disintegration of the family, abortion, abused children, drug addiction, millions of uneducated youth, and rampant corruption? What foreign country can we blame? How can the citizens of the United States justify the social, moral, and spiritual disrespect and decay of so many adults and children? What foreign country can we hold responsible?

The answer is painfully clear. To quote Shakespeare, "The fault, dear Brutus, is not in our stars. But in ourselves." Or phrased another, more brutal way (via *Pogo* cartoonist Walt Kelly): "We have met the enemy and he is us!"

(2006)

Diamond Cutters

I love baseball. Every facet of the sport intrigues me, especially as I've come to view baseball as a chess-like game played on a diamond. With its own unique lexicon, rules, and attitude, baseball is a cerebral sport and the only one where the defense controls the ball. Players need gifted athletic skills, physical stamina, good hand-eye coordination, and imperceptibly quick reflexes. But most importantly, the intangible quality that every successful player brings to baseball is pure passion—the joyful desire to excel, display maximum on-the-field effort, and never to entertain even the possibility of defeat.

By the time I turned 11 in 1952, I was hopelessly addicted to baseball. Sharing this insatiable hunger for the game with my classmates, we played at every opportunity. Even when Little League was in full swing, sandlot baseball was king, serving as bonding headquarters for friends and buddies. Without uniforms, using rag-tag equipment, and governing ourselves, countless hours of baseball-centered camaraderie ticked by in the thick of summer.

Pickup games were the norm, with sides formed by classmates and neighborhood kids. Our equipment typically consisted of coverless baseballs wrapped with layers of friction tape and previously cracked and discarded baseball bats mended with nails and screws (and like the baseballs, bandaged with friction tape). Even a proper baseball diamond wasn't a requirement: We'd play in spaces ripe with territorial plant life, cinders, broken glass, stones, gravel, and dirt much too depressed to grow vegetation. Pieces of wood or markings in the dirt served as bases.

Because there were rarely enough kids for two full teams, sandlot rules applied. With no first baseman, pitcher's hands were out. With a majority of right-handed batters, right field was out. No stealing, no walks, no leading off. Such restrictions were in place because teams used an unofficial catcher: Whoever wasn't batting that inning caught the ball and returned it to the pitcher. We umpired ourselves and group consensus ruled.

Cautious parents, wary of heavy Calumet Avenue traffic and our youthful derring-do, withheld permission to go to Forsythe Park. Sometimes we'd scale the locked fencing at Clark Field to gain access to the baseball diamond. Using an old coat to cover the barbed wire on top, kids would toss gloves, bats, and ball over the fence and then climb up and cross over the treacherous wire protected by the now punctured and torn coat.

Over at Whiting Park, the baseball field was always accessible, if otherwise minimally maintained. We'd scrape and smooth out the ruts and hindrances that interrupted grounders and one-hoppers. The fields at Standard Diamonds proved the most challenging. Cat-like reflexes were necessary to thwart potential dental visits as baseballs ricocheted off numerous impediments ingrained in the ground cover.

Several sandlot notches down, vacant lots throughout Whiting-Robertsdale provided unofficial venues for us to choose sides and play. The community played home to two particularly noteworthy fields of dreams: Kaiser Field and Sticker Stadium. Kaiser Field, favored by Robertsdale kids, was located just north of Federated Metals behind Lakeview Avenue and just west of Indianapolis Boulevard. Sticker Stadium was between the New York Central and Pennsylvania Railroads, bordered by Atchison and Cleveland Avenues in Whiting. Both of these unkempt, weed-infested parcels of real estate were transformed into mecca by the sandlot boys of summer.

Because these diamonds in the rough required considerable groundskeeping to allow game play, every couple of weeks a solitary, baseball-loving kid could be seen tending to these forsaken neighborhood parcels. These "diamond cutters," equipped with a push reel mower (sans grass catcher), plowed their way through stubborn weeds, wild grasses, sticker plants, and patches of poison ivy. Then base paths, a pitching mound, and a home plate area were marked out by eye before being shoveled, raked, filled in with dirt, and graded to suit. With mower, time, and no small amount of effort, a reasonable baseball field eventually emerged from the weeds. Diamond-cutter work was passion personified.

None of the sandlot boys of summer or diamond cutters at Kaiser Field or Sticker Stadium ever became professional baseball players. But through personal motivation and initiative, each learned the importance of commitment, a strong work ethic, and the joy and satisfaction of a job well done—nourishing what would become a lifelong love for baseball.

Such were the lessons instilled the summer I served as the diamond cutter for Sticker Stadium. With some creative license at play, the old adage that "Diamonds are a girl's best friend" also holds true for the boys of summer, particularly the diamond cutters who transformed vacant, scraggly lots in Whiting-Robertsdale into local fields of dreams.

(2017)

Diamond Masters

August 2012 marked the 60th anniversary of the greatest baseball team in history, the 1952 Whiting Little League All-Stars of Whiting, Indiana, who played in the Little League World Series in Williamsport, Pennsylvania. Let's return to the summer of '52.

It was a banner year for the Whiting Little League All-Stars. Superbly coached by Bruno Coppi and Walt Muvich, the 15 members of this team set standards of excellence that have rarely been matched. The members of the All-Stars squad included: Dan Adzia, Jack Duray, Joe Dybel, Charles "Joe" Elibacher, Rich Gaskey, Marty Jamrose, Tom Justak, Tom Kujawa, Jack Mateja, Art Mehuron, Pat O'Keefe, John Shields, Rich "Shemo" Szymanski, Steve Vrlik, and Bob White.

These young men were the cream of the crop. They earned the title "All-Star" with bat, ball, glove, and guts. Whenever they showcased their talent, spirit, and cohesive single-mindedness for victory, the ballpark's diamond dazzled with 15-carat brilliance. They were the best!

During that memorable first week in August, Whiting won the district meet in Kokomo by recording double victories over Hammond (17-2) and East Chicago (8-1). The next week in Fort Wayne, for the second consecutive year, Whiting's "Mighty Mites" (a nickname coined by the local *Hammond Times* sportswriters for reasons unknown today) dispatched all opponents in the Indiana-Michigan Sectional Tournament.

In the semi-final game against Jeffersonville, Whiting was down two runs with two outs, and on three occasions had two strikes on the batter in the last inning. Whiting rallied to tie the score, then won the game in extra innings, 13-10. For the sectional title, they defeated Sacred Heart of Fort Wayne, 2-1.

The juggernaut continued the following week, again in Fort Wayne, as Whiting won the Midwest Regional, defeating Harvey, Illinois, 5-1. This victory qualified them for the Little League World Series. From a field of 7,362 North American teams, Whiting's bubble-gum battlers were just one of eight finalists to vie for the championship prize in the single-elimination tournament.

On Tuesday, August 26, 1952, despite an early 6-0 lead over Norwalk, Connecticut, the kids from Norwalk came back to win the game 10-7, and ultimately the World Series.

Here's more about the Whiting Little League All-Stars' impressive roster:

Lead-off man **Marty Jamrose** bunted, ran, and used his quickness to get on base. He was the rally starter. He lit the fuse, knowing his teammates would supply the explosion. On defense, he patrolled left field with uncanny efficiency.

Jack Mateja played second base with a contagious confidence that solidified a remarkable infield. As a hitter, his bat control enabled him to move anxious-to-score runners along.

Charles "Joe" Elibacher was the hard-hitting catcher who anchored the all-star infield. Base runners quickly learned this masked-man behind the plate would throw them out in a flash.

Clean-up hitter was the multitalented **Bob White**, whose leadership and gameplay as co-captain and shortstop/pitcher was executed with laser-like precision.

Rich "Shemo" Szymanski, the other co-captain, was the field general. His intense, aggressive style challenged teammates to excel. As centerfielder/pitcher, his rocket-like throwing arm gunned down opponents in the batter's box and base paths.

Right field belonged to **Tom Kujawa**. His razor-sharp eyes, reflexes, and knowledge of the strike zone provided the team with another power hitter. His disciplined intelligence was evident in his strong and consistent performance.

First baseman **Dan Adzia** stretched and scooped his way to defensive superiority. He made tough plays look easy.

The "hot corner" was the domain of **Joe Dybel**. Tenacious on defense, he'd turn a hot smash into an ice-cold out. With cat-like reactions and his own special radar, Joe's fielding gems added luster to the diamond on which he played.

Pitchers **Art Mehuron** and **Steve Vrlik** hurled lightning-quick fastballs and tantalizing curves, keeping opposing batters baffled until the umpire ended their guesswork by calling them out. The entirety of the All-Stars' pitching staff had more called strikes than disgruntled unions. Their collective achievement—as 12-year-olds!—would have made Cy Young smile.

Backed by reserves prepared to the same degree of readiness, the Whiting Little League All-Stars acquired their outstanding reputation the old-fashioned way: They earned it! Even though the record book lists the 1952 New York Yankees as baseball's top team, don't you believe it! The best team that year—the number one, all-around, All-American, unequaled, unsurpassed, superior, championship outfit—was none other than the Whiting Little League All-Stars.

Along with their coaches, these 15 boys of summer from Whiting, Indiana, wore the uniform proudly, represented their hometown with honor, and performed like seasoned veterans on the field of dreams. Truly, they were Diamond Masters.

(2012)

Difference

How often do we hear the expression, "What difference will it make?" Countless conversations both public and private use these words when discussing issues of importance. In many cases, the likely answer is it *does* make a difference. But for any positive result, difference needs to be accepted and appreciated.

Human history has countless episodes of conflict and hurtful action against people suffering because of differences, continuing still today: territorial, cultural, political, religious, racial, and sexual orientation. For those guided by religion, even numerous scriptures have proven insufficient to set aside trepidation and embrace those who are different. Often difference means challenging the status quo, disrupting traditional mindsets, and threatening the security of an already uncertain future.

Today, specific terms define discrimination against those who challenge existing systems and frameworks: profiling, labeling, and bullying. And there is, of course, a plethora of hurtful terminology used against people, wholly unfit to print here. The media display images of violence, destruction, vulgar signage, and personal behaviors directed at difference. Protesters use constitutional rights to promote contrived wrongdoings, distort historical events, and fictionalize narratives to fit a skewed mindset designed to denigrate differences. Fed by 24/7 outlets of cable television and social media, these "anti-different" messages are elevated to a frenzied level of phony magnitude and importance.

The fundamental question is this: When will we, as citizens of the United States, respectfully accept and appreciate diversity and difference? When will civil debate and reasoned discussion become the priority to resolve differences instead of turning to inflammatory, derogatory rhetoric? Opposing viewpoints—regardless of content—warrant consideration. Affording such courtesy respects the spirit of democracy.

Because no two individuals are the same, difference is the norm. Within families, each member has their own unique personality and characteristics. And outside of family circles, we encounter habits, beliefs, and behaviors that differ from our own throughout our lives, contrasts that demand understanding, and at the very least, tolerance.

Regardless of age, gender, or station in life, how often are individuals derided, belittled, bullied, shunned, ridiculed, or denigrated because of their opinions, economic or cultural status, political preference, religious affiliation, or sexual orientation? When confronting difference, why is there a tendency to become uneasy and apprehensive—to reject rather than accept? And why do some individuals appear to derive pleasure from diminishing another's reputation?

Sadly the lack of acceptance and appreciation for personal differences, coupled with perceived detrimental imperfections, permeates society at all levels. This dynamic insidiously inserts itself into families, schools, churches, workplaces, and the government. No one is born to denigrate: Someone has to teach these hateful lessons of intolerance. Like an infection, "anti-different" sentiment spreads when people choose ambivalence and indifference rather than reasoned discussion.

When good people are reluctant to challenge voices of disdain, tacitly accepting these boisterous expressions of denigration, the seeds of discontent take root and grow into disorder, instilling fear and fostering dehumanizing mindsets. As a result, resolve is weakened as timidity erodes courage and trepidation silences voices of thoughtful consideration.

We must remember this: We are all the same, bestowed with the gifts of difference. These exceptional characteristics define who we are. We each wish to be valued, accepted, and loved. We have the capacity and potential to learn, grow, and build a life. Barring life-altering maladies, we have the opportunity to make choices, fulfill hopes and dreams, and enrich all our days. And we can, in turn, use our gifts of difference to improve the quality of the lives we touch.

We must each understand that our vision and demeanor improve when the heart fills the eyes. Consciously deciding to see with the heart, differences are no longer felt as threats or viewed as signs of inferiority or weakness. Rather, differences are seen as welcome signs of diversity and strength to be treasured and celebrated. Recall that difference is at the core of the United States of America, a founding principle celebrated in one of our nation's mottos: *E pluribus unum*—"Out of many, one."

What difference will it make? You decide.

(2017)

DIY Driving Lesson

I grew up in a family that never owned a car. My parents did have a Studebaker in the late 1930s, but by the time I was born in January 1941, that automobile was a distant memory. Instead, our mode of transportation in Whiting, Indiana, was bus, bicycle, or foot.

Because of high school course requirements and other scheduling conflicts, I didn't take driver's education. Consequently, I hadn't had any formal instruction in the operation of a motor vehicle. The one and only time I had driven an automobile was when a friend of mine asked me to turn his Ford station wagon around on New York Avenue while he made a pizza delivery. It was early December 1958, and I was 17 and scared to death. Somehow during those 25 seconds, I managed to safely negotiate a U-turn in front of Standard Oil's Research Lab to the residential side of the street.

The following May—now employed at Inland Steel's Indiana Harbor Works in East Chicago but still bereft of driving skills and license—I purchased a used, white-over-green 1954 Oldsmobile Rocket 88 from a neighbor. The four-door sedan had an 8-cylinder engine with automatic transmission (I didn't know how to use a stick shift, and have never learned). Plated and insured, the Rocket 88 was a sleek-looking street sled, but I still continued to ride the bus to and from work. And because I didn't know how to drive and was without a license, my Olds only hit the streets at nightfall with my friends behind the wheel as we cruised the area drive-ins.

So when U.S. steelworkers went on strike in mid-July 1959 (shuttering nearly every mill in the country), I used the downtime to hone my driving and parking skills. One late summer night, with neighborhood traffic at a minimum, I decided it was time for a do-it-yourself driving lesson. Wishing to steer clear of oncoming traffic, I planned to drive only on one-way streets. Feeling both excited and anxious, I started the car, put the transmission in drive, and eased away from the curb in front of my house on Cleveland Avenue.

Cautiously crossing 118th Street's two-way intersection, I continued north. At the two-way intersection of 117th Street, I made a right turn and drove east. At the next corner of 117th, Central Avenue is one way going south, so I turned right toward 119th Street, Whiting's main thoroughfare. Using my directional signal and following posted speed limits, my confidence grew. But at that moment, having never experienced the nuance of power steering, I momentarily over-steered and had to brake hard to avoid colliding with the cars parked along the curb. I quickly straightened out the Olds, resuming my route.

By the time I completed the turn onto Central Avenue, I had made a relatively smooth transition, and was heading south. No other vehicles were behind me, thankfully. Feeling self-assured, I drove two blocks south to 119th Street, stopped at the stop sign, checked for oncoming westward traffic, and carefully turned onto it.

The intersection of 119th Street, Cleveland Avenue, and Indianapolis Boulevard was always busy. I was stopped at a red light in the far right lane, in front of Owens Funeral Home, with my right turn signal engaged. I glanced to my left and noticed a Whiting Police car had pulled up next to me in the left lane. We both waited for the traffic light to change. I tried to appear calm, but inwardly, I was near total panic.

Did I commit a violation? Would I be arrested? Clearer thinking overcame nervous anxiety: How could the cop know I didn't have a license? I was following all the rules of the road. (For a number of weeks prior, I had carefully read and studied the Indiana Driver's Manual. I knew the rules well.)

When the light turned green, the police car continued westward and I turned on to Cleveland Avenue toward home. I parked the Rocket 88 by the curb and savored the success of my DIY driving lesson. Intoxicated with confidence, I continued to hone my driving and parking skills further while the steel strike continued into the fall.

That Labor Day weekend, I decided to travel with two friends (both licensed drivers) to the Detroit State Fair where Dick Clark was hosting his Caravan of Stars road show, promoted via *American Bandstand*. With guidance from above, I drove license-less to Detroit. Once we neared the fairgrounds, my buddies handled driving duties and also took turns at the wheel on the return trip home.

Called back to Inland Steel shortly before Thanksgiving (the steel strike lasted 116 days), I began driving to work though I remained license-less. It wasn't until a few weeks after my nineteenth birthday, when I visited the Whiting License Bureau and passed both the written and driving tests, that I finally earned my license.

In retrospect, it was pure adolescent foolishness to drive without a license. So many detrimental consequences could have resulted from such a cavalier mindset. Thankfully, my DIY driving lessons were under Heaven's watchful and protective kindness.

Years later, as a parent, classroom teacher, and dean of students, I listened to moms and dads' concerns as this milestone of teenage independence approached. Based on personal experience, I wrote a poem to help lessen this parental anxiety. Printed on 5x7 index cards, it was to be placed on the steering wheel prior to their teen's inaugural solo drive:

> The automobile I drive can be foe or friend,
> And how I control it will determine my end.
> So when I'm driving for work, school, or a date,
> I must always remember to concentrate!
> The instant I let my car try and think,
> I'll be injured or killed—quick as a wink.
> But I'll keep safe and sound
> When I'm out driving around,
> If I remember this simple refrain:
> "The car I drive has the power,
> But I have the brain!"

(2018)

Drive-In Vespers

When I was growing up in the 1940s, 1950s, and 1960s, there were two types of drive-ins: restaurant and movie theater. Here my focus is on the movie variety, specifically, the 41 Outdoor Theater in Hammond, Indiana, once located at 2500 South Calumet Avenue, adjacent to Sheffield Avenue and just north of 129th Street in the city's Robertsdale neighborhood. It's the setting for a true story about friendship, coming of age, and the indelible experience of a Catholic priest taking three altar boys to their first drive-in movie.

From early spring through late autumn, patrons arrived in sedans, coupes, convertibles, and station wagons for a night's entertainment at the movies. Couples and families with small children chose the 41 Outdoor Theater because it provided several advantages over traditional movie theaters: casual dress (families often arrived with youngsters clad in diapers or pajamas), fussy babies wouldn't disturb other moviegoers, romantics could enjoy several hours of togetherness in the privacy of an automobile, and carloads of buddies could indulge in adolescent antics and capers.

Setting the scene, it's mid-August 1948, and summer is in full flower. Three friends—Thomas McHale, Robert Babbitt, and Norman Koch— are grade school classmates and recent graduates of Sacred Heart School. Tom and Norm were soon-to-be freshmen at Whiting High School. Bob would enter the seminary that coming September to study for the priesthood. As buddies, they hunted, fished, and enjoyed a full measure of youthful adventures. The priest in this story is Father John Daniels, the assistant pastor at Sacred Heart Parish and the celebrant conducting the 7:00 pm Friday evening novena to the Blessed Mother.

This was the summer of transition from grade school to secondary education, so as graduates they were no longer obligated to be altar boys. Still Tom, Bob, and Norm volunteered to serve for Father Daniels when the scheduled servers were no-shows that Friday evening in August. As experienced altar boys, they provided efficient ecclesiastical support for scheduled liturgical services.

To express his gratitude for serving the just completed novena service, Father Daniels offered to take the altar boys to the 41 Outdoor Theater. None of the three friends had ever been to a drive-in movie and readily accepted.

Father Daniels slid behind the wheel of his recently purchased four-door Plymouth sedan. Tom and Bob sat in the backseat and Norm rode in the front. Unhurried, they had ample time as there was still too much daylight for the movie to begin, though the drive from La Porte Avenue to the theater's Sheffield Avenue entrance took but a few minutes. Father D paid the four admissions, drove along the roadway, and parked a few rows from the front of the screen.

With late seasonal sunsets coupled with daylight saving time, outdoor theater moviegoers had to wait until sufficient darkness had arrived for proper viewing. As twilight dimmed to dusk and silently tiptoed toward evening, a number of patrons left their cars and walked to the concession stand, where both snacks and restrooms awaited. Other ticket-buyers, especially families, often brought their own food and implements to ensure convenience and comfort without having to leave their vehicle, while starry-eyed couples took full advantage of darkening skies to pursue other pleasantries.

But instead of joining the moviegoers taking advantage of the opportunity to buy popcorn, sodas, and assorted goodies from the concession stand, Father Daniels turned towards the three boys and said, "We have time before the movie starts to pray the Rosary."

The trio's startled, unspoken response was "What? Pray the Rosary at the drive-in?!" Norm mentally calculated how long it would take him to walk home to Oliver Street if he left the car. The increasing darkness added to the impracticality of that thought, so he decided to stay and pray.

And so it was on that warm August evening, while the melodic refrain of "Let's all go to the lobby!" filled the drive-in speakers, the sounds emanating from within a certain Plymouth sedan consisted of the Our Father, Hail Mary, and Glory Be prayers as the four occupants traversed the beads of the Rosary.

I suspect this was the only Rosary ever prayed at the 41 Outdoor Theater. The movie watched by Tom, Bob, and Norm has long since been forgotten—odd because details of first-time experiences are usually vividly recalled. But the indelible memory of this night wasn't the film. It was an outdoor theater, three friends, a priest, and a sedan filled with drive-in vespers.

(2017)

GUEST CHECK

TABLE	PERSONS	46394	SERVER
E	2		S-9

The Elixir of Spring
Empty Promises

TAX

THANKS FOR VISITING THE MIND CAFETERIA

The Elixir of Spring

Serving as spring's welcoming committee, hours of daylight increase, winds display a repertoire of choreographed vigor, and warm droplets of rain baptize the landscape. Remnants of winter take their cue and fade out of prominence, yielding to the sights, sounds, and scents of another vernal equinox. Stimulated by the perfume of emerging greenery, songbirds advertise and audition for companionship, awash in rays from the sun's benevolence. Refreshed by nature's gifts to enjoy outside activities once again, spirits soar with youthful anticipation, hearts celebrate with appreciation for conquering another winter, and exuberant thoughts serve as incentive for tackling honey-do lists with adolescent-like alacrity.

In delicious celebration, spring exclaims, "Open for business!" Shovels and snow blowers are stowed away, swapped out for gardening tools and lawnmowers. Sprinklers are connected and at the ready. As spring unfolds, energy bursts from all living things—grass turns green, trees bud, and flowers blossom, hanging virtual vacancy signs that beckon creatures of the air, water, and land to partake of nature's bounty.

Schoolyards and neighborhoods that were muffled during winter weather now pulsate with activity. Children's voices fill the air with joyful laughter and play. Homeowners exchange conversation while going about outdoor chores. Garages doors are left open, driveways showcase vehicles fresh from the car wash, and any stubborn winter grime is hosed away from windows, decks, and walkways to welcome in spring.

One of the season's fringe benefits for *Homo sapiens* is a renewed spring in their step. This unmistakable good feeling about life adds buoyancy to our outlook and attitude. Romantics of all ages enjoy the sweetness of spring. For seasoned human units, chronic aches and pains are temporarily forgotten, allowing a full measure of sunshine to flood mind, body, and spirit. Regardless of age or station of life, the elixir of spring nurtures all. In addition to external calendar reminders, each of us experiences seasonal change within and reacts to these sensory messages that affect emotions and activities.

This time of year signals beginnings and renewals, and brings back memories of growing up in Whiting, Indiana. I vividly recall the city's annual spring Clean-Up Week sponsored by the Chamber of Commerce that encouraged residents to employ copious amounts of soap and elbow grease to clean both interiors and exteriors of hearth and home. School-aged kids, released early from class, paraded down 119th Street promoting the initiative's "Clean-up, Paint-up, Fix-up" slogan. Companies, businesses, and merchants offered incentives and targeted specific areas for improvement: parking lots, alleys, delivery areas, and vacant properties. Before-and-after photos were published in the *Times Grafic*.

Each cycle through the parade of seasons elicits thankfulness, appreciation, and gratitude for the days of our lives. As freshmen (childhood), sophomores (adolescence), and juniors (adulthood), we're not fully aware that ordinary minutes will season to become extraordinary moments to remember. Seniors—borderline magnificent human units—savor and cherish these transitions of time from mundane to magic! Now treasures of the heart, they're the prized gold of the golden years.

I freely admit I'm addicted to spring, one of my four favorite seasons of the year. Every now and then when I'm watching younger, more agile athletes, a little voice whispers to me: "You can do that!" But almost immediately, a louder voice in my head yells in response, "No, you can't! What are you thinking?!" Reality arrives to remind me of my now permanent spectator-only status.

The days when this particular arrangement of geriatric bones and protoplasm overflowed with energetic intensity are long past. Still, it's nice to recall moments when the wind was green and springtime meant classrooms, sandlots, beaches, street-corner seminars, and Whiting Park. Sharing laughter and blessings with family, friends, and classmates, we enjoyed the elixir of spring to its fullest.

(2016)

Empty Promises

It seems we're in the midst of the empty promise era. Time and time again, our televisions, radios, and computers transmit details of individuals' inability, unwillingness, or deliberate disregard to keep a promise. In every country, in every walk of life, and at all levels of social strata, we're confronted with consequences resulting from the aftermath of empty promises. Once upon a time, a person's word was their bond—no longer.

How many marriages are put asunder because the parties involved spoke empty vows on their wedding day? Unfaithfulness, mistrust, dishonor, lack of commitment, and irresponsibility doomed their nuptials from the "I do."

In the working world—blue-collar, white-collar, or no collar at all—an epidemic of meaningless words floods workplaces as individuals at every level say things knowing full well their words are devoid of truth. Too many institutions are infected with greed and use deceptive words to manipulate trusting employees and entice unsuspecting consumers to participate in questionable practices. When called to account, often their fabricated testimony mirrors any previous pledges: empty.

The most fertile arena for hollow promises is politics. Instead of misspoken oratory being an occasional (if not accidental) occurrence, empty promises have become candidates' everyday currency. Untruths are ingrained in today's elective process, tacitly accepted as the price of running for, getting elected to, and/or serving in political office.

Candidates are so focused on garnering enough votes to achieve personal priorities, they make promises they know they'll never keep. In the heat of a campaign, contenders pose, posture, and prattle to fit a particular agenda and attract certain voting blocs in order to win election or re-election. Their words are solely designed to garner support, often at the expense of factual integrity.

Promise-makers forget that truth always has enough dignity of its own to justify itself. The human brain is designed for truth. When we speak truthfully, we never have to worry later about remembering what we said—the truth always comes back automatically!

So many fall prey to false narratives rather than subscribe to honorable forthrightness. Whether obvious or subtle, the results are always the same: the erosion and decay of personal character and the total devaluation of self-worth.

Most damaged, however, are the countless children who become victims of phony commitments. Lacking any economic or social power, children are therefore most at risk and easily manipulated by unprincipled adults. Used as pawns by family and society, such mistrust causes indelible damage to children's physical, mental, and emotional well-being.

Without a secure and loving environment in which to grow and learn, children miss out on educational opportunities, lack necessary nurturing, and feel unsafe or insecure, creating indelible emotional scars they'll bear for a lifetime. Many, by necessity, learn how to fend for themselves through trial and error. Without positive examples, they struggle to develop survival strategies and coping skills, and also suffer from a lack of self-worth and self-confidence. Missing meaningful adult guidance, mentoring, and parental affection, the most defenseless become the most vulnerable. The vacant look in these children's eyes reflects the shameful assurances made to them that were never honored.

What gives a promise such profound importance is not the magnitude, circumstance, or subject of the promise. It's the character of the person making the promise that carries the real weight. Taken by themselves, words don't mean—people mean! The very same words spoken in a different manner or by a different person can have divergent meanings.

"Put it in writing" is common practice to provide legal assurances about an obligation, but the most meaningful promises are those made in person. Regardless of the particular words chosen, the strength and bonding of a spoken truth have the power to make heart, mind, and spirit soar! A verbal oath to fulfill a pledge becomes a personal contract.

Making and keeping a promise demonstrates the highest quality and integrity of our character. Fulfilling our oath validates qualities of trust, honor, respect, and responsibility. Every promise made, to whomever it's made, carries the highest degree of importance because it defines who we are.

Whether we stand before a child, a board of directors, a church altar, or voters, this importance should never be denigrated or diminished. A promise is a promise. A person's word is their bond and so much more.

(2019)

GUEST CHECK

TABLE	PERSONS	46394	SERVER
F	8		S-9

Familiar Names and Unfamiliar Places
Father of the Carpenter
Favorites
February's Invitation
First Miracle
Forgiveness
The Fragrance of Remembrance
From Green and White to Gold

TAX

THANKS FOR VISITING THE MIND CAFETERIA

Familiar Names and Unfamiliar Places

I don't travel well. Given the choice between a luxurious hotel and my home, I'd rather stay at home. Even so, there are times when a road trip is necessary and we must adapt to unfamiliar surroundings.

Years ago, when traveling Route 66 was the epitome of a westward automobile trip, part of the adventure was the variety of motor lodges and eateries encountered in each state. Route 66 began in Chicago, Illinois, and ended in Los Angeles, California, with truck stops, diners, restaurants, and countless mom-and-pop motels lining the original highway. Familiar gasoline brands (Standard Oil, Shell, Sinclair, Gulf, Mobil, Cities Service, and Sunoco) offered comfort stations for both vehicle and persons—a place to fill the tank and drain the family!

Such early roadways, whose traffic was once the lifeblood of cities and communities, gave way to interstate highways and toll roads. These modern thoroughfares offer drivers convenient border-to-border and shore-to-shore navigation without traffic lights, speed traps, local traffic jams, or other delays. With a pocketful of change or an electronic toll transponder, we can drive without interruption until hunger and fatigue demand attention. Then a convenient exit leads us to fuel, food, and lodging.

Today, hungry travelers look for favorite fast-food brands while en route to distant destinations. McDonald's, Burger King, Wendy's, Taco Bell, and Kentucky Fried Cluck-Cluck entice motorists to use drive-thru windows or dine inside. National motel chains have replaced family-owned lodging, offering comfortable accommodations with technology unheard of in pre-interstate days. But even with flat-screen TVs, deluxe room service, and complimentary continental breakfast, most patron-pampering amenities are poor substitutes for the familiarity of home and the comfort of our own bed.

From June 1969 through June 1971, I was under contract with the Vigo County School Corporation, serving as a Curriculum Specialist for the Indiana Department of Public Instruction. Based at Indiana State University in Terre Haute, I was responsible for reviewing vocational machine trades programs throughout the state, meeting with teachers and providing instructional materials. So I was on the road several days a week, visiting different towns and cities before driving north back home to Whiting for the weekend.

For some, visiting new places and staying at different hotels and motels is exciting and filled with unexpected adventure. But even today, Indiana is home to a plethora of small rural towns where eateries and businesses close shortly after sundown. For food, you tried your luck at the vending machines in the motel office, though many snacks were past their sell-by date.

Back in the room, motel TVs typically offered just two channels—there was no cable or satellite service—and local television stations signed off at midnight with a test pattern and the national anthem. Turning to the radio for entertainment would also prove frustrating. Clear-channel stations would often be unavailable and local station transmitters were woefully underpowered, with reception fading in and out.

I remember coming across a community AM station in downstate Indiana, owned by a local funeral home, that ended the broadcast day on a somber note: Muted organ music meant it was pajama time. At 5:00 am, that same station signed on with soothing organ music and the dulcet tones of the funeral home representative reading recent obituaries. I'll never forget hearing that Sycamore Pflug fell from his tractor and passed in his bean field. Neighbors were called upon to help the Widow Pflug with the harvest now that poor Sycamore was pushing daisies.

Driving north on county roads and rural highways led back to civilization. I couldn't wait to get home to the Calumet Region. My spirits brightened as the car speakers were filled by 50,000-watt AM powerhouses WLS and WGN, respectively offering the familiar voices of Larry Lujack and Roy Leonard. "East of Midnight" personalities included Don Phillips presenting hit songs from the latest WLS Silver Dollar Survey and Eddie Schwartz taking calls from fellow WGN night owls.

Traveling along Northern Indiana highways, recognizable topography, road signs, places, and names come into view. Crossing the Kankakee River Bridge on US 41 signals my entry into Lake County, with the towns of Schneider and Lowell preceding the Region's core communities of the Region. Cedar Lake and St. John are further welcome sights of being homeward bound.

Heading northward past Route 30, through Schererville, Highland, and across Ridge Road, I follow the ribbon-like asphalt welcome mat of Indianapolis Boulevard that continues through Hammond and over the steel Nine-Span Bridge to East Chicago. Driving across the railroad tracks and over the Indiana Harbor and Ship Canal Bridge, I think about the Sinclair and Standard Oil refineries standing sentry, lining the boulevard where Stieglitz Park and Goose Island had previously flourished.

Moments and memories, past and present, blend into a single thought: Home.

(2015)

Father of the Carpenter

Long ago, more than 90 generations in the past, the world struggled with power, money, and greed much as it does now. Historically, there's limited information about the daily activities of those who lived in New Testament times, but like today, most of these early inhabitants were occupied with the daily tasks of providing food, shelter, and making ends meet. Any money earned was taxed by the governing power and whatever remained was used to maintain standards of living.

There were fishermen, farmers, beekeepers, barbers, hairdressers, merchants, seamstresses, winemakers, and gardeners. Others tended livestock, raised poultry, herded sheep, or operated grain mills. Some were slaves. A small number of gifted citizens were artists, sculptors, writers, and musicians. Some worked for the government as census takers, tax collectors, or accountants. Many were craftsmen: shipbuilders, blacksmiths, metalworkers, and carpenters. These individuals took raw materials of nature and transformed them into necessary, useful items for both home and work. The story that follows reflects conditions known at that time, and its focus is a woodworker.

He was known as Joseph, son of Jacob. Though born in Bethlehem, no one knew exactly when he had arrived in Nazareth, only that he had been there for a number of years. Perhaps it was a favorable place to ply his trade and family financial circumstances necessitated earning a living. A polite, quiet, and righteous man, Joseph went about his work with dispatch and efficiency. By trade, Joseph was a *tekton,* a mechanic of sorts, but in particular, a carpenter. Most of the houses in town showcased his craftsmanship, with tables, chairs, bed frames, and cabinets of various sizes and design all a testament to his skills.

Joseph was well into his maturity when he announced his intention to marry a young woman from Nazareth. Years later, learned men would write about the circumstances surrounding this engagement, marriage, and birth of a son, but at the time it went nearly unnoticed. A God-fearing servant, Joseph was most troubled when it became known to him that the young woman to whom he was betrothed was with child. He quietly made plans to separate himself from her. But after Joseph was informed by an angel to be not afraid and take Mary as his wife, for that which is conceived in her is of the Holy Spirit, Joseph did as the angel of the Lord commanded him.

A few months later, a decree issued by Caesar Augustus required Joseph and his expectant wife to travel to Bethlehem to be counted in the census. Arriving in the town of his birth, Joseph found no room for them in the inn. Imagine how troubling it must have been for this holy man as the hour of his child's birth approached. What were his thoughts about the coming of shepherds and the wise men? But whatever worries, anxieties, and uncertainties Joseph faced, he never spoke about them. The historical record is silent.

Following the birth of Jesus, Joseph was told by an angel to flee to Egypt to escape the jealousy and wickedness of a ruling tyrant. Later, Joseph would wait once more until directed by angels to return to Palestine, eventually settling again in Nazareth. With sublime simplicity and obedience, Joseph returned to his trade and supported himself and his family by skillfully crafting useful objects from wood. He spent time teaching his young son the skills of his trade, not fully understanding all that would be asked of the boy named Jesus. As a devout and pious man, Joseph observed what the law commanded, living out his life in an uneventful manner. He would die before Jesus began his public ministry.

How many people alive today would have followed the example set by Joseph? So many individuals seek prominence and celebrity, preferring to live a flamboyant lifestyle. Too many misuse their talents, abilities, and skills. Rampant in today's society is the "me me me" mindset, with selfishness the norm rather than the exception.

When the final accounting of our days is made, what will our permanent record reveal? Will it be one of a faithful servant: compassionate, understanding, obedient, and full of charitable goodness? Will the performance of our duties serve as a guide for those who follow?

The father of the carpenter would have it no other way. He understood that those who build and those who teach use many methods and materials. He understood, too, that when a lesson is well designed and presented, the strength, purpose, and beauty of one's life would endure. And though historical information may be limited, remembrance of the father of the carpenter remains vibrant and strong over 90 generations later.

Again, the question: What will a review and remembrance of our permanent record reveal to those whose lives we touched?

(2009)

Favorites

As life unfolds, an automatic compilation of people, places, and things that shape, affect, and mark our journey are recorded into indelible memories. Each experience enriches and adds meaningful moments. As time moves along, we're consciously aware of the residue from these encounters and the degree to which they've added to the fabric of life. Some are welcome, positive recollections, while others initiate less favorable thoughts and awaken unwanted feelings that burden and detract enjoyment from our personal inventory of living.

As humans, we live on memories. They're our most treasured keepsakes, for it's our memories that define, connect, and nourish us. We use these recollections to reinforce linkage to ourselves. They become a major portion of our identity, value, and definition of our humanness. Our experiences bond us in friendship, solidify relationships, and fuse the mosaic we display each and every day of our lives, providing us with the courage and confidence to trust, risk, and love.

From our earliest days through adulthood, we learn to depend on our experiences—they literally become matters of life and death. The people, places, things, and events we integrate within ourselves over our lifetime serve as our physical, social, and moral compass. Each item in our cognitive file carries useful information: guidance, safety, lessons, goodness, sorrow, success, failure, happiness, advice... the list is quite extensive. These items prepare us to confront challenges and changes presented daily in our lives.

We may wonder how places and things—inanimate objects—could have such a profound effect on our lives. They do because they serve as the arena for the interactions that occurred within their boundaries and as the props for the happenings generated by people sharing that space at that time.

As children we are acutely aware of our surroundings, soaking up impressions of where, what, why, and how. Often these childhood inputs of life stay dormant until appropriate processing organizes and catalogs them into usable data. Some are so subtle they take years before the impact is fully understood and savored. Others are so overpowering we store them in places far within us until we have sufficient courage to confront, conquer, and understand their importance.

Early in life, the people, places, and things we confront are not of choice. So much of our early impressions are due to the choices made by others much older than we are. But as we mature, we learn about power, control, and choice. Most importantly, we learn about sovereignty—to be in command of ourselves and to understand the power of individuality. What follows is a small sample from the wonder years of this writer, from the neatest little hometown ever, Whiting, Indiana!

In February 1949, when I was 8 years old, our family moved from my grandma's house on Oliver Street to Cleveland Avenue. Strategically located in the 1800 block, our new home was a gateway to 119th Street's business district. Because our family never owned a car, my main mode of transportation was walking, and later, bicycle. Both methods for getting from here to there turned out to be a godsend.

It's difficult to name all my favorite places in this industrial Mayberry, but the ones listed here have stood the test of time. Every time I visit one of these locations in person or recall events from my life, the movie that plays in my mind touches my heart in magically wonderful ways. Granted, many of these places are varnished with the idealism of youth, preserved in childhood and adolescent memories, and viewed as hallowed locations brimming with fond memories—so be it. This is *my* movie, and watching it through ancient rose-colored glasses suits me just fine. Get the popcorn!

Whiting High School, my dream factory. Within the confines of this educational palace, I met classmates who became lifelong friends and teachers who believed in me and changed my life. It's where I learned the power of possibility.

Whiting Public Library, a wonderful, castle-like structure that became my Adventure Land starting in first grade. Within these walls, the magic of words fired imagination and adventure, opened new horizons, and filled my mind with knowledge, understanding, diversity of thought, and human expression.

Whiting Community Center, the mecca of industrial Mayberry, a place where kids were not only welcomed, but appreciated. Sports activities, recreational pursuits, field trips, social gatherings, theatrical productions, municipal exhibitions, corporate presentations, and a myriad of community functions were headquartered in this marvelous architectural structure. I literally grew up in this building. As a teenager, I worked as a pinboy in the bowling alley. The Community Center is a museum for the mind.

Neal Price's Firestone Store, where the wide variety of goods sold made music for the senses.

Dave's Drug Store, serving a perfect menu: root beer floats, potato chips, and Dave's wisdom.

Whiting Park, a place for all seasons: baseball, ice-skating, playground, picnics, and the beach. And the little stone houses always had their welcome mats out for visitors.

Sacred Heart Church and School, offering lessons for heaven and earth. No free passes!

Whiting Post Office, headquarters for 46394. There's no better zip code for cards and letters.

Nick's Pool Room, an adolescent male oasis featuring snooker, pinball, and verbal expression.

Hot Dog Louie's, offering gourmet dining at its best. Germs never stood a chance!

White Castle, the Hamburger Hall of Fame. Nourish your body, cleanse your pipes, and so much more. I just love 'em!

What are your favorites?

(2009)

February's Invitation

February has always been the runt of the calendar. Beginning with the reign of King Numa Pompilius (715-673 BC), the second king of Rome, and then during both Julius and Augustus Caesar's turns on the throne, February has been included, demoted, and promoted to fill out the required number of days in a year.

Honoring the Caesar cousins, the Roman Senate renamed the months of Quintillis and Sextillis as July and August with an equal number of days to each. But to boost these royal egos, the allotment for February (Februarius) had to be adjusted, forever after numbering just 28 days. Following additional calculations to improve the accuracy of Numa's 12 lunar cycles—and to bring mathematical and astronomical harmony to the Roman calendar—February was partially compensated with one additional leap year day every four years.

Much later, in 1582, Pope Gregory XIII introduced the Gregorian calendar, further refining the Julian calendar (named for Julius Caesar) in use since 46 BC. It standardized the number of days in a year, and defined the formula and calculation for both Easter Sunday and leap years.

Though February has long suffered such shortcomings, the month enjoys unparalleled admiration. Forty-one days into winter, the year's second month offers opportunities for both indoor and outdoor activities: Basketball and hockey season are in full bloom, and when the weather gets creative, there is sledding, skating, and shoveling.

One of the most welcomed attributes of February is that hours of daylight increase as the earth spins and orbits toward spring. But the month's most attractive feature, perfectly placed at the center—its very heart—is Valentine's Day. The holiday is February's invitation for romantics of all ages to express unabashed affection and love toward others, focusing on matters of the heart.

We give and receive gifts that mark Valentine's Day and other special occasions, but as we grow older, we realize the most meaningful gifts are those things that we cannot touch. How can this be? Early on, we learn to value things and to convey appropriate thankfulness and love for them. And too often we use the word "love" like a one-size-fits-all garment. But as we go through life, we discover there are degrees and varieties of love, and within the nucleus of love is an essential core too often neglected: appreciation.

Appreciation is recognizing the quality of character and personal regard we hold for each other. Expressing it is a symphony for the spirit, whether rendered by word, touch, body language, or loving eyes. Appreciation is the invisible connection we use to bond family, friendships, and relationships. Regardless of age or station in life, the reinforcement garnered by both giver and receiver enriches self-worth, gladdens the heart, and nourishes human interaction.

While Valentine's Day is celebrated just once each year in February, ideally every day should be Appreciation Day. Doesn't there seem to be a shortage of appreciation? We encounter countless opportunities to express our gratitude for another's consideration, kindness, thoughtfulness, and love. But we often neglect to take advantage of these emotionally nourishing moments. Every display of human pleasantry should be welcomed, recognized, and acknowledged as we go through the day. Dispensing the gift of appreciation makes hearts smile and spirits soar.

In keeping with February's invitation, here's an expression of appreciation to my favorite Valentine:

When you adjust my collar or fix my sweater's tag,
When you hold my hand,
For all courtesies big and small,
The smiles and kind words,
Reassuring gestures and looks of approval,
For changing ordinary moments
To extraordinary memories,

For overlooking missteps along the way,
For teaching me how to see with my heart
And sharing the story in your eyes,
For your trust in me,
For providing the sunshine that keeps doubts at bay,
For prayerful petitions in times of uncertainty,
For togetherness that requires no words,
For tears of sorrow and joy
That both renew and strengthen soulmate vows,
For today, yesterday, and once-upon-a-time,
But most importantly, for all our tomorrows,
Know that you are cherished, appreciated, and loved beyond words.

(2017)

First Miracle

Once upon a time, long, long ago, at an oasis several miles from a desert town called Sidon, a slave girl gave birth to a baby boy. The boy's father was a nomad merchant who traveled from settlement to settlement—oasis to oasis—with any convenient caravan. But when he discovered his newborn son was disfigured, he disavowed any kinship or responsibility and abandoned them both.

The boy's mother awoke one morning to find both the caravan and the baby's father gone. Left behind at the oasis to fend for herself and baby, she remained there, working long hours sewing and mending blankets and robes for meager scraps of food. She soon realized, however, that both of them could not survive on what little nourishment she provided.

In desperation, she convinced a couple on their way to Tyre to take her child. Cradling the baby in her arms, the wife noticed his malformed leg and disfigured face. "What's his name?" she asked. With eyes downcast and filled with tears, the baby's mother whispered, "Joseus."

The couple took Joseus to Tyre, but left after a few months to live in the town of Nazareth. There, the boy was teased and ridiculed. His withered left leg gave him an awkward gait, and his hair lip, a grotesque smile. The couple, who were of some wealth, had been married more than ten years but had not been blessed with a child. Now she unexpectedly became pregnant, making Joseus an embarrassment. They'd initially accepted the child out of pity, but after several years of caring for the slave girl's illegitimate son and with their first child on the way, Joseus was both a social and financial liability. One day, without warning, the couple sold Joseus to nomads on their way to Ramallah.

Ramallah was a disheartening and foreboding place. Joseus was bought and sold three more times. Now 8 years old and having never been schooled, he was conscripted by a camel trader to clean livestock pens and stables. Joseus worked long, hard hours. His compensation included discarded clothing and leftover foodstuffs. Sometimes, hunger would be so great that he'd poach animal feed from the bins inside the barn. More often than not, Joseus still went to bed hungry, sleeping on straw alongside the animals he tended.

One evening, Joseus overheard his master's plan to sell him. Filled with fear, he fled—first to Jerusalem, and then, after begging in the streets, made his way to Bethlehem. It was a difficult journey. His withered leg often broke out in pus-filled sores that only hindered his movement even more. Joseus' life was in disarray. He faced more shadows than sunshine. He was alone, unwanted, and unloved—a spirit-crushing feeling for the now 12-year-old.

By chance, Joseus found work at an inn. In the adjacent stable, he cared for both the innkeeper's livestock and those belonging to travelers. Occasionally his duties included sweeping the storeroom and entryway in the evening. For his toil, Joseus earned two silver denarii. Late at night, seated at a bare wooden table in the inn's storeroom, he supped alone. His diet consisted of lentils or greens boiled in water. Leftover corn porridge, heavily salted and buttered, was sometimes scavenged from the cookery. He sated his appetite with cakes made from crushed and malted grain, and sometimes scraps of moldy bread quieted his hunger. He slept upon a straw mat in a corner of the storeroom.

One unusually busy day, which found travelers from near and far filling every vacant room, Joseus limped up and down narrow stairs assisting with their satchels and belongings. The knee of his withered leg throbbed and ached, and scratches to his leg sores burned and itched. He also endured taunts from unkind customers who mocked his features and speech.

By nightfall, Joseus was exhausted, too tired to attend to the inn's livestock. He sank to his mat, and despite a blinding headache, fell fast asleep. Almost immediately, the innkeeper kicked him awake. "Go put clean hay in the stable," he commanded. "The inn is full, and I told a couple they could spend the night there."

Joseus dragged himself to the stable. As quickly as his fatigue and pounding head allowed, he placed new straw and fresh hay in a manger near the center. He was struggling to keep his balance with a large bale when a kind voice filled his ears. "This will do fine, son." Joseus turned and looked into the gentle eyes of a man leading a donkey. Seated on the beast of burden was a beautiful young woman, great with child. Carefully, the man helped her down. With unimaginable peacefulness, the mother-to-be reclined on the straw blanket next to the manger. Joseus overheard the husband's prayerful whisper, "The time is at hand."

For what seemed like only a moment, Joseus turned away. When his eyes next fell on the lady, he was awestruck! There, lying in the manger, wrapped in swaddling clothes, was a newborn baby boy. An all-encompassing love filled the stable. The boy's mother beckoned Joseus to come close to the manger. Gently, she lifted her newborn son from the manger, and guiding his tiny hand, touched Joseus' face. She smiled and cradled her son close to her bosom. Joseus withdrew to a corner of the stable, and using his hands like a rake, made a haphazard bed of straw and fell fast asleep.

Sometime during the night, Joseus was made whole. He awoke to find his withered leg fully developed and strong. Catching his reflection in a trough of water, the image was that of a handsome young man with near-perfect features. Joseus felt unrestrained forgiveness and unfathomable love. He sensed a learned awareness. He bore no anger to those who had been unkind. For the first time in his life, he was at peace. From that moment, Joseus promised to serve others with kindness, decency, and love.

Joseus was present when regal travelers arrived to pay homage to the blessed child. One of the Magi offered him a position of authority within his household. Joseus grew in stature and prosperity, spending his life sharing the gifts of the first Christmas bestowed on a lowly disfigured stable boy through the touch of a newborn cradled in his mother's arms. In the silence of the stable, under a heavenly night sky, a single star filled the manger with light as the world welcomed the Prince of Peace.

Today, more than 2,000 years later, the gift of the first Christmas is given to us—the charity of His love. May the gift of Christmas enrich and nourish all our days.

(1994)

Forgiveness

One of the most difficult life lessons is learning how to forgive. Forgiveness is a uniquely personal decision that cleanses emotions, promotes love, and renews the spirit. On the surface, forgiveness seems easy. But we quickly realize the difficulty in activating this most important human process. Forgiveness opens us to uncomfortable vulnerability by generating an internal power struggle between reluctance and willingness.

A whole range of incidents can precipitate the need to forgive: hurtful words, unkind deeds, insensitive actions, personal attacks, disrespectful conduct, reckless anger, inappropriate behavior, premeditated evil, meanness, ignorance, stupidity, arrogance, pride, prejudice, selfishness, violence, abuse, and omission to respond in a time of need.

Lessons of forgiveness begin early and often. We're taught as children to accept an apology after suffering from the actions of someone who then says, "I'm sorry." But what's clear in one case becomes cloudy in another when prompted by adults to apologize at times when we feel we've done nothing wrong ("Tell your brother you're sorry").

Granting forgiveness at any age can be a difficult task. Length of time and degree of affront crystalizes and hardens a reluctance to forgive. Some think that to forgive is a sign of weakness—backing down or giving in shows a lack of resolve. Likeminded folks feel it's better to hold a grudge and maintain animosity, therefore exercising a skewed concept of power, dominion, and authority. In their view, withholding forgiveness gives them license to gossip and demean, belittle and degrade, and wallow in self-righteousness.

At the heart of any hesitation to forgive is a fear of letting bygones be bygones—that a pardon could be taken advantage of, misinterpreted, and misused. But such perceived fearfulness is unwarranted because just the opposite occurs. When we willingly and unconditionally forgive, pathways are opened for love to flood our heart, mind, and spirit. This isn't a sign of weakness, but of strength. Offering forgiveness enriches and elevates our stature rather than diminishing it.

We all have experienced unkindness, thoughtless actions, and hurtful words directed at us by family, friends, classmates, coworkers, and complete strangers. Typical everyday interactions can elicit unexpected reactions as emotions supersede rational thought, resulting in personal affronts and hard feelings. What begins as an insignificant or unintentional oversight can fester and grow so big that it gnaws at the human spirit, eroding and damaging relationships.

Throughout our days, the chance to forgive, clean the slate, and begin anew is presented. Holidays, special occasions, and other social gatherings on our calendar encourage us to seize the moment to reconcile damaged feelings, write off negative emotional debts, and let thoughts turn kind. The Christian season of Lent offers one such opportunity.

The traditional purpose of Lent is to take spiritual inventory of our lives. For 40 days, believers prepare for Easter through prayer, penance, fasting, and self-denial. It's also a time for forgiveness. Faithful followers offer prayers of petition, intercession, reconciliation, and absolution. Those who kneel humbly ask for their misdeeds and sinful acts to be forgiven, praying for exoneration and asking to receive a full measure of Heaven's abundance. Prayerful words are offered to "forgive us our trespasses as we forgive those who trespass against us." Forgiveness is a gift that must be received and, in turn, presented to others—without condition.

As personal inventories are scrutinized, we must understand that before we forgive others, we must first forgive ourselves. As humans, we are imperfect, flawed, and prone to making poor choices and bad decisions. As children of God, we fully realize the gift of Baptism—a cleansing of the soul. It is left to us, however, to periodically cleanse our spirit, mind, and heart with forgiveness.

And so another season of Lent has begun. May it be filled with prayerful preparation that cleanses, renews, and nourishes all that is good and decent in humankind. Over 2,000 years ago, at a place called Calvary, we were taught the ultimate lesson of forgiveness and love. Those ten words continue to resound throughout the world: "Father, forgive them for they know not what they do."

Forgiveness—pass it on.

(2012)

The Fragrance of Remembrance

Memory is treasured above all other attributes of humanness. Along with good physical health, having a vibrant memory fills each day with feelings of unmatched richness and joyfulness. Recalling past moments is the one ability we draw upon every moment of our lives in order to grow, achieve, maintain, and learn. Memory dysfunction due to disease, injury, or aging is devastating beyond description and can render one frozen in the here-and-now, devoid of what occurred in the past and unable to imagine future experiences. Without memory, personality withers and slips away—eroding identity, removing awareness, and emptying the eyes, leaving these windows of the soul vacant.

We take memory for granted, even though from the moment of birth, its importance increases exponentially. Not an isolated function of the brain, memory is a team effort, with everything transmitted by our senses to our neurons affecting it in some way. It's our personal filing system. Consciously and subconsciously, memory is used for reference, decision-making, and reaction. We determine what is meaningful and therefore what to keep. Simultaneously, we develop cognitive compartments where this information is stored.

In our very early years, we don't realize there are different kinds of memories. Our cerebrum is on autopilot, using memory for reference, retrieval, and response to stimuli. The process is emotionally straightforward: tears, smiles, laughter, anger, fear, and safety. But as we transition from childhood through adolescence to adulthood, memories reflect a multitude of shades, each with differing intensity: happiness, love, anxiety, fear, failure, and sadness, as well as degrees of uncertainty regarding personal image, confidence, self-worth, ability, and achievement.

However, as the parade of seasons marches along year after year, a subtle, wonderful transformation occurs to our memory and recollection. Like fine wine aging to perfection, past experiences mature. And as each memory is subpoenaed for review, it arrives exuding an exotic fragrance. Random moments of days long since passed are summoned to the mind's forefront and become a cherished homecoming. Thoughts from younger times arrive with unaccustomed clarity, filling the mind with details as vivid as though they just occurred. This harvest of memories ushers in a peaceful sweetness.

Messages from our senses trigger the fragrance of remembrance. Hundreds of ordinary, taken-for-granted moments now return as extraordinary memories from childhood, adolescence, and adulthood. Activities and adventures—private and public, solitary and shared, poignant and painful—are accompanied by scores of sweet-sad beginnings and goodbyes.

A desirable fringe benefit of aging is having time to reflect upon and reminiscence about the times of our lives. Inwardly we celebrate achievements and happily recall delightful moments, while also contrasting these positive memories with regrets—the should-haves, could-haves and what-ifs. We ponder potential and absolutely life-changing choices, decisions, and windows of opportunity that were accepted, ignored, or refused for reasons that today seem impulsive and immature. At times, such remembrances are so compelling that our eyes fill with tears. There's an inexplicable yearning for another chance to do things over, but reality quickly sets in, leaving a sense of emptiness and loss in its wake.

Alone with our thoughts as the setting sun turns the sky apricot to announce the evening's arrival, these moments of reverie provide an occasion to inventory and savor days past. Without hesitation, treasured ruminations gain entrance and play subconscious movies. People, places, and events we haven't thought about for years unexpectedly fill the mind. Yet all too soon, memories of indelible life moments take leave and quietly return to their keeping place.

What remains is a pensive, melancholic glow of those who have touched our heart and taught life-changing lessons. And like a favorite perfume, the sweetness of these moments becomes a symphony for the senses.

Cherish these special gifts bestowed by the fragrance of remembrance.

(2015)

From Green and White to Gold

A 50th Reunion Tribute to the Whiting High School Class of 1958

Tonight we mark the milestone that once seemed so far away at Commencement—our 50th anniversary of graduation. In the past half-century, we've gone from green and white to gold! Along the way we've processed life and life has processed us. We've been tempered, ground, sharpened, and honed. Occasionally we've been dulled and needed a touch-up or some repair and refurbishing. At times we've had to sail against the wind, but nevertheless we've stayed on course, focused on our journey.

Through good times and not-so-good-times, happiness and sorrow, laughter and tears, and triumphs and defeats, we've remained true to ourselves. We wear our scrapes and blemishes like badges of honor. We've paid our dues and we've earned this time to celebrate. Like a fine wine, we've been aged to perfection. We may be creased and folded, marbled and mellowed, but in short, we've endured. Tonight we're here to hit the pause button and rewind the tape. It's time to open the memory vault and enjoy some long ago moments.

Over 19,000 days have passed since that September morning in 1954 when we came together as Whiting High School's newest freshman class. A number of those who began the adventure with us that day are not here tonight. Twenty-three of our classmates have passed away, their life songs ending much too early. Others have been unable to make the journey due to health issues, and a select number decided to forego this opportunity for personal reasons. Regardless of rationale or circumstance, know that they are with us in spirit.

Arriving at Whiting High School as old eighth-graders, we were determined to make our mark within its halls and classrooms. Those freshman days were good days, a time when the wind was green, a time of beginnings. Days filled with potato chips and a Pepsi, of a first girl with perfumed hair. They were the days of warm autumn rains, a time of expectation and apprehension, eagerness and enthusiasm, hopes and dreams, and the indescribable feeling of just being part of it all.

Being a freshman was work. Going through registration and getting schedules so we'd be in class with our friends, there was also orientation, having lockers assigned, and buying supplies—books, paper, pencils, erasers, pens, notebooks, and folders. And there were always fees to pay: locker fee, class fee, gym fee, shop fee, and band fee. Some say that money talks, but all mine ever said to me was, "Goodbye!"

1954 was a year for Levis and loafers, bobby socks and long skirts, a year for football supremacy and Chili Bowl victory. There were Friday night dances and basketball tickets at 35 cents. There were club initiations, assemblies, pep rallies, and picnics. There were Christmas parties where some of us sang songs in Spanish but sounded Polish. It was a time for nicknames and fads, career plans and Cokes, days to build friendships and hold hands at the game (or at the show or on the way home from wherever), and seasons to go skating or swimming, play ball, or just loaf. It was a time to share and a time to belong. Freshman can be an attitude or an age. For us, these were the early days, a time to be young.

We went to classes to learn about geography and history. We struggled with Civics and algebraic equations, murdered English, and took Spanish or Latin and have never been the same since. We had difficulty remembering how to use an adverb, with Mr. Taylor cringing when someone spoke in the wrong tense. Our minds failed us when we were asked to list the Bill of Rights, and many a piece of chalk was dropped in frustration when the X's and Y's didn't equal the Z's.

We had our problems, no doubt about it. But what was amazing about us freshmen was that we could sing from memory every Top 40 hit without a single mistake, yet could not distinguish a noun from a pronoun.

We closed out our first year with a picnic at the park. Yearbooks were signed, and we tried to get as many autographs in our *Reflector* as possible—especially a long note from a favorite classmate. After 180 days, we'd survived the scourge of being an underclassman and were on our way up. Building in confidence and eager to get on with the summer at hand, we departed Whiting High School with our heads held high, the *Reflector* jammed under our arms, and our nostrils filled with the scents of Pine-Sol and soap, thanks to school custodians cleansing classrooms and hallways of dirt and grime that had escaped notice during the year.

The sound of the dismissal bell was still in the air when we headed down Oliver Street, crossing 119th Street and stopping at Hot Dog Louie's for a quick snack. Then it was on to Walgreens to secure more autographs. Ten or so signatures later, we made another pit stop, visiting Dave's Drug Store for a malt or one of his giant root beer floats and a bag of Mrs. Klein's potato chips, whose slogan "Untouched by human hands" also became the battle cry of adolescents continually battling bad breath, body odor, and foot fungus. When it was time to head home, there was a final pause to say, "See ya' around," and then it was summer 1955.

But before it began, it was over, and summer had faded into fall. Beach towels, bathing suits, and suntan oils were put away for another season. In their place came haircuts, daily showers, clean clothes, brushed teeth—and school. By now we were full-fledged members of the teenage generation with all the privileges appertaining thereto. It was autumn 1955, and as sophomores in high school, life was sweet.

These were the days when boys turned into football players after practicing in the late August sun under the watchful eyes of a coach who they said had no mercy. We were the same kids as last year, but in many subtle and not-so-subtle ways we were different. Now a year older with our beginning behind us, we were more self-assured and more confident of the course to follow. Our year began with registration, schedules, lockers, renewed friendships, and conversations about the summer past and the year ahead—180 days of homeroom and classes.

In 1955, we listened and danced to the sounds of The Penguins' "Earth Angel" and Bill Haley & His Comets' "Rock Around the Clock." The latter became a teenage anthem, having been introduced in the soundtrack to the movie *Blackboard Jungle*. We were part of a new generation of teens that became an economic force, adopting fads, foods, music, and clothing as statements of our youth.

As sophomores, we replaced given names with nicknames like Yags, Mrz, Spanky, Buck, Beaky, Juicy, Gizmo, Scottie, and Riggsy. There were catchy names like Kujie, Krev, Dutch, and Dee Jaye, plus all-American names like Willie, Peanuts, Cookie, and Charley. The kids that came together as freshmen the year before were now a unit, a team, a class.

Those were the days of open-necked sport shirts and crew cuts, ponytails and crinoline petticoats, crewneck sweaters and poodle skirts, and penny loafers and bobby socks. We sported blazers, Jantzen sweaters, blue suede shoes, and ducktail haircuts. We accessorized with bracelets, watches, and class rings. It was a time to be young and think April thoughts.

Who remembers the titanic struggle between ignorance and knowledge? Why was it so difficult to draw a circle in geometry class with just the chalk and string? How many times did we have to bisect and trisect that anemic-looking frog in biology? Or listening to the challenge offered by Mr. Stoffer, "Bet you a dollar to a donut?"

To defray classroom tedium, certain students played practical jokes in biology class: a spider on a girl's leg, a garter snake placed harmlessly on a girl's shoulder, a mouse in a desk drawer, or the secret potion in chemistry class that ate the sink's plumbing. Remember the fire extinguisher that "accidentally" discharged in the hall? When the culprits were caught—and they were almost always immediately caught—they'd plead coincidence! It was to no avail. Many young lads became intimately acquainted with our beloved class sponsor, as his seasoned walnut paddle of iniquity reverberated with the resounding crescendo of a buttock caress. Offenders always received the standard penance: two swats!

Some things continually perplexed us. Why did our locker open every time except when we were running late for class? Why did the talker always get caught and not the talkee? (The least they could have done was penalize the other guy for reckless listening!)

Sages tell us that life is a series of hills and valleys. In 1955, I resided in a valley devoid of intelligence. Philosophers say we can easily forgive a child for being afraid of the dark, but what about those who are afraid of the light? I have never been afraid of the light. I simply cannot find the switch!

One day we turn around and it's autumn, and the next day we turn around and it's spring. All too soon our second year at Whiting High School was coming to a close and there was so much more to do.

If there's a turning point in adolescence, a stage between not having to shave and shaving every day, a time when bobby socks are replaced by nylons, it's junior year. It's a year of emerging independence, an escalation of self-assurance and confidence. The junior year is that delicious stage of youth when all nonsense and adolescence silliness slams headlong into the torrent of teenage hormones and intoxicates them to the degree that they stagger under their influence in a state of befuddled amusement.

This third year of high school is the final plateau before reaching the summit of secondary education—base camp one. To all who reach this lofty status come new privileges and rights. Having survived two years of being underclassmen, we had earned the spoils of victory.

Being a junior in high school is ridiculous at times. You're at what they call the "in-between age"—too old for the kiddies, but too young to run with the big boys and girls. Being a junior, for some boys, is learning that maturation doesn't always arrive at the same time and place with equal prominence. Looking in the bathroom mirror, you discover only one side of your face needs shaving!

Being a junior is learning that "going steady" refers to relationships and has nothing to do with prunes or laxatives. Being a junior is learning you have sweet breath for kissing but rancid armpits. Being a junior is often frustrating, but it's also a joy. It's like being a hitchhiker who sucks his thumb—one finds it difficult to make any progress. Such is the lot of the high school junior, and this is how it was in September 1956.

Like most years, each day brought adventure, unexpected events, laughter, and tears. It was also a year of new words like Sputnik and rocket, launch and re-entry, satellite and outer space, and another word that caused much apprehension and anxiety: Russian.

But while the outside world clamored about the launching of a foreign satellite into space, the members of the Class of 1958 continued to demonstrate their spirit and strength while focused on their scholastic, athletic, and social goals. We continued to be faithful to our duties of holding up the radiator in the main hall. As scientists and engineers directed their collective energies to conquer gravity for the weightlessness of outer space, we remained down to earth, relaxing while anchored against and leaning on walls, water coolers, doorways, railings, lockers, fences, pool tables, trees—anything solid. Whenever you saw a junior boy, they were desperately clinging and grasping to some fixed object lest they slide to the ground like jelly.

The 1956-1957 school year ushered in white buck shoes and V-neck sweaters. It was a time when girls all dressed in coordinating colors, turned their sweaters around, and spoke in Pig Latin. It was the age of ducktail haircuts and greasy heads, knock-knock jokes, and slang expressions. Entering our lexicon were now classic phrases like, "See you later, alligator," "There's a fungus among us," and June Rowe's favorite, "Easy greasy, you gotta long way to slide." Don't forget "daddy-o" and Hank Plawecki's favorite, "Some-ma-na-gun." Steve Linko combined strategies of skill and psychology by singing "The Purple People Eater" for three consecutive hours while playing snooker at Nick's Pool Room.

The soundtrack of our sock hops featured Elvis Presley, Ricky Nelson, and Pat Boone. Television screens were filled with *American Bandstand* and *The Mickey Mouse Club*. It was an age where youth was king, and the music belonged to us! Feeding our almost insatiable teenage appetite for rock 'n' roll, established stars and newcomers released records only to find themselves dethroned overnight by a fresh sound or a new dance. Popular songs by The Diamonds, Danny and the Juniors, Dion and the Belmonts, Johnny Mathis, Duane Eddy, and hundreds more filled jukebox speakers at Whiting's favorite teen gathering place, The Oil Can.

The sounds and the sound-makers became a vital part of our lives in the season of 1957. Pool rooms, bowling alleys, pizza parlors, drugstores, street corners, and the Community Center— these were the hangouts, the places to be, where homework was forgotten and assignments set aside. Those were the scenes, sights, and sounds of our junior year at Whiting High School. Together, the class of 1958 made it a very good year.

Senior year started in early September. The playboy of the seasons winked one last time at suntanned faces while falling leaves bid farewell to their branches after being painted by the flame of an early autumn sun. It was the beginning of the end, but also the end of the beginning.

Our senior year was a year for formulas and facts, Bermuda shorts and car coats, knee-length socks and chemise dresses, the holiday basketball tournament and the sub-deb winter formal. These were the youthful days for snapshots and soft drinks, street corner seminars, and jokes about Ida's New Location. For the Class of 1958, this was the year of years, a good year, the last-time year.

During these final 180 days of our high school career, we had many memorable moments. In our own words and in our own ways, we each could share favorite stories and memories. Tonight we've come together to celebrate and share a number of these remembrances. This was our time, an evening for white sport coats and pink carnations. There were pre-prom parties, ballroom dancing—and later on—late evening dining and a show in Chicago. Clutching souvenirs and listening to favorite tunes on the radio as the Chrysler Windsor cruised southward on Lake Shore Drive. Before returning home, prom couples parked at Bobby Beach to watch the moonlight dance on Lake Michigan. With the radio playing Dean Martin and Tony Bennett, starry-eyed adolescents shared soft quiet kisses at 4:00 am.

We picnicked at the Dunes, played softball with the girls, took photographs, signed autographs, and listened to phonograph tunes. There were moonlit walks and quiet talks with gentle voices in the night. The final days of our year were filled with the traditional Bum's Day assembly, a hayride at twilight, open house at Mr. Fowdy's, Class Night, and then Commencement.

The crisp twilight of an Indian summer silently gave way to the fragile patter of windblown snowflakes. Icicles drying in the sun nourished the buds of a new season as winter melted into spring. Ninety days later, spring returned the favor and matured into summer. Then, in what seemed like a moment, it was no more.

The strains of "Pomp and Circumstance" have long since faded into time. The Class of 1958 graduates went their separate ways to make their marks in a world that's difficult, challenging, complex, and ever-changing. More than half a century has passed since that June evening, and tonight we've come home to renew friendships and share memories about our magical, once-upon-a-time experience at Whiting High School.

Like the fabled land of Camelot, let us resolve that from this night on, and each evening before the flames of faraway stars flicker darkness into dawn, we'll think back on all the tales we remember of classmates and teachers, of those whose voices have been stilled, and of family and friends who touched our lives along the way and helped bring us to this time and place.

We celebrate with heartfelt appreciation, knowing our journey through life has gone from green and white to gold. May God always bless the Whiting High School Class of 1958.

(2008)

GUEST CHECK

TABLE	PERSONS	46394	SERVER
G	5		S-9

The Geriatric Adventure
Gifts of Christmas
Golden Moments: A Love Story
Graduation Thoughts
Guns vs. Causation

TAX

THANKS FOR VISITING THE MIND CAFETERIA

The Geriatric Adventure

Throughout life, there's a progression of events, happenings, and adventures. During our childhood and pre-adult years, these moments are often accompanied with anticipation, excitement, and an impatient eagerness that engenders fond remembrance of these various milestones. In adulthood, this continuum is amplified by responsibilities, promises, and necessities.

But as we accumulate years, confronting this procession signals the onset of what I call the Geriatric Adventure. Unlike earlier times, this stage of life generates degrees of uncertainty, reluctance, and hesitation, plus a fearful realization that we're facing limitations of capability, self-reliance, and choice. There's a troubling awareness these advancing golden years will menace our independence, control, and sovereignty.

Hallmarks of the Geriatric Adventure are surprise and unexpectedness. Ordinary routine tasks, once quite easily completed, now require additional strength and effort if not also extra concentration, struggle, and frustration. This manifestation of change fatigues mind, body, and spirit. Disquieting feelings about physical health and emotional well-being—not to mention increasing anxiety toward driving and after-dark outings—conspire with unexpected aches and pains and seemingly arbitrary unsteadiness.

Although age-related, the defining characteristic of the Geriatric Adventure is the randomness of arrival. There is no set year, specific time, or calendar date. Its onset can be gradual or accelerated by age, environment, injury, malady, or simple genetics.

We learn early that life's journey is not a sprint but a marathon. By the time we've become mature adults, we need to have acquired beneficial lifestyle habits, like good decision-making skills, choosing healthy options, and keeping a positive mindset. To ward off unpleasant aspects of the Geriatric Adventure we need to be joyful, to laugh, to participate, and to celebrate—appreciating each and every moment of every day without regret.

But the Geriatric Adventure is not dark clouds and gloom—far from it! Speaking as a participant, entitlements like senior discounts and coupons, designated parking places, and special accommodations from sundry businesses and establishments enrich our social rank. Some seniors, though no longer licensed to drive, have abundant gas. And we become extremely knowledgeable of pharmaceuticals, ensuring to keep a current edition of *The Pill Book* within reach.

In our younger days, we socialized at pool halls, bowling alleys, and bars. Today, it's drugstores, doctor offices, and funeral homes. As soon as we're seated in the doctor's waiting room, geriatric strangers readily reveal their latest diagnosis and medical history. With uninhibited exuberance, narratives about urinary tract infections, varicose veins, bowel disorders, digestive issues, and aching joints are shared like party hors d'oeuvres. These impromptu merry medical seminars only pause when the next patient is called. Then, almost boastfully, someone else volunteers to detail his or her latest procedure.

Lined up along a waiting room wall decorated with advertisements for compression hose and absorbent garments are supportive devices for the Geriatric Adventure: canes, wheelchairs, and walkers. One upscale walker sports turn signals, curb feelers, and a horn. Talk about celebration!

In spite of their eccentricities, Geriatric Adventurers are a delight to talk with and listen to as they convey moments of their life's journey. When I was much younger, I wondered why God let people get old. I found an explanation in John Powers' book, *The Unoriginal Sinner and the Ice-Cream God*: "God answered, 'I let people get old because they are my human sunsets: the most beautiful part of the day.'"

I believe the most important benefit of the Geriatric Adventure is that it teaches us to cherish the gift of being and appreciate all who have touched our lives with goodness, thoughtfulness, kindness, and love. It does seems like time has sped up. As teenagers we took time for granted, spending days with carefree abandon as though we had an unlimited supply.

Today, as seasoned citizens, that supply is diminished. We know that most of our life has become the past. Each new day arrives as a gift from Heaven, so we treasure it like a precious gem, protective as to how we spend the smallest snippets of time. Even so, when another week has passed, it seems as though we've expended a fortune. For those of us who are ancient, a day doesn't go as far as it once did.

If Heaven is kind, the majority of us will join the Geriatric Adventure. We need to welcome and celebrate this passage of life with acceptance and courage for whatever is presented along the way. There are lessons to learn, tests to past, and knowledge to add to our personal inventory and destiny, remembering that the sunset is the most beautiful part of the day.

(2016)

Gifts of Christmas

In December 1951, I was in Sister Mary Applesauce's sixth-grade class at Sacred Heart School in Whiting, Indiana. I was also a member of the boys' choir that would sing Christmas carols at Midnight Mass on Christmas Eve. Joining voices with seventh- and eighth-graders, the choir formed an angelic sound. For the better part of the year, we were mischievous, free-spirited youths, but at Christmastime we transformed into pious, dignified, well-disciplined Catholic lads.

We practiced daily in the downstairs parish hall, giving us an hour's respite from our daily diet of Applesauce and salvation. Sister Melody guided and directed our voices into a heavenly chorale of altos, sopranos, and tenors. During rehearsal, we were all business. We took Sister's direction without nonsense or challenge. Vocal warm-ups, breathing exercises, and melodic variations were practiced over and over. Suffice it to say that as Christmas approached, the Sacred Heart Boys' Choir sounded magnificent! Even so, once school had ended for the day I focused on more pressing secular matters.

Excited with anticipation for Christmas and full of the holiday spirit, I wanted to buy my mother a special gift. Though money was scarce, by age 10, I'd become financially resourceful, having found a dependable supply of revenue.

As a fifth-grader, I'd discovered people threw away soda bottles and metal coat hangers. Each empty pop bottle was worth 2 cents, while Kinanne's Cleaners offered 1 cent for every two coat hangers. Several times a week I'd scrounge my neighbors' trash, searching for discarded bottles and hangers. Occasionally, a Canfield's bottle—worth 5 whole cents!—would be discovered. Dozens of searches through neighborhood garbage cans over the summer and autumn had generated a tidy sum. Kindly merchants were always generous, knowing I hadn't purchased the soda in their store but paying out the deposit anyway.

Comic books and small toys filled the bill as gifts for my older brother Ron and younger sister Barbara. Dad would get a carton of Old Gold cigarettes, but I wanted to buy Mom something special. In spite of frugal budgeting, my Christmas funds were nearly depleted. By the time I arrived at Sherman's Indiana Supply, I was down to my last dollar and a few coins. Sherman's had a bright new store along 119th Street at Central Avenue, where they sold hardware, paint, plumbing, and housewares. The salesperson, Mrs. Parker, helped me select a nice "mom gift"—a 10" Pyrex pie plate. With its scalloped edge, the glass dish resembled the one I'd broken while washing dishes.

I handed Mrs. Parker the last of my funds, $1.50. Along with the receipt, she returned 11 cents in change. Wrapped in holiday paper printed with green holly and red berries the pie plate made an elegant gift. I took it home, and after writing "For Mom" on a gummed sticker, I placed it under the tree when no one was watching.

Our family always opened gifts after 6:00 pm on Christmas Eve. I learned later that this was so we could wear something new to Midnight Mass. Mom said all the right things as she unwrapped my present. Later, after I put on my brand new white shirt and dark trousers and was bundled against the cold, Dad walked with my brother and me to Sacred Heart Church, arriving around 10:00 pm.

My brother and I went to the sacristy, each putting on a white cassock and surplice, and took our assigned places. Sister Superior, who was in charge of the entire choir, monitored our progress and behavior. We lined up according to grade, and Sister distributed booklets with the words to the carols. A small pump organ was placed in the sanctuary. One of the parishioners, Melvin Schaffer, would be the choir's accompanist.

At 10:30 pm, we silently marched out and took our place behind the communion rail. A single blue votive candle was positioned at selected intervals as a marker indicating where to stand: sixth-graders in the front row, seventh-graders in the middle row, and eighth-graders in the back row. Sacred Heart Church was beautifully decorated for Christmas. The

Nativity scene was on display to the side. Blue light bulbs formed a heavenly glow around the crib and figurines. Fresh evergreen trees decorated with lights and tinsel filled the sanctuary, the pine-scented perfume adding to the ambiance and majesty of the moment. The church was filled to capacity.

On cue, the organ played and we sang. We opened with "O Little Town of Bethlehem" and closed with "Silent Night." Our English and Latin were flawless. The packed church beamed as our voices presented ageless Christmas hymns. Following our presentation, we walked silently to the sanctuary where folding chairs were set up facing the main altar. Glancing at the congregation, we saw proud parents and parishioners smiling through teary eyes, the looks on their faces conveying approval and appreciation.

So many years ago, I learned the most important gifts in life are not things but matters of the heart. As proud as I was of the pie plate I'd purchased from Sherman's, it was the giving that became a treasure. Faith, goodness, kindness, thoughtfulness, friendship, peace, generosity, time, and love become cherished gifts of Christmas. All who touched my life gave me these gifts.

Merry Christmas, everyone!

(2007)

Golden Moments:
A Love Story

Golden moments are the handiwork of Heaven. Every now and then, like a wonderful surprise, unrelated random events arrive at a predestined locale, gather like playful children, and transform mundane moments to extraordinary, life-changing experiences. Words like "destiny" and "fate" and phrases like "It was written in the stars" and "It was meant to be" are used to explain and dispel the improbability of coincidence or accidental reasons for such occurrences.

But as we accumulate seasons of maturity, we gain a personal wisdom and reverence for mystical forces that were custom-designed for us before we were born. When the stars align, celestial gymnastics release mind-dazzling benevolence like an avalanche of benedictive blessings, filling the heart, mind, and spirit with joy. This is what we humans call love.

Of all the emotions and feelings we experience, love is the one most sought after, cherished, coveted, and treasured above all others. If we try to describe this all-consuming feeling of delicious attraction, yearning, and attachment for another, there's always the difficulty of explanation. Attempting to describe how we pursue, capture, and physically embrace life's most important emotional bond of exhilaration is like trying to tame lightning, hug moonlight, or describe the geometry of thoughts: It's too intangible, elusive, and fleeting.

Still, I can't help but make an attempt as I share one particularly special gift of golden moments that was fully revealed to me 55 years ago. Several events conspired together in 1960 to set in motion a love story that continues to this very day.

Nineteen years old and in my second year of a four-year apprenticeship at Inland Steel in East Chicago, Indiana, I often took the bus to work even though I had a car. One early spring night after working the 4:00 pm to midnight shift, a couple of carpooling buddies of mine, Paul and Don, offered me a ride home. But first, wanting to grab a bite to eat, Paul drove south to the Hessville neighborhood in Hammond.

Turning from Kennedy Avenue onto 169th Street, Paul guided his 1956 Pontiac two doors west to a drive-in restaurant whose roof featured a revolving multicolored neon rainbow and flashing bands of pink neon that illuminated the white building's perimeter. Just above the front windows facing 169th Street, a white painted sign with large black letters spelled out the establishment's name: POW-WOW.

The Pow-Wow Drive-In was open daily from 4:00 pm to 1:00 am, beginning in early April through October. Set back from the street, the location gave drivers ample room to circle around, check out the street sleds and carhops, and select their preferred parking space. Two carhops were assigned at each corner of the drive-in to take orders from those who parked in their service area.

Sitting in the back seat, I surveyed the various hot rods on the premises but my focus was on the carhops, many of whom were students at nearby Morton High School, located just a block south of the Pow-Wow on Marshall Avenue. Giving our order to one of these young ladies, Paul, Don, and I each asked for a burger, fries, and a Pepsi.

Enjoying the ambiance, the neon-light show, jukebox selections, and most of all, the carhops, I was immediately hooked. Following this first visit, whenever I was scheduled to work the 4:00 pm to midnight shift, I'd skip the bus and drive to the mill so I could stop by the Pow-Wow afterward for a late-night snack.

One particular carhop at the Pow-Wow, whose number was S-9, had caught my eye. A senior at Morton, Suzanne stood 5 feet 4 inches tall with an unforgettable smile and a ponytail that kept cadence with her movements as she carried trays to and from waiting cars. To me, she was Debbie Reynolds from *Tammy and the Bachelor* in living color, a vision of happily-ever-after that literally took the air out of my lungs. S-9 was, quite simply, A-D-O-R-A-B-L-E!

Suzanne took my order on several visits and we exchanged small talk, but a classic case of apprehension and fear of rejection took over in me. Often I was too timid to park in her assigned area. Still, little by little, as spring turned to summer, we became better acquainted. My visits to the Pow-Wow increased as my confidence grew, and I routinely parked by her assigned station. Captivated, I decided that S-9 and the steelworker would somehow become a couple.

The problem was that I wasn't looking for a steady girlfriend. Upon completion of my apprenticeship at the steel mill, I expected to be drafted into the military for two years so I didn't want to get involved in a serious relationship. I was emotionally conflicted, to say the least. As the summer progressed, my visits to Pow-Wow decreased.

Late one Saturday afternoon, my mom wanted me to deliver some gifts to my brother and his wife who were living in Hessville. Traffic, trains, and the hassle of being the family's delivery service tested my patience. Additional aggravation ensued after finding no one home and having to bring the packages back—wasted time, gasoline, and effort. Plus I'd missed lunch because I was busy with chores earlier in the day, so now I was a very hungry, not very happy camper.

Driving north on Kennedy Avenue, I caught the light at 169th Street and on a whim, decided to turn west. Pulling into a spot at the Pow-Wow, I waited for a carhop to take my order. I looked up to see S-9 approaching my car, her ponytail swinging in time. Seeing Suzanne again took my breath away and made music for my eyes, pausing euphoric heartbeats as the stars aligned and Heaven smiled.

After we quickly caught up on current affairs, I impulsively asked, "So when are we goin' out?"

"I don't know," Suzanne replied. "When are we?"

"Next Saturday. We can go to your homecoming game."

She hesitated, and I waited for the pain of rejection.

"I have to ride on a parade float because I'm one of the homecoming queen's attendants, but we can meet at the field before the game."

Though somewhat skeptical, I agreed.

True to her word, Suzanne and I met at the Morton High School homecoming game as planned, where we held hands, joined hearts, and shared thoughts of togetherness. Ordinary minutes became extraordinary moments to remember.

As our first date came to a close, I looked into her eyes and saw the rest of my life. How lucky I was to find someone who became both ends of my rainbow. That night, under a sky quilted with stars and bathed in autumn moonlight, September 24, 1960, became Magic Day, henceforth forever remembered and celebrated.

Our courtship continued, blossoming into marriage on June 19, 1965. This year we celebrate our golden wedding anniversary. The magic of Suzanne's love taught me how to see with my heart and treasure the gift of Heaven's golden moments. She is amazing!

(2015)

Graduation Thoughts

A Letter to My Graduating Seniors at
Lake Central High School, Class of 2007

Dear Graduating Seniors:

When we complete high school and prepare for graduation, we pause to reflect on the past four years and give some thought to what future endeavors await along our journey. As your teacher, I've been privileged and honored to have shared with you a portion of your high school career. In a few days you'll receive your diploma and cross the threshold to young adult.

As my gift to you, I offer just a smidgen of wisdom about lessons I've learned with the hope that you'll embrace the future with the same energy, enthusiasm, and passion you did as a high school student. Here are my graduation thoughts.

Each of us learns early that life is a series of beginnings and goodbyes. And no matter the number of our years, we never quite get used to it.

Four years ago, we shared a beginning, and today we share a goodbye. Fortunately, this melancholy is short-lived as you begin a new phase of your life. Whatever bittersweet memories remain from your high school days will be quickly replaced with anticipation and excitement of future endeavors as your life unfolds.

May every wish become a star to follow. May every hope become an adventure to pursue. And may every dream enrich and enhance your life's journey. As one of your teachers, let me add my congratulations for a job well done and best wishes for your future success.

Teachers touch the lives of students in many ways, and students touch the lives of their teachers—all in all, a pretty good deal. By now you know the important things in life are not things, but people. The sign in my classroom said it all: "Trust, Honor, Respect, and Responsibility."

Before the chalk dust settles and the classroom door closes for the final time this year, here's my graduation wish for you:

> May each day be filled with laughter, love,
> good health, and good fortune.
> May Heaven's angels guide you every step of the way.
> May the good Lord keep you close to Him forever.
> May you always take time to help Mom with the dishes.
> And may you always remember to convey appreciation
> to all the good people who touch your life.

Take care, be well, stay safe, and God bless.

Sincerely,

Mr. Koch
Lake Central High School

(2007)

Guns vs. Causation

Another mass shooting in a school by a demented, heavily armed young man has resulted in the deaths of young children and their teachers, once again bringing the question of gun control and Second Amendment rights to the forefront of national news. This latest violent rampage only adds to the growing list of senseless acts of human destruction. And as before, blame is focused on readily accessible firearms: assault rifles and high-capacity magazines.

Voices of political leaders, law enforcement officers, and sundry gun control advocates are calling for more gun laws and additional federal and state regulations, bans, and restrictions. Without question, guns and the bullets therein served as the instruments for this latest act of insanity, but the core reasons for such repulsive violence are much more disturbing and profound.

A number of factors serve as catalyst and contributors that manifest into such twisted, terrible acts of human behavior:

- The deterioration of virtuous individual character
- The decay, ridicule, and diminished importance of spiritual values, religious beliefs, and prayer
- The erosion of family: fractured, acrimonious, and broken homes
- The cavalier disregard, devaluation, and destruction of life
- The loss of direction and corruption of America's moral compass
- The acceptance of flagrant violence and repugnant behavior as entertainment in movies, video games, music, and society
- The wanting education of children: academic, social, and moral
- The lack of priority for mental health care and maintaining mental health wellness

- The detrimental effect of our nation's dysfunctional elected officials and their inability or unwillingness to resolve issues that adversely affect citizens. Instead they focus on special interests, political ideology, and personal political careers. As a result, our national security, American exceptionality, and our quality of life are diminished, causing erosion to America's core values.

For too many years, we've witnessed the declining influence of the family, church, and school. This societal triad nurtured, taught, built, and sustained positive, constructive values—individually and collectively—since America's founding. It strengthened, supported, and propagated our nation's exceptionality. But all too often today, this triad is attacked, ridiculed, disrespected, and devalued.

As a public school teacher for more than four decades, I observed far too many children with empty eyes and vacancies of the heart. More often than not, students arrived at the school doors undervalued, poorly parented, spiritually malnourished, and ill-equipped to effectively cope with the process of growing up and becoming an adult.

From infancy on, too many children aren't being taught what is kind, good, thoughtful and decent. They haven't captured the essence of trust, honor, respect, and responsibility. They don't value their spirituality, the necessity of prayer, nor the sacredness of life. Most importantly, they don't feel cherished, valued, or loved. When things get difficult, they lack the capability to resolve problems appropriately. They don't know how to make good decisions, handle adversity, or employ successful problem-solving strategies. Lacking these skills, their personal struggle leads to frustration, anger, acting out, and in some cases, violent behavior.

Without question, firearms in the hands of discontent, angry, mentally unstable, or antisocial persons are dangerous and deadly. But the root causation is founded in economic and education deficiencies, poor parenting, dysfunctional families, spiritual starvation, lack of self-worth, and not treasuring the sacredness of life.

What will it take before we as a nation understand that our most important task is the well-being of children? What needs to happen before we as individuals realize that people are more important and valuable than things?

No one grows up in a straight line—it's a series of advances and retreats. We all need someone to celebrate our triumphs and be supportive and nurturing when things don't go so well. We need each other. We are all teachers—we learn from each other by word and example. Children must be taught lifelong lessons of goodness, thoughtfulness, kindness, compassion, appreciation, and love. They must be guided and strengthened with examples of trust, honor, respect, responsibility, faith, and prayerful reverence for things we cannot see.

We already know the root cause of violence. We also know that until each of us fully captures the sacredness of living within our heart, mind, and spirit, there will be destruction of life. The choice is ours.

(2013)

GUEST CHECK

TABLE	PERSONS		SERVER
H	4	46394	S-9

Have a Good Day!
Here and Gone
He Was My Brother
Hometown: Yesterday and Today

TAX

THANKS FOR VISITING THE MIND CAFETERIA

Have a Good Day!

As we go through our daily routines, it's common to hear someone say, "Have a good day!" Most of the time, the words bounce off without impact and are dismissed without much thought. But every now and again, those words stick like Velcro and their meaning gives us pause to consider and reflect: Just what is a good day?

When I was a kid, a good day was finding enough discarded soft-drink bottles in neighborhood trashcans and alleys. Each bottle was worth a 2-cent deposit, and converting glass to cash was crucial to a 11-year-old who needed 24 cents for the Saturday matinee at the Capitol Theater in Whiting, Indiana (covering admission, a small Coke, and a box of Jujyfruits).

A good day was discovering a discarded cereal box with its valuable box top undamaged. These all-important cardboard flaps were necessary for procuring any number of premiums offered by radio programs. Along with a few coins, a kid could send box tops away to Battle Creek, Michigan, or Checkerboard Square in St. Louis, Missouri, for badges, signal rings, and secret decoders. Heroes of the radio airwaves, like Tom Mix, Sergeant Preston, The Lone Ranger, Little Orphan Annie, and Superman invited faithful listeners to join their inner circle by using these official gadgets and gizmos.

Later, as a teenager, a good day was having the means to replace the well-worn heels on my only good pair of shoes and the skills to sew buttons and color-match thread on the hand-me-downs that comprised my school wardrobe. A good day was saving a dollar in advance to pay one-third of the cost of my high school yearbook or scraping together the price of a 35-cent basketball ticket. A good day was being able to set a double-double bowling match at the Whiting Community Center—earning $6 in one evening was something special! (Being 16 meant that discarded soft-drink bottles were now left to younger entrepreneurs.)

There were times when good days were few and far between. But when they did arrive, those moments were delicious and savored like an elegant banquet.

As we age, our experiences temper and tone memories. The very structure of our lives is altered and modified. Our perspective is broadened or narrowed and strengthened or weakened by events from our formative years. It is this seasoning that determines the number and quality of good days. Though each day is a gift, we know too well that it can also be a challenge. For too many, a good day is one with bearable discomfort or tolerable pain, having some food in the pantry, or enough money to fill prescriptions and pay household bills.

A good day is relative. A good day is one when loved ones remember and appreciate us. A good day is when thoughtfulness and kindness are in abundance. Good days are better than bad days. Most of us have lived long enough to know that good days are optional. In many cases, we determine the number of our good days.

As we mature, we learn how to make our own sunshine. By thought, word, and deed, we can create goodness. And if we're generous, our homemade supply of sun-drenched goodness can be shared and given to others as a gift. When all is said and done, we understand that there is never any excuse for not being kind. Have a *good* day!

(2003)

Here and Gone

Over the years, many things that were commonplace are now gone. Some disappear due to technological advancements, others fade away thanks to lifestyle changes, and some simply vanish because it was time.

In no particular order, here's my list of products, places, items, and activities once here and now gone. Many will be familiar to those who also call Whiting, Indiana, their hometown. Some entered our lives in other ways and for a variety of reasons.

Automobile seat covers. Fender skirts. Tire inner tubes. Whitewall tires. Vinyl tops. Steel license plates. Ditto and mimeograph machines. Rooftop TV antennas. Black and white TVs. Soda fountains. Jukeboxes. White Rain shampoo. Toni home perms. Submarine races. Tinsel for Christmas trees. Merthiolate. Airmail stamps. C.O.D. packages. S&H Green Stamps. E.F Hutton. Foreman Motors. The *Chicago Daily News* and *Chicago Herald-American* newspapers. Liberty Head dimes, Buffalo nickels, and all coins made with silver. DuMont, Muntz, and Admiral television sets. 78 rpm records. Cassette decks. The Bell System. *McCall's* and all other now defunct magazines. Beatniks and greasers. The Henry J automobile. Floppy disks. The carousel slide projector. The military draft. Radio adventure programs. Jim Moran, the Courtesy Man.

Ironing clothes. Rabbit ears. TV trays. Kellogg's Pep breakfast cereal. Cigarette ads on radio and television. Streetcars. Shoreline buses. Steam locomotives. Elevator operators. Reel-to-reel tape recorders. 8-track tapes and cassettes. Top 40 radio disc jockeys. Fountain pens, ink wells, and blotters. Slide rules. Typewriters. Complimentary road maps from gas stations. The Robert Hall Clothing Store with plain pipe-racks. The *Morris B. Sachs Amateur Hour.* Record players. VHS and Beta. Foot X-ray machines when buying shoes. *American Bandstand*. Bowling alley pinboys. IBM punch cards for data processing. Corsets and girdles. Television test patterns. Duz, Rinso, and all of their soapy and sudsy cousins, plus laundry's big three: clothesline, clothespoles, and clothespins.

Party lines and telephone operators. Leo P. Kneozer Oldsmobile & Cadillac. Broadway Oldsmobile. Station wagons. Automobile carburetors, engine chokes, and side vent windows. Writing J.M.J. at the top of parochial grade school assignments. School desks fastened to the floor. Latin Mass. The *Baltimore Catechism*. Radio program premiums for box tops and coins. Lionel trains. The Mr. Machine robot toy. Jarts. Chemistry sets. Erector sets. Knickers. Crinoline petticoats. Fedoras. Movies without swear words and vulgar language. The 41 Outdoor Theater and other drive-in movie theaters. The Paramount and Parthenon Theatres. Karmel Korn. Steel soda cans. J.C. Higgins and Whizzer bikes. Silvertone, the Sears store brand for radios and televisions. Autolite car batteries and sparkplugs. D.A. haircuts on guys, and French twist, bouffant, and pageboy hairstyles on gals.

Kaiser-Frazer, Hudson, DeSoto, and Studebaker-Packard. Coal bins. Glass deposit bottles. Wire coat hangers. Playing in the street. Western Union telegrams. Home delivery of milk, baked goods, and almost everything else. GM's Fisher Body. Quarantine signs posted on homes with measles, chicken pox, and other communicable diseases. Fallout shelters. Carbon paper. Hubcaps. Fog lights. Pinto. Corvair. Wire wheels. Jalopies. Hot rods with steering wheel spinner knobs. Push reel lawn mowers. Cannon towels. Charles Antell's Formula No. 9 hair cream, Wildroot hair tonic, Hair Arranger paste wax, and Bryll Cream. Individual prices stamped on canned goods. Bobby socks. Babushkas. Hallicrafters radios and TVs. Fox Deluxe, Tavern Pale, Primo, and other once-upon-a-time beer brands.

Howard Johnson motels. AMC. Oldsmobile. Pontiac. Standard Oil. Sinclair's Dino. Service station attendants and pump helpers. Gasoline for 20 cents a gallon. Leaded (ethyl) gasoline. Chicago's Last Department Store. Chicago's Last Liquor Store. Thunderbird Motel. *The Mickey Mouse Club*. Mail-order catalogs from Sears, Roebuck & Co., Montgomery Ward, and Spiegel. Polk Bros., Goldblatt's, Minas, Millikan's, and Nagdeman's department stores. Browsing for bargains at Venture, Topps, Shopper's World, Shopper's Fair, F.W. Woolworth, E.J. Korvette, J.J. Newberry's, Jupiter, and Kreske's. Rosalee's, Joe Hirsch Store for Men, Jack Fox & Sons, and the Army-Navy War Surplus Store.

Door-to-door salesmen offering encyclopedias, pots and pans, vacuum cleaners, brushes, and notions. Pan Am. TWA. Rotary-dial phones. Telephone booths. Princess and Trimline push-button phones in designer colors. Hair curlers and rollers. RKO Radio Pictures. The Saturday Movie Matinee for kids (two feature films, stage games, cartoons, action serials, coming attractions, and "News of the Day" reels). 8mm Bell & Howell family movies. 16mm film projectors operated by AV students. Argus cameras. Kodak's Brownie and Instamatic cameras. Sylvania Blue Dot Flashbulbs, Flashcubes, and Magicubes. Polaroid. Listening booths to audition the latest 45s. Action Comics. Vacuum tubes for "hand-wired" Zenith radios and TVs.

Mrs. Klein's and Red Dot potato chips. Burger Chef. The Calumet Region's drive-in restaurants: Art's, Dog 'N' Suds, Fat Boy, Hoppe's, Hutsler's Frostop, Kelly's, Patio, Pow-Wow, Serenade, and Son's. Grocery stores: A&P, Condes' Grocery, IGA, National Tea, Park View Foods, and Weiner's. Gold Crown and Red Crown gasoline. Martin's service stations. Burgess batteries. P.F. Flyer gym shoes. Dr. Lyon's tooth powder. Holy Childhood stamps. *Dig* and *Teen* magazines. Milkshakes in a glass topped with whipped cream and two cookies. Gregg shorthand. Kayo syrup. Bubble Up, Wink, and B-1 soda. High school homerooms. Friday night-after-the-game high school sock hops in the gym. Clean-Up Week ("Clean-up, Paint-up, Fix-up"). Standard Diamonds. Pick-up sandlot baseball games. Crane Lake.

Recall hometown names from yesteryear: Whiting News Company. *Main Street Digest, Whiting News Life,* and the *Times Grafic.* Nick's Pool Room. Hot Dog Louie's. McNamara's. Burton's. Lewin-Wolf. Hob-Nob Restaurant. National Dairy. Gyure's Recreation. Neal Price's Firestone Store. Western Tire & Auto. State Bank of Whiting. Bank of Whiting. American Trust & Savings Bank. Chilla's Bank. Schlater and Spanburg Funeral Homes. France Ford. Kinkade's Bicycle Shop. Hansen Buick and Ciesar's Chrysler-Plymouth.

Latiak's, McLaughlin's, and all Whiting-Robertsdale Standard Oil service stations. Victory Restaurant. Bezan Photography. Slovak Dome. St. Mary's Hall. Stieglitz Park. Goose Island. Towne House Lanes. Dave's Drugstore. Ida's New Location. Central Drug Store. The Capitol Theater. Seifer's Furniture. Orr's. The Standard Hotel. Brown's Apparel. Winsberg's ("The Store for Young Men"). Glenn's Shoes. Richard's Pharmacy. Ande's Pizza. Sunday night dances in St. John's Panel Room. The Spot Diner. Gambini's. Jansen's Fruit Market. Plus countless other neighborhood gathering spots, stores, and businesses.

Now it's your turn. Add to the above or start your own list of forgotten favorites while remembering the people, places, things, and happenings brought to mind at the recollection of each "here and gone."

(2014)

He Was My Brother

We all experience the loss of a loved one or dear friend. Whether their passing is expected or sudden, the emotion and remembrance left in a person's wake provides an opportunity to pause and recall personal and private moments.

My older brother Ronald, two and a half years my senior, grew up with me in Whiting, Indiana, and lived the majority of his life in the state's Calumet Region. For the last 25 years, he resided in Morocco, Indiana. On February 8, 2007, Ron died from complications of diabetes. He would have turned 69 years old on August 4.

Because most of our family albums were accidentally discarded shortly after my father's death in 1965, few photographs remain. When we were growing up, personal cameras were rare, home movies too expensive, and videos non-existent. Most of the snapshots we do have were taken with inexpensive Kodak cameras, and many of the monochrome images have faded with time. Aside from high school yearbooks, the pictures I remember of my brother Ron are stored in my heart.

In recent years, when someone passes away, family members display photographs of various events and milestones in the deceased's life on poster boards at the wake. Ron decided against a public viewing. No matter, as I have my memories of him to treasure. Because of the way he hopped around the house when he was very young, he was nicknamed Bunnie. By the time he was eleven, he was Ronnie, and from a teenager on, Ron.

I can picture Ron as a kid playing in the sand at Whiting Park, as a teenager setting pins at the Whiting Community Center, and playing the drums in the 1956 Whiting High School homecoming parade. I recall images playing softball on the playground by McGregor School before Whiting's gymnasium was built.

One memory from my time as an altar boy at Sacred Heart Church stands out. Serving the Saturday night Holy Hour with my classmate Jim Harmon, we prepared the censer and vestments for the closing benediction. No one from the choir was there to sing the designated hymns but as Father Miller elevated the Host, we heard Ron's tenor voice coming from near the sacristy, singing "O Salutaris Hostia" and "Tantum Ergo." I served many times at Sacred Heart, but the remembrance of this particular summer evening is special.

In high school, Ron excelled in music. He was also very skilled in the machine shop and was a gifted bowler, carrying a 190 average. He was voted "Most Talented" by his fellow classmates. Upon graduation, Ron enlisted in the navy, serving three years overseas. He returned home in 1959 and began a career in banking. A year later, in 1960, he got married. As his life unfolded, Ron changed occupations and employers with uncommon frequency. He always pursued financial dreams, seeking the good life.

He spent a number of years trying to find life's shortcut to grasp the golden ring. From banking to refineries, refineries to businesses, businesses to steel mills, and steel mills to local government, Ron finally settled on being a county worker. Along the way, he and his wife had four children. Moving from the Calumet Region to a more rural setting, he had acreage and a new home close to schools for the kids.

But circumstance, coupled with Ron's characteristic inner restlessness, eventually led him to sell the property and move to a mobile home park in Newton County. By now the kids were grown, married, and on their own. Sometime in the early Nineties, he was diagnosed with diabetes. Over time, the disease progressed and took its toll on his health. Following the death of our mother in 1990, my brother didn't speak to me for 15 years. Countless attempts at reestablishing communication were unsuccessful.

About two years ago, at Christmas time, I heard that Ron had surgery due to diabetes, resulting in the amputation of his left leg below the knee. By now he was a resident of the county care center in DeMotte, Indiana. I picked up the phone, and Ron was receptive to my call. We talked for about an hour. I asked if it would be okay if I came to visit him, and he said yes.

What began as a single stopover became a twice-weekly occurrence. Every Tuesday and Thursday, I visited Ron and we'd catch up on old times. When the weather was good, I took Ron shopping in adjacent Rensselaer or out for lunch at his favorite diner in Roselawn, the community next door. In August 2016, I drove him to the Hammond Marina so he could attend his 50th high school reunion (Whiting High School Class of 1956). Reminiscing with classmates buoyed his spirits and gave him an opportunity to share youthful memories.

Ron's eyesight was failing and his health continued to deteriorate, eventually requiring the use of a wheelchair. His son offered to move his father to Dallas, Texas, so he would be with family and loved ones. After the move, I continued to call Ron twice a week and we'd talk about good times. He asked me to come see him one last time.

Early in February, I flew to Dallas and visited with Ron at his son's home. His days were numbered and he struggled for awareness. When it was time for me to leave, I told Ron I loved him. I felt his tears on my cheek as we hugged goodbye.

A few days later, Ron passed away. Now he belongs to the stars. May he dwell in peace in the house of the Lord.

So much has been left unsaid and unwritten. I prefer to remember good moments and fond memories, for this is about caring, compassion, and love because he was my brother.

(2007)

Hometown: Yesterday
and Today

I've said many times that growing up in the industrial Mayberry of Whiting, Indiana, was the best thing that could happen to a kid. Coupled with the adjacent Robertsdale neighborhood, my hometown was a marvelous full-service community that allowed for youthful hopes, wishes, and dreams to come true. Equipped with quality churches, public and parochial schools, businesses, theaters, parks, and other social gathering places, Whiting residents thrived, and families enjoyed amenities that enriched and enhanced each day. This is about those places of the heart.

As a school kid in the 1940s and 1950s, I was amazed that a city the size and population of Whiting had such a variety and diversity of establishments. There were seven major supermarkets (A&P, IGA, Jewel, Kroger, National, Park View, and Weiner's) and several dozen corner grocery stores in Whiting-Robertsdale. Various civic organizations and neighborhood taverns offered places to meet and enjoy libations. Banquet facilities provided venues for weddings, birthdays, and other celebrations. Long-time residents remember St. Mary's Hall and Slovak Dome, and countless activities were held at St. John's Panel Room, Sacred Heart's Rose Room, Knights of Columbus, Whiting Moose Lodge, Elks Lodge, Eagles Lodge, Sokol Club, the V.F.W., and the American Legion. The Whiting Community Center also hosted a variety of social and athletic activities.

Whiting didn't suffer for a lack places of worship—a total of 22 by a 1956 tally. The city had no less than six Catholic churches—Immaculate Conception, Sacred Heart, St. Adalbert, St. John the Baptist, St. Mary, and SS. Peter and Paul—with only the last not having a parish school. There were also several Protestant denominations (Baptist, Lutheran, Methodist, and Presbyterian), plus a Jewish synagogue, a Masonic Temple, and various places of worship for ethnic nationalities, all helping to fill residents' spiritual needs. And to serve families in time of bereavement, Whiting counted five funeral homes: Baran, Kosier, Owens, Schlater, and Spanburg.

Whiting was also home to a large number of banks and a whole range of retail and service businesses: restaurants, diners, dime stores, drugstores, newspaper/stationery stores, flower shops, dry cleaners and laundromats, jewelry stores, furniture stores, shoe stores (and shoe repair shops), men's and women's clothiers, barber shops and beauty salons, doctor and dentist offices, utility companies, insurance agencies, and even lumber yards and bowling alleys. Automobile dealers included Ciesar's Chrysler-Plymouth, Hansen Buick, Lake County Motors, Schlatter Ford (later France Ford), and Swarthout Chevrolet. For tune-ups and fill-ups, we had our choice of Standard Oil service stations (which dominated Indianapolis Boulevard and Calumet Avenue) as well as Shell, Sinclair, and Sunoco.

Municipal buildings dotted throughout Whiting-Robertsdale shone like gems in a custom setting, serving community residents and visitors alike: Whiting City Hall, Whiting City Schools, Whiting Post Office, Whiting Library (a Carnegie Library), the Whiting Fire Department, and the Whiting Police Department, along with the Standard Hotel and Central States Bank buildings.

Safety and security were hallmarks of Whiting-Robertsdale neighborhoods, and families thrived in an environment with easy access to playgrounds, parks, and recreational areas and facilities. These included the aforementioned Whiting Community Center as well as Whiting Park with its lakefront and beach, Standard Diamonds, Forsythe Park, and Bobby Beach. Complementing city-maintained offerings were numerous empty lots that served as playing fields, neighborhood gardens, and places where kids could dig up a healthy supply of worms on their way to fish at Wolf Lake.

With geography that combines Norman Rockwell and Currier and Ives paintings into a living portrait, it's really no wonder that "The Little

City by the Lake" engenders such heartfelt emotions and allegiance from its residents. This one and a half square mile municipality has it all, making this Mayberry of the Midwest the complete package. Residents and business owners showcase civic quality and character through well-kept neighborhoods and a business district that reflects pride of stewardship. Whiting was—and remains—the capital of Indiana's Calumet Region.

Today, Whiting is in the midst of a renaissance. Thanks to astute organization, effective management, financial prudence, insightful planning, and high standards of performance by those in positions of responsibility—coupled with the enthusiastic support of residents and business owners—Whiting is moving forward.

In addition to other annual and seasonal offerings adding renewed vibrancy to the city, Pierogi Fest has become an internationally famous food extravaganza drawing thousands of visitors each summer. The city is focused on building new infrastructure, attracting new construction projects, guiding architecturally sensitive renovations, and creating environment friendly landscapes. It's a clear commitment to residents, business owners, visitors, and community neighbors that the core values upon which Whiting was founded are being reaffirmed.

Each generation captures and keeps personal memories of experiences derived from growing up and living in their hometown. Those times fill countless pages of life's scrapbook with delicious images and recollections. I've always been grateful to the people who helped me along the way, for family and friends who shared these times, and for the hometown that made such a positive, constructive difference in my life.

(2011)

GUEST CHECK

TABLE	PERSONS	46394	SERVER
1	2		S-9

If You Had to Choose
iPods, Cell Phones, and Earbuds

TAX

THANKS FOR VISITING THE MIND CAFETERIA

If You Had to Choose

One of Nat King Cole's classic recordings is the 1963 hit, "That Sunday, That Summer," which tells of having to choose a single day in life to celebrate forever.

Listening to the song, I wonder what day I'd select. Of the more than 24,000 days of life given to me thus far, which one do I treasure above all others to relive? Which 24 golden hours, which 1,440 minutes would I pick? It's not an easy decision. Would my selection come from childhood or adolescence? Is the choice governed by age, circumstance, or happenstance? Was this a day shared with others or a solitary expenditure of personal time? Were these hours part of a birth, beginning, culmination, or farewell? Did these golden moments involve triumph, success, wonder, romance, melancholy, awe, or an unexpected turn of events?

Each of us gathers personal keepsakes of the heart. Among our memories, we store images, sounds, scents, and feelings that prompt extraordinary emotional reactions. Within an instant, tears of recollection fill our eyes, feelings of contentment flood our senses, and an unexplainable serenity saturates our conscious awareness.

What is this magic? How does one explain the mechanism that provides these microseconds of cognitive luxuriousness? Like a shooting star, they blaze brightly for the briefest of moments before returning to a place that remains secret even to ourselves. What would we do if we could capture and keep for one day such personal magic?

As we inventory our precious moments, would you zero in on a particular season or a certain turning point in life? Perhaps you'd choose an unexpected outcome from what began as an insignificant occurrence.

Or maybe you'd pick something that was meticulously planned and came to desired fruition. What moment would you want to relive?

Consider how many nights we drift off to sleep recalling our favorite memories. Who hasn't had dreams so vivid that the emotional afterglow lasts hours after awakening? And how often during our waking hours, do subtle sensory stimuli trigger random flashbacks about events that have enriched our lives? Maybe in some mysterious way, our mind automatically searches for life's sweetest nectar, knowing those remembrances will invigorate our spirit, refresh our thoughts, and revitalize our very humanness.

As humans, we share a common bond and purpose. Each of us wants to be valued and appreciated. Each of us wants to be connected, to belong, and be part of emotionally nourishing relationships. We flourish in communities and thrive when validated by family and friends and respected by strangers. Knowingly and unknowingly, we build memories in others as they also build memories within us. And each of us wants to be loved and to love someone in return.

So if you had to choose just one day to enjoy and savor, what day would that be? What if you could assemble a week? What if you could collect a month's worth? Which days would those be? What are your special moments?

Every time I hear "That Sunday, That Summer" (it's one of the selections on the jukebox in my rec room), I recall a special Friday in September 1960. It was one of those ideal late summer days drenched in sunshine and canopied with blue sky. A particular young lady had caught my eye and our first date was her high school's homecoming football game. Chosen as a senior class attendant, she arrived with the queen's court. At game time, we sat together in the stands. Forty-eight years later, we're still together.

If I had to select a moment in time, it would be the one when I looked into her eyes and saw the rest of my life. That memory lives in my heart, for it's how we began our journey of togetherness toward happily ever after. If I had to choose, it would surely be September 24, 1960, the day the magic began.

What day would you choose?

(2008)

iPods, Cell Phones, and Earbuds

As humans, we crave contact. Since prehistoric times, our species has used drawings, sounds, and words to communicate. With each technological advance, we readily embrace and integrate the latest gadgets that put us in touch. At times, communication is one way—listening to recordings, watching television, and viewing movies and videos. But interactive devices remain popular because humans love to exchange ideas, thoughts, and news in the moment.

As someone who grew up in the 1940s and 1950s, communication consisted of books, radio, records, television, and face-to-face contact. The telephone was available, but its use at home by children and teenagers was closely monitored by parents who restricted it to calls deemed necessary. Instead our primary means of interactive communication was our daily togetherness at school. We couldn't wait to see and talk to our friends and classmates, hearing what they had to say. Sharing hallways in school between classes, cheering at sporting events, walking home from school, and engaging in informal street-corner seminars were all part of our social and communicative development.

Later, when separated by geographic distance, phone calls helped supplement our need for contact until our next in-person visit. And when phone calls weren't possible, we sent cards and wrote actual letters to loved ones and friends. That was so long ago.

Today, immersed in technology, we use electronic gadgets and devices to communicate. In school, during passing periods, students fill hallways with their ears plugged with earbuds. Though walking side-by-side with peers, they prefer to listen to other sounds rather than friendly voices.

In this self-imposed solitary confinement, students shun opportunities to socialize, trade comments, and share memory-making moments with classmates. Some are so offended and self-centered they engage in argumentative outbursts when told in classrooms to turn off their electronic toys, de-bud their ears, and pay attention.

Regardless of circumstance or distance, someone is always in contact with someone. But many are so addicted to self-importance they always have a phone hanging on their ear! Others multitask in a desperate attempt not to be alone with their own thoughts—whether driving, shopping, or walking, their phone is glued to their ear.

Sometimes in church, a congregant's purse or pocket will signal an incoming call. Not too long ago at a wake, someone's cell phone provided a musical interlude in the middle of the memorial prayer service. Occasional forgetfulness forgiven, such examples of inconsiderate self-importance boggle the mind. Should they try to contact Heaven one day, I hope they're not greeted with a busy signal!

Now that computers, cell phones, iPods, Blackberries, iPhones, television, GPS, and cameras are all integrated into unified communication devices, what will become of individuality? People are so enamored with themselves that they even share their most intimate thoughts and photos without a second thought, perhaps hoping to gain notoriety, recognition, or fame, unaware of the repercussions and personal damage caused by such action.

This unsavory information inundates the internet along with the benign. Non-erasable data floods Facebook, Twitter, YouTube, message boards, cell phones, and countless computer screens. Personal electronic devices are wonderful but they don't come equipped with common sense. Avoiding overuse, misuse, and unnecessary use requires responsibility, courtesy, and intelligence. Unfortunately, ego typically trumps common sense. Addiction to these devices has placed personal privacy, safety, and security in jeopardy.

Consider public safety, too. Talking on the phone while driving is understood as risky behavior, yet there are folks who go further—by texting while driving. Periodically taking their eyes off the road to punch in their vitally important message, these drivers jeopardize the safety of themselves, their passengers, and others on the road in order to satisfy an egotistical mindset. Truly, they're legends in their own minds. Texting has also become a major distraction in classrooms. Kids definitely learn by example.

One disturbing outgrowth of our constant attachment to electronic devices involves earbuds. Kids walk around like marionettes attached by droopy strings, glued to whatever is being pumped from their devices to their audio receptors. Often they'll remove one of the buds from an ear and place it in a friend's ear so they both can share the current selection. Once done, it's returned to the owner's ear.

Now we were taught as kids not to share toothbrushes, combs, hairbrushes, cosmetics, and other personal items to prevent the transfer of unwanted bacteria and germs. But today the exchange of earwax particles, bacteria, sweat, and unknown microbes are part and parcel of every cool kid's Earbuds Profit Sharing Plan. Can an increase of ear infections be far behind? It's a budding question.

(2009)

GUEST CHECK

TABLE	PERSONS		SERVER
J	4	46394	S-9

January
A Joyful Lesson
July
Just Thinkin'

TAX

THANKS FOR VISITING THE MIND CAFETERIA

January

January believes it has squatter's rights to the calendar because it's first in line. With a full month of 31 days, the first holiday of the year (New Year's Day), and a menu of weather-related entrées, who can argue with such chronologic arrogance? Janus, a Roman god of beginnings and endings, openings and closings, gives the month its name. Always portrayed as having two faces—one looking forward, one backward—January is his month because it's the time when the sun starts to return. Janus is the doorkeeper who watches over the entrance of the year.

Part of January's prominence comes from the ritual of formulating personal intentions and plans for the new year. Amid celebrations with noisemakers, confetti, and renditions of "Auld Lang Syne" at the stroke of midnight, people across the globe usher in the latest allotment of days by making resolutions, commitments, and hopeful toasts for laughter, love, good health and good fortune. Party hats and libation-filled glasses complete a list worthy of January's namesake. Such frenzy at the start of a new year, looking both forward and backward, is enough to give a Roman god whiplash.

But January is more than just a party and pretty faces. It's a time when winter displays its full strength and control of all living things. Freezing temperatures, icy roads, cold and gloomy days, crystal clear dark nights, and occasional visits of bright sunshine fill this initial cluster of days.

January is both predictable and erratic. As the earth continues to orbit around the sun, daylight lengthens—first by a stingy few minutes, then toward the end of the month, more generously. But January exacts a price for this additional sunlight by delivering only brightness while holding back warmth. And on a moment's notice, as if to remind us of its adventurous nature, January whips up icy soufflés, snow drifts, and pellets of crystalized rain that cover cars, sidewalks, and roadways with an abundance of freezing skid-stuff that challenges both ambulatory and driving skills. Such immature behavior keeps insurance agents and body shops well supplied with patrons who literally meet by accident. All these fender benders make Janus smile.

January is forever trying to stay young, with thermometer readings usually in the teens or twenties. At times it regresses to single digits and even below zero, displaying a total disregard for maturity. And every now and then, just for laughs—a blizzard!

Such behavior makes January a difficult month to endure. It's also the time when we receive our W-2s, which means tax season is upon us. If January wants a little more respect, it could offer an annual tax freeze while deducting some ice and snow and returning a little warmth. But those of us who celebrate our birthdays in January somehow appreciate the antics of this month. It's difficult to explain, but January makes us smile.

For residents at the 42nd parallel north, January is the add-an-extra-blanket, turn-up-the-thermostat, wear-layers-of-flannel, and get-dressed-*before*-going-to-bed month. Cuddling and snuggling is mandatory nightly behavior.

January is a steaming hot cup of coffee before dawn, hot soup at lunch, and supper served on heated plates. January is scurrying from store to warm car, car to warm house. January is when shoppers use extra gas searching for parking spaces closer to the mall's entrance. January is watching wildlife enjoy the bounty at feeders we keep filled. January is when school kids return to classrooms and parents regain the sanity of the daily routine. January is when everyone considers heating their garages.

January is the time when landscapers offer discounts for mower tune-ups and lawn care service. January is finding the courage to face both darkness and cold to fetch the morning paper, set out the trash and recycling, and let Fido do his business. It's also a time when residents battle nasty conditions taking down outdoor Christmas decorations.

January is chapped lips, dry skin, red noses, watery eyes, cold feet, and chilled bodies. January is wool hats, mittens, and boots. January holds the mystery as to why kids are impervious to frigid temperatures, revel in the snow, enjoy sliding on ice, and rarely have their scarf tied or jacket fully zipped, while seasoned human units hunker down, stooped-shouldered and shivering to keep warm. January is a geriatric obstacle course. January teases and taunts us to move to lower latitudes.

By the end of the first 31 days, January is spent and willingly turns things over to February. As daylight increases, January's envious look betrays the knowledge that there will never be a request to serve another monthly term until the next year comes around.

January is my favorite month—enjoy.

(2011)

A Joyful Lesson

Every year on my birthday, I ask myself two questions: Am I satisfied with my life? Am I happy?

One year, I really thought about the second question and realized I was relying on luck or chance because that's what happy means: an unplanned happenstance. Having discovered that happiness is an accident, the question I now ask instead is: Am I joyful? Because joyfulness is a choice.

I recommend having fun. Life is a gift, and we should try to be joyful each of the 1,440 minutes of every day. Sometimes we're so focused on our journey that we fail to notice the more important gifts of life. We're so preoccupied with things we need to get done that we forget that it's our connections with each other that really matter. We're so driven with career and personal goals, and often get competitive as we aim to achieve them. We must remind ourselves that in addition to a career, we each have a calling. A career is what we get paid for, but a calling is what we're made for.

We learn early on that everyone gets fouled in the game of life, so we need to make our own sunshine and share it with those who touch our life. In spite of tough times and difficult days, we must forgive, pardon, let bygones be bygones, and be magnificent to one another. That's the essence of our calling: kindness, compassion, forgiveness, and love. Total realization of this calling came to me when I wasn't paying attention. Thanks to Heaven's benevolence, I learned a joyful lesson that changed my life.

When I was young, my mom taught me how to do laundry. Every Monday evening after the dishes had been washed, I'd be in the basement, stationed alongside our Sears & Roebuck Apex top-loading washing machine and flanked by three large wicker baskets of soiled clothes. My mom's sorting method was whites, colored garments, and outerwear (delicates were washed individually by hand and thus never placed in a basket). She also explained the difference between detergent and soap: Detergent is low suds, made from chemicals, while soap is bubbly, rendered from vegetable oils or animal fat. Therefore, her #1 rule for laundry: Always use detergent!

Years later, at age 23, I was a college freshman, living in the first coed dormitory on the campus of Indiana State University. A coin-operated laundromat with automatic washers and dryers for students was located two blocks away, but I wasn't about to lug my laundry two blocks there and back. There had to be a better way! Late one night, doing some investigative research in my dormitory, I discovered the basement utility room. There was a single laundry tub, a top-loading Whirlpool washer, and an electric dryer for the housekeepers and maintenance staff to launder uniforms, towels, and cleaning cloths. The best discovery of all? The machines were not coin-operated!

So around 12:30 am the following night, barefoot with my laundry in tow, I quietly made my way downstairs to the utility room. I switched on the light, closed the door, and loaded the washer with my jeans, khakis, and shorts. Time was of the essence: no sorting, no problem. Unfortunately, I'd forgotten laundry detergent. However, on the shelf near the laundry tub was an almost full bottle of Joy dishwashing liquid. I set the washing and rinse cycles, water temperature, and then, since I wasn't quite sure how much soap to use, emptied the bottle of Joy into the washer. Closing the lid, I fired up the Whirlpool.

Amid the hum of the electric motor, the sound of agitating water, and the steamy humidity, the lid of the Whirlpool started to flutter. With each agitating motion of wet clothes, bubbles began oozing out from under the lid. At first, there were a few clusters. Then a couple of seconds later, a kinetic eruption lifted the lid, freeing millions of soapy spheres!

Flowing aggressively from the top of the washer over the edge, the slippery tsunami cascaded down the front of the machine, met the floor, and made acquaintance with my toes. Warm, cleansing bubbles shampooed my bare feet and pooled around my ankles. From washing cycle through rinse cycle, they continued their escape. I was entranced. With the bubbles now several inches deep, the utility room floor resembled a foamy carpet.

Near panic, I looked around for something to corral the encroaching suds. In a small closet-like recess was a floor mop and wringer-bucket. I grabbed the mop and tried to capture the bubbles, but the motion of the dry mop against them only made the soapy spheres go airborne! Quickly, I soaked the mop with water in the utility sink and launched another frontal attack. With each thrust and sweep of the mop's absorbent braids, I vanquished the soap-bubble carpet, revealing the tile floor. Mopping up the last of the overflow, I had a eureka moment when I remembered Mom's laundry mandate: Detergent, not soap!

The Whirlpool finished its cycle and stopped. I raised the lid and peered inside. Even after a number of rinses, my jeans, khakis, cutoffs, and Jockey shorts remained intimately entwined in a bubble-rich embrace. I knew from that moment on, I would never be able to get the Joy out of my pants!

(2016)

July

July arrives in Whiting, Indiana, as it does in many other small towns, with a hometown parade, patriotic displays, and fireworks at night. But "The Little City by the Lake" closes out the month with something all its own—the internationally famous Pierogi Fest, celebrating homemade dough-filled pillows of potato, cheese, and other tasty fillings with festivities galore. It's a fitting (if somewhat fattening) end to July, a month that's always one of the biggest attractions on the calendar.

Falling smack dab in the middle of the year, July proudly promenades as summertime's king, strutting along with royal attitude and confidence. With extraordinary exuberance July exclaims, "I'm here for the party!" July is playful, providing a plethora of summertime opportunities for all who relish the season. July is bathing suit month, a time when swimming pools and lakes entice youthful beachcombers and other tan seekers to savor the exhilarating enjoyment of sun, sand, and splash.

On the Fourth of July, the annual celebration of America's birthday is marked by Independence Day celebrations throughout the land. For a few brief shining hours, the Stars and Stripes are taken out of closets and attics and prominently displayed throughout the community as we celebrate our nation's sovereignty, our democratic system of government, and the spirit of America. From border to border and shore to shore, we pay homage to all who those who have served, fought, and died to protect our freedom, liberty, and independence. (How fitting would it be for us to show additional respect for this great country by flying the flag each and every day? Find something else to put in the closet or attic.)

Although June presents the solstice, July takes full control of summer. Casual, comfortable fashions become the norm: flip-flops, tank tops,

T-shirts, light and airy fabrics, and clothing that encourages both head-to-toe tans and sunburns. Sunglasses and floppy hats become part of the uniform when shopping at open-air malls, attending recreational events, and tackling everyday tasks outdoors.

Out of garages and carports come convertibles, motorcycles, and sun-roofed vehicles, gliding down streets in celebration of summer. Lawn mowers, weed-whackers, trimmers, and edgers join the chorus of gas-powered and electric motors as residents cut and prune landscapes to desired standards. Insects thrive and birds gorge themselves, feeding their young with the latest supply of food on the wing. Mosquitoes fortunate enough to escape feathered hunters find summer revelers to pester at picnics, playgrounds, and parks. During July, sales of insect repellent, bug spray, and fly swatters skyrocket!

One of July's main objectives is to make August jealous. As each humid, sun-drenched day arrives, July is already planning for what follows: late-hour sunsets to paint the horizon with crimson and ruby rays of the setting sun, evenings flooded with moonlight, and nighttime skies embroidered with stars. As an added attraction, July serves up an occasional shower of cleansing raindrops to wash and renew the landscape.

July challenges fans and air conditioners to keep perspiration and temperatures to tolerable levels, while providing ideal conditions for garage sales, car washes, and baseball games. July knows how to heat highway roadbeds and neighborhood streets, sidewalks, and driveways. Those who enjoy going barefoot in the summer are quickly reminded to avoid hot concrete, asphalt, and beach sand. But this is the season to be outdoors, so residents and creatures alike take necessary precautions to thoroughly enjoy July's 31 days.

July is a month that changes moments to memories: family gatherings, extended vacations, special events, and the magical transformation when strangers become more than friends. Watching romantics hold hands and share laughter and smiles as they watch the Fourth of July parade or stroll through Pierogi Fest makes those of us who are comparatively ancient recall days of once-upon-a-time when we had limitless energy and were seemingly invincible to problems or vexations of the spirit. July was the elixir, the nectar that sweetened youthful days.

Which July do you remember? What ordinary moments became a treasure of the heart? What images of this month do you keep in your personal scrapbook? July affords the time to remember, recall, and reminisce. In quiet moments, invite those past times of your life to visit. Let thoughts fill your memory like a trusted friend and touch the things we used to be.

July marks the midpoint of the calendar year, making it the perfect place to pause. These are the sun-drenched days following the summer solstice. Bask in the warmth and soak up the rays. This is the gift of July, delivered via tasty dumplings wrapped in babushkas and smiles!

(2011)

Just Thinkin'

Humans, time, and technology cause constant change. People continually affect our lives, while time moves along at a constant rate. Technology's impatience, however, accelerates at mind-boggling speed. Every so often, we pause to take stock of this transition from present to past and new to old, reviewing our circumstances and pensively measuring what's been gained and what's been lost to time. As the years accumulate, thoughtful visitation of past moments becomes more frequent as we informally inventory the treasures of our personal library.

It's sobering to realize that knowledge and skills once deemed essential have been rendered obsolete, and many of the people who touched our lives have passed. In concert with such obsolescence and loss, other things once considered important have since been devalued or replaced with state-of-the-art newness that demands adoption.

A parallel reality to change and the passage of time is the parade of seasons. As we age, the parade lengthens and ushers in a cataract-like condition that clouds the lenses of memory, reducing sharpness and clarity of remembrance. And then there are sinister mental maladies that decay memory, rob identity, and freeze the mind to the present.

So much of what we once used to define and enjoy earlier days is now passé or discarded like outdated grocery items. Remarkably, every second of living adds to our inventory of lessons, experiences, and knowledge. Subconsciously, as the present transitions to the past, some past moments become poignant cherished memories.

What's striking about these experiences is that they reside securely in our thought-storage comfort zone. No matter the number of years that have passed, we can still recall—with absolute clarity—specific events as if they occurred an instant ago. Arriving in no particular order, emotions blend with sights, sounds, and a fragrant bouquet of scents to fill our cognitive landscape with images mirroring those of the original encounter. Meandering through a network of reasoning and intellect, thoughts and images cascade across the mind's geography like photographic slides revisiting emotional milestones and heartfelt episodes. With willing approval, we open our mind's repository and reunite with forgotten moments of yesteryear.

Sometimes we revisit past events where regretful choices or decisions still trouble the mind. We think, "What if...," and then imagine different outcomes. Memories of lost opportunities, unrequited love, unpleasant relationships, and unfulfilled hopes and dreams are edited to more desirable scenarios. Though these visits to our own private fantasy island are short-lived and quickly fade away, they leave in their wake both wistful and joyful afterglows of once-upon-a-time.

Regardless of whether these thoughtful remembrances are mundane, ordinary, or extraordinary, each arrives with ancillary cognitive baggage. Thoughts never travel alone; they're group-oriented. What triggers this reflective thinking and retrieval remains a mystery. Somewhere deep inside our wired gray matter, interconnected circuits receive signals from a variety of stimuli. These signals are decoded and directed to a particular area as the mind browses through its memory bank, instantaneously activating remembrance.

Life is God's gift, bestowed with ordinary and unexpected moments both present and past, and enriched by years and gratitude for all who touch our lives. By energizing both heart and mind, we're able to savor and retrieve memories of childhood, adolescence, and adulthood—beginnings, endings, achievements, struggles, failures, successes, regrets, adventures, relationships, and love. Each musing strengthens and nourishes our spirit, and enables each of us to celebrate life with renewed thankfulness and appreciation.

(2017)

GUEST CHECK

TABLE	PERSONS		SERVER
K	2	46394	S-9

Key Man
Kramden and Norton

TAX

THANKS FOR VISITING THE MIND CAFETERIA

Key Man

At some point, everyone dreams of being a star. Thoughts of being in the limelight conjure a heady exuberance as our imagined celebrity draws adoring fans wishing to catch a glimpse of their hero.

I experienced a collision of fantasy and reality early in life. Raised on radio adventure programs and Saturday movie matinees at the Capitol Theater in Whiting, Indiana, I was totally in awe of these fictional heroes. Before drifting off to sleep each night, I'd imagine myself as the good guy in the white hat saving the day.

Whether such fantasies were set somewhere rural or urban, I always triumphed over evil and would saunter off savoring victory with class, bravado, and enviable skill. By the age of 10, I was truly a legend in my own mind. Maybe it was the Cheerios, Ralston, Wheaties, or Pep that caused this mental malfunction. Perhaps it was due to the theater popcorn, Milk Duds, Jujyfruits, or Dots, or the hundreds of gallons of sodas that slid down the funnel connected to my bottomless pit of a stomach, sending all those chemicals to my brain—I really don't know. What matters is that by the time I was in fourth grade, I was addicted to celebrity. And I was about to learn a valuable lesson for indulging in such vanity.

It didn't take long for me to get my comeuppance. Early in 1950, the pastor of Sacred Heart Parish, Father Herman J. Miller, had installed an electric bell system to signal the end of class as well as dismissal and special announcements. Prior to this technological modernization, a student would go out in the hall at the appointed time and hand-ring a single bell. Ringing the bell was the domain of brown-nosers in the eighth grade. Saturated with their own self-importance, they would fawn over Sister Bruiser and vie for the privilege of being the bell ringer.

The bell ringer enjoyed a level of celebrity status later reserved for high school AV assistants who set up projectors and screens in classrooms for educational films, a task that transformed humble schoolboys into chick magnets. Teenage girls swooned in awe as Mr. AV deftly threaded the projector and brought film reels to life on the screen. Such technological proficiency was intoxicating and filled timid boys with the courage to do brave things.

As if to set the stage for the predestined lesson I needed to learn, Father Miller had the control switch for the bell placed in the fourth-grade classroom. To prevent pranksters from setting off unauthorized ringing, the switch was recessed and required a miniature forked key. Once inserted into position, the key was used like a standard toggle wall switch. The bell ringer would ring the bell for three seconds, then shut it off.

The privilege of being the bell ringer was earned by merits, and somehow I had earned enough to qualify. (To this day, I believe in miracles!) At the beginning of the day, Sister gave me the key for the bell's switch. Just before dismissal, I returned the key to her desk.

On the second day of my tenure, while in the process of ringing the bell for hourly aspirations at half past the hour ("Everything for Jesus, Mary, and Joseph"), one of my classmates distracted me. Instinctively turning to look at him, I lost focus and inadvertently let the key slip out of the switch and fall to the floor. I picked up the key, and in a panic, was trying to reinsert it in the switch so I could shut off the bell. See, a continuous ringing of the bell was the signal for a fire! School children were to evacuate immediately!

Sister rushed over to where I stood frantically trying to refit the key. Out of the corner of my eye, I saw her beet-red face wearing an expression that signaled trouble. She grabbed the key and shut off the bell. Then she went out into the hall and told everyone to go back to class—there was no fire.

Some students had already cleared the building and were out on the playground waiting for the fire engines to arrive. A number of seventh-graders cheered because school would be closed for repairs, while sixth-graders lined up like soldiers, prepared to march out through their assigned fire exit. In the excitement, three second-graders threw up on classmates still seated at their desks and then three others barfed in the hallway. Every first-grader in row four panicked and wet their pants.

Without a moment's hesitation, as a result of the chaos caused from my error, Sister de-keyed me and replaced me with Mary Margaret Saccharin! I went home that day embarrassed and considerably more humble. I learned a valuable lesson about self-importance and celebrity. Being a key person is not all that great. To this day, that reminder rings in my ears!

(2007)

Kramden and Norton

Over 40 years ago, a college education was expensive, not unlike today. But in the 1960s, it was possible for a college kid to earn enough money during the summer to pay next year's tuition. (The good ol' days.)

Having entered college at Indiana State University in Terre Haute, Indiana, in September 1964, and then marrying the following June, I needed additional funds to help maintain the apartment my wife and I were renting in Robertsdale and cover my on-campus expenses downstate. So in the summer of 1965, I took a job as a machinist at GATX (General American Transportation Company) in East Chicago. That fall, I accepted an offer to return to Inland Steel's Indiana Harbor Works (also in East Chicago), where my machinist career had begun. However, to accommodate my schedule at ISU, I'd now be working holidays, weekends, and summers as a general laborer at the mill.

Finishing classes by 2:00 pm on Friday, I'd drive the 158 miles home from ISU, work Saturday and Sunday in the mill, leave our apartment at 2:00 am Monday morning, and drive back down to campus in time for my 8:00 am class. Carrying 18 to 21 hours per semester as an undergraduate, my schedule was full and free time non-existent, but I was determined to earn my degree and become a teacher. I accepted inconvenience and was determined to overcome whatever obstacles there might be to achieve my goal. This was my schedule throughout the summer of 1967.

My job at Inland Steel involved a wheelbarrow, shovel, broom, and other conventional maintenance tools. Luckily, my coworker Jerry was also a college kid, attending Purdue University in downstate West Lafayette. Our foreman, Leo Noel, teamed us together and dubbed us "Kramden and Norton." Being the taller of the two, I was Norton and Jerry was

Kramden. As weekend warriors, we cleaned offices on Saturday and sewers on Sunday.

Now for those too young to know, one of the most popular sitcoms of the 1950s was *The Honeymooners*, starring Jackie Gleason, Audrey Meadows, Art Carney, and Joyce Randolph. Set in Brooklyn, New York, Ralph Kramden (Gleason) and his wife Alice (Meadows) lived in a bleak walk-up apartment, where their upstairs neighbors were the Nortons, Ed (Carney) and his wife Trixie (Randolph). Best friends, Ralph was a bus driver and Ed cleaned sewers.

And so it came to be that Inland Steel's dynamic duo of Kramden and Norton plied their labor skills in the mill each and every weekend. We were assigned the 24" Bar Mill sewer in Plant 1. Over our regular work clothes, we suited up in non-slip black boots, bright yellow rain gear, safety goggles, a hard hat, and heavy-duty insulated rubber gloves. The sewer was under the runout tables and had to be flushed weekly. Grease and debris from the rolling process formed gooey, malodorous black taffy that clung to the walls and equipment along the full length of the sewer. High-pressure nozzles, fixed at various intervals, directed streams of water along the trough and helped move the sludge toward the settling basin several hundred feet away.

As sewer engineers, our task involved driving waste materials off the underbelly of the runout table as well as the bevel gears and steel latticework supporting the table. With limited headroom, we performed our task bent over with our boots splayed against the curved bottom of the sewer, guiding the high-pressure stream from a fire hose against the steel structure and upper portion of the sewer, loosening sludge and sewage, while simultaneously directing the flow to the catch basin at the end of the sewer.

In the summer, hot air triggered aromas that only added to the nastiness of the job. In winter, below-freezing temperatures made the job absolutely brutal! Hoses were kept flowing to prevent freezing nozzles, but every now and then the high-pressure stream would hit stubborn pockets of sludge and splash back, covering us with contaminated sewer water.

Wrestling a fire hose in limited space was always a challenge. But Kramden and Norton joked and laughed through any and all discomfort.

By day's end, we welcomed the opportunity to discard our subterranean uniforms and get clean. Before removing any equipment, we had to degrease our boots and gear with solvent. Then we made our way to the locker room for a much-needed shower. Even after copious amounts of soap, hot water, shampoo, and some serious scrubbing, we carried the scent of the bar mill sewer with us. Several days later, the lasting cologne of the previous Sunday's sludge fest didn't escape detection.

One particular Monday morning before driving downstate, I stopped at White Castle for a large coffee and a half-dozen belly-bombers with extra onions and pickle. Now road ready, I was heading south on Route 41 in the freezing cold darkness of a new day with the car's heater set at blast-furnace levels. Remnant bar mill sewer perfume mixed with the signature aromas of the sliders' steam-grilled beef and onions and the fresh hot coffee.

A few miles further into my drive, having ingested my early morning feast, a gaseous compound of unimaginable intestinal potency percolated with an urgency for release. Once liberated to the car's interior, driver asphyxiation became a definite possibility—one of the few times that both the car and driver were full of gas! Ventilating the car by lowering the front side windows, the good news was that by the time I reached the town of Kentland, the air quality improved and the remainder of the trip was uneventful.

When Jerry and I graduated college with our respective degrees, Kramden and Norton officially retired from weekend work at the mill. Jerry joined the managerial track at Inland Steel, becoming a supervisor in the rolling mills, and I became a high school teacher, just as I'd always dreamed. But recalling those days together always brings feelings of satisfaction and good times. I earned every penny of the $2.20 hourly rate, dealing with adversity, overcoming obstacles, tolerating inconveniences, and laughing all the way back to campus.

To Jerry, the Ralph Kramden to my Ed Norton: Thank you, my friend.

(2007)

GUEST CHECK

TABLE	PERSONS	46394	SERVER
L	3		S-9

Lessons from Life's Classroom
Life's Field of Dreams
Lookin' Back

TAX

Lessons from Life's Classroom

Most of us think that after eight years in elementary and middle school, another four years in high school, plus any time spent completing undergraduate, graduate, and post-graduate degree programs, that our essential learning is pretty much accomplished. But we soon realize that learning is actually a lifelong endeavor with each new lesson adding to the quality of life. Moreover, a number of the most critically important life lessons aren't learned in school.

A schoolhouse education and what's learned via life's classroom are completely opposite from one another. In school, we're exposed to a variety of subjects, taught lessons, and then tested to see what we've learned. But in life, we're tested first—then we learn the lesson!

Some of these life lessons are sobering, some poignant. Others are filled with uncertainty, struggle, and challenge. But each lesson enriches and enhances our existence, adding quality, value, and meaning to it. Every experience we have allows us to grow individually, socially, emotionally, and spiritually. Life lessons also pay us valuable currency, giving us the tools necessary for fruitful daily living: unclouded judgment, coping skills, survival strategies, creative thinking, task analysis, effective decision-making, and personal fulfillment.

We all have our own inventories of lessons learned, both scholastically and simply by living life. What follows is a partial, random list of lessons I've learned during my time in life's classroom:

> Life is a series of beginning and goodbyes, and no matter the number of our years, we never quite get used to it.

We set our priorities and only do what's important to us.

Plan the work, then work the plan.

The triumph over sadness isn't easy.

What happens to us as a child stays with us all of our life.

Loneliness is a threat to good health.

Knowledge is power: personal, social, economic, and spiritual.

Education is the key that unlocks the door of opportunity.

There's no more powerful force than the written or spoken word.

Ignorance is understandable. Stupidity is inexcusable.

Each day is a gift containing 1,440 minutes. Use this time wisely. There are no returns.

Asking for help isn't a sign of weakness. Rather, it's a sign of strength.

It's difficult to learn anything positive when we're angry or hungry.

Forgiveness is more rewarding than getting even.

No one grows up in a straight line. It's a series of advances and retreats. We need someone to celebrate our triumphs and be supportive when things don't go so well.

Time places a halo around things.

We must learn to see with our heart.

We need to believe in sunshine during dark, cloudy days.

If we put junk food in our body, we'll have a junk body. If we put junk in our mind, we'll have a junk mind.

By always telling the truth, we never need to remember what we said because the truth always comes to mind automatically.

Forgiveness is easier to get than permission.

Of all living things, only humans pray—or need to.

The only person we can change is ourselves!

There are many types of love.

We must learn how to use money and never let money use us.

There comes a time when we can't take our stupid back. We'll be held accountable for our actions.

Never be so bold and ask God to make things easy. Be humble and pray that He makes things possible.

Friends help us get through difficult times. Their support reflects the quality of friendship.

Always help Mom with the dishes!

Strive to capture the essential elements of character: trust, honor, respect, and responsibility. Bond these elements with kindness, thoughtfulness, goodness, faith, compassion, forgiveness, appreciation, charity, and love.

Many ordinary moments become extraordinary memories.

We can't do much about the hand we were dealt at birth, but throughout life we can decide how that hand is played.

We all want the same thing: to belong, to be valued, to be necessary, and to be successful. We want to find someone to love and cherish. Most importantly, we want someone to love and cherish us in return.

We don't have to be born rich to live a rich life.

Appreciation engenders love.

Words have shadows.

Laughter is therapeutic. It nourishes mind, body, and spirit. It's the melody of our humanness.

One of the most valued gifts we can give to a loved one is sovereignty.

Unconditional love makes the heart soar!

(2014)

Life's Field of Dreams

I love baseball. Not just the game itself but what it symbolizes and the impact it's had on my life. Much more than nine players between the lines trying to best an opponent, baseball is emotion, dedication, and commitment. The game is an individual challenge fused to team effort to achieve victory. Baseball provides kids of all ages with dreams. Regardless of your talent, ability, or skill, the welcome mat is always on display at home plate.

What boy hasn't fantasized about hitting one out in the bottom of the ninth, snatching triumph from the jaws of defeat? What kid hasn't pictured himself leaping to make a game-saving catch against the outfield wall or spearing a sizzling liner just as it tries to leave the infield? What tousled-haired slugger hasn't dreamed of stepping up to the plate with the game on the line, the roaring crowd in his ears, and the winning run on base? Let's take a trip into the mind of a pint-sized all-star at the plate:

Facing an opposing pitcher who throws baseballs that shatter the sound barrier, our hero narrows his eyes to laser-sharp focus, tightens his grip on the bat, and coils his muscles like overwound clock springs. The pitcher sends the horsehide sphere spinning toward the plate. In the blink of an eye, the diminutive DiMaggio senses this fastball is destined for outer space, sending signals to his body.

The sound of a swinging bat colliding with the ball fills the stadium with an exhilarating crack! Like a true major leaguer, the little guy hesitates for a brief moment before beginning his home run trot around the bases. Displaying

no outward evidence of his feat, inside his heart is bursting
with pride. He acknowledges his accomplishment by tipping
his cap to an imaginary crowd as he returns to the dugout
where his teammates wait to greet their champion.

How many times have boys played the greatest baseball game of all time in their minds? Soaring like some invincible mythical Olympian against outfield walls and hearing a welcome thud as their glove interrupts the flight of a would-be home run, turning it into an instantaneous inning-ending out.

No other game requires more individual preparedness or presents such personal challenge as baseball does. Simultaneously, it demands continuous mental concentration and physical prowess. Baseball engenders such fervor in young boys that they clear vacant lots, mark off bases, tape a coverless baseball, mend cracked bats, and fill sandlots with their spirit.

Why do thousands compete every year to earn the privilege of wearing a Little League uniform, to be part of the team? It's because the game of baseball offers them the chance to perform on the field of dreams. Baseball encourages dreams. It stimulates the imagination, exercises the mind, touches the heart, and leaves an indelible mark on the spirit. Baseball is more than just a game—so much more.

There are baseball players everywhere, with various levels of ability, talent, and skill. Some make it all the way to the majors, with just a few entering the Hall of Fame. Most, however, exhibit their limited talents in sandlots and local parks. The important thing about baseball is not the level of achievement or whether we make it to the big leagues, but the quality of play.

To the field of dreams that is life itself, every individual brings a uniqueness that's unmatched in the entire world. As in baseball, we're granted a certain number of times at bat in life. Our chances for success are limited and the opportunities to advance life's teammates even more so. There are times when we're called upon to sacrifice ourselves for the good of the team. Once in a while, we're given the green light to swing away—to do whatever we can for others. And there are times, in spite of our most valiant efforts, we're not successful and fail to make a difference. And sometimes we commit errors.

A productive life, like baseball, demands personal dedication, preparation, and energy to meet unforeseen challenges. At times we're on the defensive, perhaps beyond our range, trying to keep opposing forces from victory. Even so, we're held responsible for our actions and expected to do our best. Life's Manager has done everything to prepare us for the game. By word and example, He taught what must be done to win, to achieve victory, and make it safely home.

In spite of our fragilities, our Manager readily forgives errors and overlooks our shortcomings. He keeps all the records and always knows the score. His coaching staff does their best to keep us alert, in the game, and watchful. Occasionally we lose our concentration, resulting in miscues and injury. When we get down, He's there to renew our spirit and strengthen our will to win.

And when He decides we've played enough innings, He takes us out of the line-up. When that day comes, hopefully our scorecard will reflect our best efforts, with our fellow teammates applauding our performance and long remembering our contribution.

Baseball mirrors life. Regardless of what position we play, what role we fill on the team, and what order we're assigned in the lineup, each of us wants to make it home safely and hear our Manager say, "Well done! You've been a credit to the team, an outstanding player, and gave a good account of yourself during your time on the field of dreams."

(2009)

Lookin' Back

A Poem for the Whiting High School Class of 1958's 25th Reunion

Lookin' back and what do we see?
Images of what we all used to be,
Of times and events with joy and tears.
Only traces remain of our high school years.
We're now so much older as we recall what we did
Back at the time when we were just kids.
The words printed here are about me and you,
Filled with memories when everything was new.
Those times of our lives, the way we were,
Are kept locked in our treasury, safe and secure.
We know those moments are forever past,
But sharing together, we make them last.
Still and all, we're lookin' back
To see what we can see.
And it warms the heart
To touch those things of what we used to be.

(1983)

GUEST CHECK

TABLE	PERSONS	46394	SERVER
M	8		S-9

Making New Out of Old
Making the Grade
A Matter of Commitment
May: Prelude to Summer
Melancholy Moments
Money
A Moving Experience
Musical Notes

TAX

THANKS FOR VISITING THE MIND CAFETERIA

Making New Out of Old

One of the courses I wish I'd taken as a postgraduate student was Ideation Techniques. The syllabus of the course focused on improving, adapting, and expanding the versatility and value of technology and products now considered outdated or obsolete. A sign on the classroom wall read, "If it works, it's obsolete!" (a phrase credited to media theorist Marshall McLuhan). In Ideation Techniques, obsolescence was viewed as the beginning of a challenge, not as a conclusion.

From early on, we're required to learn skills. We perform tasks, pursue jobs, and utilize sundry ancillary applications to increase our quality of life. We're encouraged to accelerate economic worth, promote self-reliance, refine personal independence, willingly welcome change, and embrace emerging technology. By doing so, we're told this will solidify our personal and social value and add to our overall daily enjoyment of living.

The problem is that everything moves so fast. Even as we master current technology, it's very quickly rendered obsolete and must be set aside to make way for new methods or applications. I have a whole list of skills that have become obsolete or, stated more kindly, old-fashioned, like ironing clothes. Prior to permanent press, everything had to be ironed. By fourth grade, I was skilled at ironing towels, household linens, shirts, pants, and jeans.

My sewing skills are another example. To this day, I can reattach a button, mend a tear, and re-stitch a well-worn hem. I also learned how to cook. But today, thanks to microwaves, packaged mixes, and frozen foods, no one absolutely needs to know how to make something from scratch. From entrées and side dishes to baked goods, it's simply out of the box, into the microwave, and zap!

When I entered college in September 1964, cooking was not allowed in dorm rooms. However, the use of electric teapots or appliances that could heat no more than 8 ounces of water was permitted, enough for a cup of instant coffee. On each floor of the residence hall was a room equipped with ironing boards and irons so residents could keep shirts and slacks wrinkle free, but with the advent of permanent press, these facilities went largely unused.

Now, on occasion I enjoy starting my day with scrambled eggs and toast. As a technology education major, I noticed the unused irons and designed a fixture that held two of them side by side, upside down. Setting both to the highest heat and using a store-bought aluminum tray, I was able to make breakfast as many mornings as I liked. (I kept eggs, bread, and butter chilled in a small ice chest under my dorm room desk.) Permanent press may have rendered ironing passé, but the irons were perfect for cooking! A few years later, such ingenuity was itself unnecessary as residence halls had installed kitchenettes.

As a youngster, I learned by trial and error how to repair a Bendix bicycle brake and patch punctured inner tubes and damaged tires. I was also very good at shoveling coal into the bin, and skillful at removing clinkers from the family's furnace on frozen winter mornings. In high school, I learned how to thread a movie projector—both silent and sound—and used that skill as a chick magnet. To be an AV kid carried instant celebrity! High school was also where I mastered the operation of the ditto machine. Savoring the aroma of the activating fluid was incentive enough to run extra copies for teachers!

Another skill was the seasonal task of putting up and taking down wooden storm windows and screens. Each sash was numbered and had to be matched in order for the unit to fit properly. Unfortunately, part of that endeavor included washing the window panes with copious amounts of ammonia, vinegar, and elbow grease. That chore was an effective way to destroy an early autumn Saturday morning.

In the machine shop at Whiting High School, I discovered mechanical aptitude and developed metalworking skills. In the print shop, I learned how to set type by hand for the school's newspaper, *The Tattler*. Outside of those hallowed halls, perhaps the skill that made me proudest and taught me the greatest lessons was setting pins at bowling alley at the Whiting Community Center.

Each of these manipulative and cognitive tasks served me well. Every skill I acquired had ancillary applications that would be adapted, modified, and used innovatively for future tasks. Coupled with my college-prep courses, when I graduated from Whiting High School I had a solid foundation upon which future education would be grounded.

Not too long ago, I was musing about some of the stuff that has come and gone—technology and gadgets that made growing up such a joy. In no particular order, here's my recollection of some now obsolete items, each carrying a lifetime badge of honor:

> Payphones, rotary telephones, and cozy phone booths. Telephone operators, party lines, and push-button phones. Full-service gas stations. TV roof antennas (the ultimate social status symbol of the 1950s), and TV repairmen who came by when sets went on the fritz. Parochial grade-school nuns who dressed like nuns! Home delivery of milk (in glass bottles), baked goods, fruits and vegetables, and groceries, as well as house calls from doctors.

> Soda fountains, where phosphates, sodas, and milkshakes reigned. Church-key bottle openers for beer and pop. Push reel lawnmowers, the soundtrack of boyhood summers as they whirled around to cut neighborhood lawns. And my personal favorite, wooden screen doors that always applauded the person leaving.

> Electronics transformed lifestyles almost overnight. Transistors replaced vacuum tubes. Heavy, unwieldy portable battery packs were shrunk to a single diminutive 9-volt battery. Vinyl replaced shellac for records, and turntables featured three speeds (78, 45, and 33 1/3 rpm). When long-playing, microgroove recordings debuted, a full 15 minutes of music could be played on one side of a 10- or

12-inch album. Then there were music stores where we could audition the newest "teen operas" on 7-inch singles prior to purchase.

Other establishments had jukeboxes stocked with the popular songs of the day and stereo systems with surround sound. These precise systems featured clarity, range, and audio sophistication. Car radios boomed with Top 40 hits as hot rods visited favorite drive-in hangouts to check out competing street sleds. I even installed a 45 rpm record player in my Olds so I could listen to my favorite singles on demand. Whitewall tires, once the rage, are nowhere to be seen now, just like vinyl tops, hubcaps, spinners, and a whole catalog of chrome details and gadgets for cars.

Drive-in movie theaters were the place of choice for togetherness. Today, these outdoor venues are almost nonexistent. How does one explain the summer delight of an outdoor movie under the stars with family, good friends, or a sweetheart, enjoying the latest Hollywood films in the privacy an automobile. To thwart pesky mosquitos and insects, I made specially fitted car window screens—they were so cool!

Flashbulbs, box cameras, and 8mm film cameras for home movies quickly passed into time. Instant photography dazzled us for a second or two, eventually evolving into digital cameras and smartphones.

From the sophisticated to the sublime, these innovations, adaptions, and ideation techniques enriched youthful times, solved problems, and turned challenges into enjoyable moments.

Today, the saying "If it works, it's obsolete" still rules. And although the pace of change has most certainly accelerated, the fundamental concept remains: Progress begets obsolescence, but also initiates beginnings. Making new from old celebrates the initiative, creativity, and versatility of the human mind. And with considerable celebration and personal pride— without a smidgen of hesitation or regret—that's the way it should be.

(2018 - Previously unpublished)

Making the Grade

As recently reported in *The Times*, all Indiana public schools were recently assigned either passing or failing grades following a state review. A few schools in the Calumet Region earned an A and are being lauded and celebrated for their achievement, while others received lesser grades of C, D, and F.

There was a time when students were graded, not schools. I attended Sacred Heart School in Whiting, Indiana, for Grades 1-8 and when Sister handed out final report cards at the end of the year, there was a handwritten notation on the back. It either read, "Promoted to Grade [whichever was next]" or the dreaded "Retained in Grade [your current level]." I vividly remember those notations because Sister wanted to retain me in Grade 2 because of my stutter. Fortunately, over the summer I attended a remedial reading class at Whiting Primary and resolved my speech problem. After an oral test of my reading and speaking proficiencies in August, Sister changed the notation from "Retained in Grade 2" to "Promoted to Grade 3."

When I entered high school in September 1954, we didn't need a statewide evaluation for us to know that Whiting High School was a first-class, grade A learning environment. Since its founding in 1898, Whiting High School set standards of excellence in academics, fine arts, business and office education, industrial arts, athletics, and activities. Older family members made sure the newest freshman class of Oilers—a nickname acknowledging both the importance of the city's Standard Oil refinery and the railroad crews that had maintained "Pop Whiting's Siding"— knew the school's history, legacy, and tradition, and understood what was expected of them. At commencement in June 1958, 85 seniors of Whiting

High School's finest class proudly represented family, community, and their alma mater.

This recollection of past academic experiences also came about because of a question posed a few weeks ago in the *Chicago Tribune*: "What makes a public school a success or a failure?"

For this writer, a product of both parochial and public education, the answer comes easily: The most reliable predictors of success are family, teachers, and classmates. The teachers I respect and remember most were the ones who inspired learning, valued students, encouraged improvement, and imparted life lessons alongside academic knowledge.

And after more than 65 years, I still remember the impact those teachers made in my life. Like Miss Evelyn Stewart, the second-grade teacher at Whiting Primary, whose kindness, compassion, and encouragement instilled self-confidence and helped me conquer my stuttering. Her elementary classroom was magic! And Father John Daniels, the assistant pastor at Sacred Heart Parish, who guided me in faith and strengthened my spiritual belief. Serving as an altar boy for Father D was a privilege and honor. *Deo gratias*, Father.

There were some extraordinary teachers at Whiting High School. James Ulrich taught me a love for English and the power of the written and spoken word. Jack Taylor's pedagogy made learning joyful and meaningful. Tom Faulkner's business and office instruction emphasized preparation, quality, and accuracy of written communication. Jesse Allen's approach to algebra, geometry, and trigonometry was a cognitive symphony. Bernard Vesely's print-shop craftsmanship and teaching turned handset type into the school's award-winning student newspaper, *The Tattler*. William Buerkholtz and George McClure, mavens of the machine shop, not only taught students manipulative, marketable industrial skills but also life itself! In particular, Mr. McClure offered advice, counsel, and examples of how to make a positive, constructive difference in the lives we touch.

Other honored faculty and administrators at Whiting High School during those years included James Buckley, George Burman, Delma Byers, George Calder, Shirley Crutchfield, Joseph DePeugh, Ruth Espenlaub, Steve Fowdy, Raymond Gallivan, Norman Hall, Alice Jenkins, Alex Kompier, Henry Kosalko, Peter Kovachic, Charles Leckrone, Marie

Lentvorsky, Adam Lesinsky, Elizabeth Matson, Joseph McAdam, Michael Mihalo, Edward Pawlus, Ane Marie Petersen, Joseph Piatek, Bernard Qubeck, C. E. Riehl, Von Stoffer, Arnold Turner, Marion Wagner, and E. L. Watkins.

Over the years, I kept in touch with many of my teachers. Their letters, cards, and calls became personal treasures. Somewhere far beyond the stars, those who have passed on now enjoy the banquet from the harvest of their lives.

School days leave indelible marks on our heart, mind, and spirit. These moments are enriched by classmates and teachers who willingly gave their time, talent, expertise—and love. No one grows up in a straight line. It's a series of advances and retreats. We need mentors and friends to celebrate our triumphs and be supportive when things get difficult.

To my teachers and classmates who encouraged, supported, and believed in my efforts—and shared their gift of friendship—my heartfelt appreciation. Thanks for making the grade.

(2014)

A Matter of Commitment

Whatever happened to commitment? More and more, we seem to be witnessing the extinction of commitment. Not too long ago, a promise was a promise. When someone gave us their word, it was their bond. We could depend upon the other person to uphold their part of whatever agreement had been negotiated. Likewise, we worked to keep our part of the bargain, lest our character or honor be tarnished. And putting a pledge in writing meant it took on added importance, legally binding the concerned parties to fulfill their commitment.

Today, however, commitments are all too frequently disregarded, devalued, and set aside as circumstances change. Often we rationalize and justify our actions, fabricating a positive spin on decisions to save face. Years ago, such conduct would have been greeted with disdain and disfavor.

How often do love-soaked couples vow to remain committed to each other in marriage, only to violate or abandon those vows as soon as times turn tough? Should things get difficult, the trend is to get out and run away. These once so-in-love-can't-live-without-you couples seem to decide very quickly to devalue their nuptials, annul their promise, and deem their wedding a mistake. Instead of attempting to resolve differences, communicate better, and nurture the relationship, they choose the convenient way out. Too many marriages end in divorce because neither partner understood the meaning of commitment.

Think for a moment about the millions of discarded, abused, and poorly cared for children we read about and see almost daily on television. Every one of those children belongs to someone. Pathetically, the parents of those kids have totally abdicated their responsibility. News reports tell of abused children, with some incidents so brutal they defy comprehension. We learn of newborn babies left in dumpsters and alleys, discarded like day-old garbage. Deadbeat parents refuse to support their children, causing defenseless kids to endure financial and emotional hardships. What causes parents to totally dismiss obligations to their children? What is at the root of such callous behavior?

Too many people subscribe to a selfish attitude of "Me first!" or "Me only!" They conveniently forget about commitment, sacrifice, and struggle. Treasured human values of trust, honor, respect, and responsibility are trampled and abandoned. If they can't have things their way, they quit.

How often have we watched major-league athletes and other celebrities whine about their multimillion dollar contracts? Having previously signed an agreement, they now feel slighted because a rival is making more money, and they want to renegotiate terms. Where's their sense of commitment? What message are they sending to fans that look up to them as role models? Where's their sense of honor? For too many people—celebrities, elected officials, business executives, and public figures—commitment has eroded into greed and selfishness.

Throughout day-to-day living, we're faced with commitments. Regardless of our occupation or station in life, we have obligations and others who depend upon us. And the degree to which we accept or reject these commitments determines the strength of our character and the quality of our lives. At work, with friends, as citizens, or at home, commitment varies. Some commitments require skill and talent, while others demand energy and involvement.

Every time we begin a task—whether alone or with others—we're confronted with commitments. We make a private contract with ourselves to perform the necessary duties to the best of our ability for as long as it takes. Sometimes circumstances out of our control can increase anxiety, causing us to feel overwhelmed and question our resolve to continue. During critical times, we must search for added strength, guidance, and support, drawing upon family, friends, and faith.

We live in such interesting times. People of different generations view similar issues with markedly divergent points of view. Those tempered by hard times and seasoned by life's struggles seem out of sync with those who have never known adversity. Some young people cannot identify with older folks' concepts of morality, work ethic, and allegiance to their faith. "What's the big deal?" is a commonly heard question when old ways are challenged.

Who knows how all of this will turn out? Perhaps one day far in the future, we'll come to a universal understanding about commitment. Until then, I suspect we'll plod along, tolerating society's pampered, spoiled whiners.

I'm reminded of the closing lines from my favorite Robert Frost poem ("Stopping by Woods on a Snowy Evening") that brilliantly distills the guiding principle that I hope we all someday follow. Although the traveler in the poem pauses, he knows he must continue his journey.

After all, it's a matter of commitment.

(2006)

May: Prelude to Summer

If we were to personify the months of the year, May has to be the all-American girl for which the remaining eleven months compete. Like a debutante or a young lady dressed for the prom, May blossoms into the beauty that becomes summer.

Amid warm spring rains and sun-splashed days, May accepts extra April showers and apprentice sunbeams auditioning for June. In the early days of the month, May teases with a roller coaster of diverse weather. On one day, balmy temperatures tantalize residents to wear tank tops and shorts, while the very next delivers chilled rain carried by rambunctious wind gusts, driving the very same inhabitants to reacquaint themselves with wool slacks and windbreakers.

In May, local garden centers display trays of annuals and perennials to lure customers to purchase a flat or two for the yard. With lengthening daylight hours, birds begin their choral practice before the sun peeks above the horizon. As a special treat, May arranges for a few mornings to look like a cozy, down-filled comforter as fog blankets the landscape. Shortly after daylight, dawn takes control like a mom waking up her kids for school, tugging at the tapestry of droplets to uncover the terrain so earth-dwellers can be on their way.

By the second week of May, birds have the notes to their songs down pat. Garden flowers face east for their morning shower of sunshine, displaying a richness of color, texture, size, and shape. As if on cue, the season of spring presents all living things in perfect harmony. Taking prompts from the birds and the bees, humans and other animals are enticed to add to the bounty and diversity of life on earth.

May is home base for Mother's Day, a time to recognize, celebrate, and pamper moms who do so much for their families. Without question, mothers know how to deliver! Thus the purchase of flowers, sweets, and other gifts from grateful spouses and children accelerates in appreciation for their time and attention.

May is permission month, featuring 31 days of "May I?" All of nature, whether people, plants, or animals, voices a similar question: "May I prepare for summer?" "Yes, you may!" The fifth month of the year offers an official welcome to blue skies, warm temperatures, extended daylight, and starry moonlit nights. May singlehandedly produces the symphony of sounds that performs throughout the day and nighttime hours, making music for both the ears and eyes and setting the cadence for mind, body, and spirit. In concert with this annual springtime soundtrack, May arranges landscapes, terrain, and opportunities for all living things to accomplish assigned tasks, fulfill responsibilities, and enjoy quiet moments of solitude or togetherness.

May is a sweet elixir for the senses. Like an exotic perfume, May exudes alluring scents that enrich the enjoyment of spring. Romantics of every age stroll along together, holding hands and sharing moments to remember. May is joyful and carefree, but raucous and rowdy too. It's a time for birthdays (Taurus and Gemini guide those who read the heavens' placement and pattern of stars), anniversaries, and all kinds of celebrations. May is also pensive, reserved, and somber. It's the month we remember those who serve in the military, and prayerfully give thanks to those who made the ultimate sacrifice for their country.

For school kids, May is the last full month of classes before summer vacation. May is the month of proms and parties, picnics and yearbooks, locker clean-out, and end-of-year exams. For parents, May is the quiet before households are filled with late-sleeping, vacation-minded youngsters. And May is another opportunity to share breakfast and fellowship with cherished colleagues, active and retired.

May mornings are delicious. Arranged like choice menu selections, the beginning hours of May days refresh, energize, soothe, and prepare all who tend the stewardship of our earthly home. May is the prelude to summer. May is simply the best! I love May.

(2011 - Previously unpublished)

Melancholy Moments

Every so often, out of nowhere, right in the middle of things, and without any forewarning, melancholy moments arrive. Little snippets of life barge into our mind, pushing aside whatever's in their way to commandeer center stage. Similar to pop-up ads on the internet, we're thinking about something or engaged in some other activity, when all of a sudden we're sidetracked by an unannounced intrusion of personal memories that grabs our attention and doesn't leave until properly acknowledged.

Melancholy moments arrive replete with personality and modus operandi. Some approach gently, like a tap on the shoulder or a gentle tug on a sleeve. Other times, they burst in like a brash relative, scattering focus and concentration to all corners of the mind, loudly announcing, "I'm here!"

At one time, these moments could be summoned in predictable, orderly fashion: looking at old photographs, re-reading cards and letters from cherished friends, and going through scrapbooks, school yearbooks, family albums, and vintage newspaper clippings. But now they present themselves whenever and wherever they please. But if I may reveal a personal secret: I now welcome and look forward to their visits.

Be aware though that many of these melancholy moments are not all sunshine and lollipops. Some fill the heart with sorrow, loss, regret, pain, and a sweet-sad poignancy. There are times when our memory is both our best friend and our worst enemy. On occasion, visiting memories can challenge our spirit, test our resolve, and initiate tear-filled eyes. But one of life's lessons is that "It always rains hardest on the people who deserve the sun." Knowing that brings comfort and incentive to continue life's journey.

In my younger years, I'd mentally fend off unsettling, uncomfortable, and intrusive thoughts and remembrances—but no longer. Today they're welcomed, embraced, and cherished as badges of honor. Alone or connected, these melancholy moments define who I am, what I've done, and validate life lessons and experiences. Even the unexplainable ache that can remain when these moments return to their keeping place can't diminish my appreciation of their visit.

As we learn to deal with the changing seasons within ourselves, these melancholy moments serve to remind us of how precious each moment is. Because time goes by so quickly, we seldom realize how meaningful, valuable, and precious these events will become. Ordinary everyday moments can transform into extraordinary remembrances. Memories are our connection with the past. Although we live in the present and plan for the future, it's our past that nourishes, comforts, secures, and serves as a personal treasure of our lifetime.

Our past is always just a thought away. Precise occurrences can be recalled instantaneously and so vividly that the past becomes present-like. Long-ago experiences assume crystal clarity as if they're part of the here and now. We continually input moments from daily living, and like a personal TiVo, we're able to store, retrieve, access, review, and remember the times of our lives. As years accumulate, memories are valued beyond words.

Autumn offers an opportunity for melancholy moments. With early evening darkness, chilly mornings, and a slower seasonal pace following summer, there are respites during the day to invite personal reflection of the times of our lives: reviewing successes and struggles, triumphs and defeats, achievements and failings, love and loss, hellos and goodbyes, and all kinds of moments in between. We have time to remember, to think about how life unfolded, and the mysteries, adventures, and wonders still waiting to be revealed.

As November's weather encourages inside activities, brew a cup of your favorite hot beverage, get cozy in a comfortable place, and remember when. So many moments, so many memories. Treasure the melancholy moments and savor the priceless memories.

(2013)

Money

All things considered, I like money. Over the years, it's been a love-hate relationship—from having no money to having enough to pay expenses and also enjoy a number of amenities. One of life's essential lessons is learning how to use money and not let money use us. Another is how to earn and make money. And the graduate school of money knowledge is acquiring the skill to grow money and build a nest egg for the future.

Investments, frugal spending, dedicated saving, and an overall mindset of financial wherewithal are necessary to meet present and future obligations without generating undue stress and uncertainty. Money can be a positive or negative in life. If we have adequate means of acquiring additional quantities of legal tender, there's a degree of satisfaction and comfort. If we're in debt, with limited or sporadic resources of income, the stress can be overwhelming.

We learn early that "Money doesn't grow on trees," a favorite retort of cash-starved parents when confronted by family members with lists of wants. There are various stages of money. Initially, it carries great importance, then becomes necessary, and ultimately, after years of struggle, is viewed casually as a means to conduct social and routine activities.

Having folding money makes wallets and purses smile: a few Georges, a couple of fivers, a ten-spot or two, some double sawbucks, and, on rare occasions, a Benjamin. Money acts as a signpost of progress along life's journey. Earning power defines accomplishment. Money is the way we measure value and keep score.

But money can have a severely negative impact. As a child, when money was scarce, holidays and special occasions were marked with memories of disappointment and doing without. Terms like hand-me-downs, second-hand, used, and patched-up were commonplace. Social events went unattended, milestone celebrations were muted, and a type of isolation was felt due to lack of economic means.

No one ever gives instructions for earning money other than the generic response, "Work for it!" Left to our own initiative, we develop strategies, logistics, and plans for eliminating cash shortages. As a kid, first I scoured alleys and empty lots for deposit bottles, and later sold old newspapers and scrap metal to local junk dealers. In the summer, I mowed lawns and pulled weeds, and in the winter, I cleared snow from sidewalks and driveways. By sixth grade, I had a paper route.

In high school, setting pins at the bowling alley at the Whiting Community Center ended hand-me-downs. Hundreds of lines and racked pins even translated into the Lewin-Wolf suit I wore at graduation. Earning money elevated my self-esteem as I became independent and self-reliant. With graduation came full-time employment at 17.

As a steelworker, the wages I earned paid for a used car, new clothes, social activities, and initiated a savings account—my work ethic was in full bloom. After six years, I transferred from the mills to a downstate university campus. But with college expenses growing, I worked weekends cleaning steel mill sewers, traveling back and forth for the next three years. And having married the summer after my freshman year in college, I learned that managing money while single is far less complicated than the responsibilities that come with marriage and family. I continued working weekends, summers, spring breaks, and Christmas vacations in order to help defray housing and education costs.

Money becomes a major concern when raising children—struggling to scrape by, living paycheck to paycheck, and barely making ends meet. Family needs, mortgage obligations, insurance premiums, monthly budget items, and ever-present unexpected expenses elevate stress levels and fatigue the spirit. Credit cards become enemies and deficit spending portends financial difficulties that produce anxiety, usher in sleepless nights, and challenge our ability to pay bills and reduce accumulated debt.

Checking and savings accounts are constantly monitored to guard against overdrafts and diminished reserves. Extra jobs become commonplace in order to supplement income. Personal wants and time with family are sacrificed in order to provide groceries, clothing, and other household necessities. As children mature, college expenses—tuition, books, room and board, and transportation—take precedence.

Then, in what seems like an instant, money loses its dominion. Seasoned by life experiences, the accelerator is replaced by cruise control. Folding money stays in the wallet longer. Wants and needs are scaled back. Personal time and good health become more important than a fistful of Benjamins.

Today, remembrance of sleep-deprived, purpose-driven, frantic schedules seems surreal. Even so, there is satisfaction knowing that lessons about money were effectively learned.

(2012)

A Moving Experience

We had been preparing to move since late spring. The process began the day we came upon the "For Sale by Owner" sign in the front yard of the newly built ranch house in Dyer, Indiana. After weeks of meetings and copious correspondence with the owners and our Realtor, we were nearing D-Day—our Departure Day.

Up until the last moment, the impact of moving out of the house that was our home for 33 years was only minimally felt. In preparing to move, we collected countless boxes, purchased packing supplies, and began the stages of organizing items accumulated over a lifetime, selecting some and discarding others. For more than 90 days we sorted, wrapped, packed, and labeled household goods, furniture, clothing, and accessories. We held a garage sale and followed that with several trips to Goodwill in an attempt to pare down the quantity and scope of the move. Still, it all changed dramatically on the first Monday in August when the moving vans and crew arrived early that morning and the totality of what was happening really set in.

It took five strong movers to load the two large vans. By 3:30 pm, our belongings had been trucked to our new home. Room after room was filled with furniture and stacks of labeled boxes. Returning north to our now-old house in Whiting, I loaded up miscellaneous items and tools from the garage. My pickup truck proved its worth as I needed several trips to complete the move.

With the house in Whiting set to close in two weeks, we spent that time thoroughly cleaning it. Each room was dusted, vacuumed, and made ready. Bathrooms were sanitized, and chrome accessories left gleaming. Even the attic storage area was vacuumed. Windows throughout the house were cleaned and wood trim waxed. Closets and pantries were dusted and vacuumed. Tile floors were wiped clean and carpeting was vacuumed with our dirt-hunting Electrolux. In the kitchen, appliances were cleaned, with the sink and countertops tended to until they glistened.

The lower level awaited the new owners to enjoy the cozy atmosphere. Completely remodeled a couple of decades ago, the once cold and uninviting basement had been paneled, carpeted, and given a suspended ceiling with decorative lighting. The antique soda fountain, wraparound bar with wood stools, and brick-enclosed alcove featuring a handcrafted trestle table and benches were included amenities. The laundry room was paneled, painted, and pristine. Without question, this old house was move-in ready.

Over the years, the house and property had been continually maintained and the quality of those efforts was reflected both inside and outside the building. The garage and adjacent storage area were also cleaned and made ready for the new owners' vehicles and accessories. At the closing, both the Realtor and buyers said it was the cleanest house they had ever been in.

I have to admit, however, that moving was very stressful. According to some, moving ranks as the fourth most stressful time in life, behind death, divorce, and illness of loved ones. Leaving our home of 33 years and a neighborhood we'd lived in longer than that—one that defined our community with collective goodness, decency, and feelings of belonging— tested heartfelt feelings. Moving from the industrial Mayberry where I spent the majority of my 65 years was both poignant and heartrending.

The day before closing, I made one last trip to the house in Whiting and gave it a final check for readiness. Alone, I went upstairs for the last time. I visually checked the attic, bathroom, and each of the four bedrooms. These were the rooms I built so many years ago. Now their emptiness was disquieting. Consciously, I confronted memories eager to flood my mind. There were so many moments to remember. I tucked them away in a special keeping place to savor at a later time.

I walked slowly downstairs and viewed the main level. Everything was in order: the enclosed front porch, front room, living room, and dining room. The kitchen, bathroom, first-floor bedroom, closets, and pantries were empty of all items and looked abandoned. One last tour of the now silent and unfurnished lower level, where laughter, love, jukeboxes, and sodas once reigned supreme, and it was time to go.

It was early evening when I closed and locked the back door for the final time. I hesitated just a moment in the backyard to take one more mental picture of the place we called home for over a third of a century. Walking up the driveway to my parked truck, I paused, looked at the front entrance of this old house, and for a private, very personal reason said, "Thanks."

(2006)

Musical Notes

A popular high school fad during the 1950s was writing notes to classmates. While this continued on for a future generation or two, such behavior now sounds quaint when viewed against today's technology of email, text messaging, and personal cell phones. But once upon a time, receiving a handwritten note from a favorite friend was the coolest. Composed during class, these teen epistles were mind dessert, offsetting dull lessons, chapter assignments, and other less-than-exhilarating academic tasks.

Along with a variety of ink colors, creative bobbysoxers added sketches, caricatures, cartoons, and flamboyant cursive lettering. Standard stationery was college-lined, three-hole, loose-leaf notebook paper. Tightly folded with interlocking tabs for ease of transfer, these saltine-sized packets were hand-delivered in hallways and restrooms as students hurriedly scurried from one class to another using the five-minute passing period to full advantage—the teenage version of the postal system. Years before Mr. McFeely's famous greeting on *Mr. Roger's Neighborhood*, Whiting High School students on their way to and from class echoed, "Speedy delivery!"

One of the more creative and enjoyable styles of note writing was the song-title letter, which incorporated titles of current Top 40 hits to add enticing meaning to the message. Dating, teenage romance, and other adolescent interests served as subject material for these frequent exchanges of written thought.

While recently working on an upcoming class reunion, I was looking through my 1958 Whiting High School yearbook, the *Reflector*. Pressed between the pages were a few sheets of creased notebook paper. Fifty plus years of seasoning showed discolored edges and faded ink, but the words of this song-title note still reverberated as if it were only yesterday.

Reading it so many decades later simultaneously elicited a heartfelt smile and a tinge of melancholy. The author passed away a number of years ago at a far-too-early age, but her youthful spirit, love of life, carefree exuberance, and joy of being a teenager at Whiting High School still glows warmly across the years. Her handwritten expression of expectation, hopes, and dreams reawakened memories of once-upon-a-time.

For those who never received a song-title letter, and to celebrate the life of a classmate who helped make me a better person, here's an edited portion of her note:

> "Hey, *Moonlight Gambler*, heard you came to school in a *Flying Saucer*! I'm in Civics class and feel like a *Hound Dog, Stranded in the Jungle. My Prayer* is that an *Earth Angel* will ring the bell before I get a *Fever*. Tried to read the assignment, but *I Almost Lost My Mind*. I feel like *Singing the Blues* on *Blueberry Hill*, but I'll settle for Whiting Park. With a little *Friendly Persuasion*, maybe we'll get to the movies and wind up *Sittin' in the Balcony*.
>
> Even though it's Thursday it seems like *Blue Monday*. My head's going *Round and Round*. Halfway through English, why does the clock move so slow? Ulrich is watching me so I'm *All Shook Up*. Hope he doesn't call on me. Really, are term papers that important? (Don't have a song for that!)
>
> Do you watch *Bandstand* after school? Would love to be on that show. Have band eighth period. Stop by, knock on *The Green Door* and say hi. You're right next door in the machine shop. Look for me through the window. If Mr. Humphrey sees you, he'll have a cow. *Chances Are* you'll get caught.

Stop by my locker after school. What should we talk about? *It's Not for Me to Say.* (You *know* what I want to talk about!) *See You Later, Alligator.* I'll be *Waitin' in School* and don't want to be *Stood Up!*"

High school years go by at the speed of life. We entered secondary school as an old child and graduated four years later as a young adult. The transition from kid to grown-up was not without challenges. The emotional roller coaster of adolescence, with all its highs and lows, filled our days and nights.

Through coursework, sports, activities, and the social naiveté of boy-girl relationships, we did our best to learn, cope, and move forward. New skills and strategies were required to understand and manage the changing seasons within ourselves and the world around us. Along the way, we confronted and struggled to accept feelings of happiness, sadness, anxiety, fear of rejection, success, failure, and sorrow, while also experiencing our share of laughter, and tears.

Innocence's last call was replaced with a maturing sweetness that included songs and musical notes.

(2013)

GUEST CHECK

TABLE	PERSONS		SERVER
N	1	46394	S-9

November Thoughts

TAX

November Thoughts

There are times I wish the month of November was just ten days long. With late autumn's onset of darkness, always-changing weather, and bleak, sunless days, it would be better to shorten the month as an incentive to encourage winter to get on with it.

Having said that, there's a stark beauty about November. Leafless deciduous trees, stoic conifers, and days attired in pearl-gray clouds have a calming effect as we go about our daily rituals and tasks. Wildlife displays an additional urgency to complete preparation for winter's harshness, challenging their safety, security, and survival.

After the "fall back" time change, morning daylight arrives earlier and late afternoons imitate evenings. When winter firms its grasp on the calendar, daylight will be rationed with a stinginess that adversely affects all living things. On days when sunshine is in abundance, it often duels with frigid temperatures. Inhabitants find themselves both buoyed by the sun's rays and taunted by aggressive winds as they scurry about tackling obligations before the curtain of night.

Nights in November encourage us to be warm, cozy, and secure in our homes. With fireplace or furnace, hot cocoa or coffee, and sweaters or fleece garments to keep the cold at bay, we nest in a favorite chair to watch TV, curl up with a good book, or cuddle with a special someone.

There are times when I want to lengthen November. The 30 days allotted to the month serve as a transition from autumn to winter. In ever-enlarging increments, darkness overtakes daylight, permitting the moon and stars some extra minutes to fill the heavens like sparkling jewels. November is a time to reflect, review, and remind. This is a time of preparation, a time of thanksgiving for the bounty we share, and a time to savor the seasons past.

Wearing a jacket to stave off the early November chill, this geriatric unit often occupies the glider on the deck to watch the trees dance and sway to November's menu of breezes. Stubborn autumn leaves hold onto branches in defiance of accelerated winds, but eventually release their grip and take flight. Blanketing the landscape, these flakes of multicolored sunshine carpet lawns, cover decks, and search for gutters to clog.

In the early morning light, clouds take shape, shadows lighten and disappear, and resident geese begin their noisy social gathering for sustenance. Sipping on the day's first cup of honeyed tea, memories and remembrance gently visit my mind. Road traffic builds with commuters going to work and school buses picking up students for school. The sight of those rubber-tired cheese wagons announcing their arrival with flashing strobes triggers memories of my four-plus decades spent in classrooms. I also recall the times my wife and I walked our kids to school, holding their hands while shuffling through autumn leaves and jabbing at winter's snowflakes, joyfully sharing a journey to the schoolhouse door. How quickly the eyes fill with tears.

Now retired and released from structured obligations, there are memories of long-ago shiftwork days when a young apprentice waited on the corner for public transportation, heading for the steel mill with a shopping bag of work clothes, a brown-bag lunch, and bus fare in hand. Remembrance of these mornings (whether sunlit, rainy, dark, or freezing) brings melancholy feelings of less complicated times. It was a time of beginnings, initial steps of the journey toward becoming a grown-up.

Day by day, as life unfolded, apprehension lessened, uncertainty faded, confidence increased, and future adventures were welcomed with passionate energy, enthusiasm, and purpose—from classroom to factory, factory to campus, and campus to classroom.

Thinking of years that have passed all too quickly—goals accomplished and ambitions not pursued, hopes realized and dreams unattained, and all moments in between—can elicit mixed feelings. Most of all, there's personal satisfaction, thankfulness, and appreciation, knowing that the items on my life's resume are the result of hard work, trust, honor, respect, responsibility, and loving prayerful support far beyond the stars. These are my November thoughts.

(2011)

GUEST CHECK

TABLE	PERSONS		SERVER
O	3	46394	S-9

October's Glory
Ode to No One (Together vs. Alone)
Outdated and Passé

TAX

October's Glory

You'd think that any month holding title to eighth place and then unceremoniously moved down to tenth would be resentful, but not October. Despite the calendar-changing shenanigans of Julius and Augustus Caesar, October accepted its new position in the solar lineup and embellished its allotment of 31 days with exuberance and enthusiasm.

As a full-fledged member of autumn's sweet-sad season, October brims with delicacies left over from summer's frivolity as well as presenting its own special menu of prepared entrées. Teasing everyone with occasional flashbacks of sun-drenched beach parties, October delivers hours of abundant sunshine and bright blue skies that make music for the senses.

Elevated temperatures give vegetation encouragement to feast on nutrients, causing lawns to thrive and mowers to mulch. Resident wildlife scurries with an added opportunity to prepare their stores for upcoming adverse weather conditions. And people display their approval by filling mall parking lots and athletic fields as well as partaking in activities that offer opportunities to commune with nature.

October is also in charge of changing seasonal scenery. Sun fades from full to partial. Sunsets arrive earlier. Fog rolls in the early morning hours. Evenings are markedly cooler. And the light from a harvest moon drenches inhabitants.

Nighttime is no longer filled with a symphony of sound. Evening hours are noticeably subdued as nocturnal activity is redirected to more pressing tasks. Leaves begin their dance with the sun and wind, simultaneously changing hue and tint as they twist and turn with every gust of wind. Witnessing such artistry on display dazzles the eye and engenders envy in those who view themselves as athletic.

When October's wind gets the jump on its cousin November, leaves are separated from their branches and sail about, floating, spinning, and displaying their aerodynamic abilities as they land on neighboring turf. Millions upon millions of leaves find rest on terra firma as their purpose is complete. Soon landscapes are carpeted with autumn leaves from every variety of tree, bush, and shrub, awaiting young-at-heart feet to shuffle through piles of these deciduous cornflakes, crunching their way to and from school and play. Only oak trees stubbornly hold their leaves fast to branches throughout autumn. In winter, the chocolate-colored vegetation from these acorn makers will afford stark contrast to the latticed, snow-covered branches of leaf-bare trees.

Upon being reassigned placement on the calendar, October decided to be a full-service participant, offering something for everyone: sight, sound, scent, and touch. The month is a sensory extravaganza. Throughout October's 31 days, the moon will take time to play peek-a-boo with precocious clouds, shining full strength, and then provide frosty, luminous moonlight while hiding behind patches of overcast skies like a bashful child.

Weather will cooperate by allowing convertibles to travel top-down, celebrating good times. Sweethearts of all ages will join hands and hearts as they journey through October days, forming bonds and sharing moments of melancholy remembrance of times gone by.

Each of us in our own way finds time to acknowledge, treasure, and appreciate October's moments to remember. Saturday afternoons in the fall are like precious jewels. Sundays have an easy, peaceful feeling as autumn beckons at a slower rhythm than summer's hectic pace.

It's the time of year when nature willingly accepts October's recycling materials, as flowers, garden remnants, and trees return their bounty to their earthly beginning. Fringe benefits include two of autumn's favorite fragrances: the perfume of burning leaves and the sweet scent of dampness when blankets of fog transition to gossamer droplets of dew by the early morning sun. Cool autumn rains baptize, cleanse, and refresh Mother Earth.

A crystal clear October night is crispy and delicious like fresh potato chips. Bathed in the moonlight under a sky twinkling with stars, romantics share their hopes and dreams, filled with wonder at the majesty of the universe.

The sight of ducks and geese winging southward toward warmer climes, quacking and honking their exuberance in appreciation for the summer is a clear signal that change is coming (these fair weather creatures determined long ago that rock salt and snow shovels weren't for them). Permanent wildlife residents, however, search out nooks and crannies in which to hunker down during the frigid, snowy winter weather to come.

Human residents begin their preparation for seasonal change, too. Lawnmowers are replaced by snow blowers, furnaces take over from air conditioners, and staying indoors becomes more attractive than being outdoors. Sweaters, windbreakers, blankets, and hot cocoa are now more prevalent than tank tops, sandals, and iced tea.

October is the time of harvest as the bounty of nature's labors is displayed for all to see and enjoy. The glory of October is that it provides the means for all of us to taste the sweetness of autumn. October can be an attitude or an age. It can be a time for renewal or reflection, continuation or beginning. Fall brings forth both memories and new adventurous moments. Such is the glory of October.

(2010)

Ode to No One
(Together vs. Alone)

No one to cuddle, no one to hold,
No one to snuggle as the weather grows cold.

In rooms of fine furniture, bedding, and covers,
No one acts like passionate lovers.

Alone in the dark and quiet of night,
No one to help chase away fright.

No hand to hold to help steady the way,
No one to hug to make things okay.

Hearts not as one send messages and pleas,
Like ships in the night adrift on the seas.

In separate beds, in separate rooms,
Unshared moments shredded and strewn.

Everything in order, everything in place,
Always important to display a happy face.

Clean and scrub, polish and shine,
Show-and-tell, everything looks fine.

Carpet and flooring and tile of stone,
Clearly remind a house is not a home.

Disarray in the kitchen, chairs not pushed back,
Shoes all askew, clothes piled in a stack.

Bathroom at times looks like a mess,
How important is all of this, more or less?

Rule of the house, no shoes on the rugs,
Instead of a look, perhaps a few hugs.

Soiled dishes and tableware, rinsed without soap,
Chided and reminded, I'm such a dope.

Window blinds improperly closed,
Do it right, or leave them alone.

Few words are spoken, minimal touching allowed,
Keep to your space, and please do not crowd.

Chat about finance, household, and food,
Togetherness moments always elude.

Public behavior, guarded display,
Private affection has become passé.

Romantic dreams, like stars in the night sky,
So far away, why even try?

One day the grave will settle it all,
One day no answer or response to a call.

Then it won't matter, shoes on the rug,
There'll be no feet or someone to hug.

Comments and complaints for wrongs that besmear,
Will it be better when no one is here?

The little annoyances, errors to atone,
Only silence and the sound of being alone.

No one to cuddle, no one to hold,
No one to share the time growing old.

A lifetime of moments and memories bestrew,
Treasure those moments, when love was so new.

An unplanned meeting—love-at-first-sight time,
Teenage love story when hearts first intertwine.

A flower in September, a homecoming game,
Soft eyes and held hands set love's heart aflame.

After decades together, love still grows,
Hearts bonded as one, with memories aglow.

Cherish the good, pray away the bad,
Learn how to laugh and never be sad.

Hold fast to gifts from Heaven above,
And hold on forever to those whom you love.

To close out the day, prayerful words are said,
That blessings and goodness and love be widespread.

May someone special always be there,
To snug up the covers and nuzzle your hair.

Wish pleasant dreams to fend away fright,
Then, sweetly and softly, kiss you goodnight.

I love you.

(2015 - Previously unpublished)

Outdated and Passé

Every now and then it's refreshing to take a few moments and review how quickly products, gadgets, activities, and customs became outdated and old-fashioned. Recalling these faded bits of living gives pause to consider that the speed of life accelerates as we accumulate seasons. As you read these items, you'll have to supply the visuals and remembrance of them before they became outdated and passé.

Whatever happened to television repairmen, C.O.D. packages, bobby pins, layaway purchases, inner tubes for bicycles and automobiles tires, seat covers, and fender skirts? When did we stop buying fancy TV cabinets that included a phonograph and radio? Radio and TV vacuum tubes were replaced with transistors and solid-state circuit boards.

At one time communities had a whole service-repair industry: shoe, television, and telephone. Door-to-door salesmen rang residential doorbells on a regular basis: *Encyclopaedia Britannica*, Fuller Brush, Watkins Products, pots and pans, and vacuum cleaners. There were even traveling photographers with a pony in tow for kids' pictures, complete with cowboy outfits and props.

There was home delivery of groceries, ice, milk, baked goods, poultry, and farm-fresh produce. For new moms, there was diaper service. Whatever happened to the trillions of safety pins we once relied upon to fasten everything from diaper flaps to torn seams and missing buttons? Doctors made house calls, and county agents visited homes and assessed furnishings to calculate residents' personal property taxes.

Gas stations had attendants who cleaned our car's windshield and checked the oil, radiator, and tire pressure while filling the gas tank with lead-based, high octane Gold Crown ethyl. Inside, mechanics tuned up sluggish street sleds by adjusting carburetors and changing plugs, points, and condensers. In earlier times, they checked the choke, advanced the spark, and added brake fluid and battery water as needed. And if we were really nice, they'd rotate our tires too! For added customer convenience, there was a vending machine with cigarettes for 25 cents a pack.

Way back when, families and teen romantics flocked to outdoor drive-in theaters and feasted on burgers and fries at drive-in restaurants. Carhops served patrons as young Casanovas cruised by to check out ponytails and other street rods. Many couples parked under starry moonlit skies and enjoyed submarine races at Whiting Park and Robertsdale's Bobby Beach. Others enjoyed impromptu beach parties, toasting marshmallows and roasting hot dogs on driftwood fires while guzzling beer.

There were Friday night sock hops in the gym after the game, homecoming bonfires, and daily street-corner seminars where classmates gathered to share friendship-enriching high school days. Teen hangouts like The Oil Can, Gambini's, and Nick's Pool Room engendered lifelong memories.

For Mrs. Housewife, there was a plethora of products to enrich and enhance her domestic duties: gaily patterned kitchen aprons and pinafores, S&H Green Stamps, Maytag wringer washing machines, Argo starch, steam and dry irons, Singer sewing machines, Sunbeam appliances, upright Hoover big-bag vacuum cleaners, Crown gas stoves with burning pilot lights, GE refrigerator-freezers that only had to be defrosted once a month, and Crosley table radios to keep her entertained while she scrubbed, ironed, cleaned, and cooked.

Somehow, she still found time to sip a Royal Crown or Tab cola and treat herself to White Rain shampoo and a Toni home permanent. Dressing tables were covered with hair curlers, rollers, bobby pins, and barrettes, Hazel Bishop lipstick, cosmetics, and Mojud nylon hosiery. She kept her smile bright with Dr. Lyon's toothpowder and her preferred perfume was Evening in Paris.

In relaxing moments, she shared telephone party-line conversations with neighbors. Then party lines gave way to private lines and operators gave way to rotary-dial telephones. Telegrams and airmail became distant memories, while black-and-white television programs opened new vistas for family entertainment.

We enjoyed America's modern lifestyle. Coal-fired furnaces kept houses warm in winter, while open porches, screened windows, and electric fans provided relief from summer's heat and humidity. Depending on the season, kids swam, skated, or went sledding at Whiting Park, fished with bamboo poles and bobbers at Wolf and George Lakes, and used Whiting-Robertsdale neighborhoods as one giant backyard for youthful fun and frolic.

The Whiting Community Center was headquarters for Halloween and Christmas parties, sporting events, swimming, social activities, and bowling. Pinboys and patrons—young and old alike—filled the Center with energy, enthusiasm, and enjoyment.

Change is constant, and we've adapted quite well to letting go of the outdated and passé, but every now and then, remembrances of once-upon-a-time moments arrive for a brief visit. Be sure to have the welcome mat ready to usher in those good times once again.

By the way, when was the last time you heard someone whistling?

(2015)

GUEST CHECK

TABLE	PERSONS	46394	SERVER
P	5		S-9

Paperboy
Parting Words
Pat Pending
Plan Period
Prelude to Winter

TAX

THANKS FOR VISITING THE MIND CAFETERIA

Paperboy

My first paying job was that of paperboy in 1952. Previous employment was self-directed, like scavenging discarded soda bottles from neighborhood alleys for the 2-cent deposit and shoveling snow in the winter. I wanted to find a job that provided consistent cash flow to meet my growing economic and social needs, but jobs were limited for an 11-year-old sixth-grader. I was too young to set pins at the bowling alley at the Whiting Community Center and lawn care jobs were sporadic (and seasonal). Money was so scarce, I was more broke than the Ten Commandments.

Gathering my courage, I walked over to the Whiting News Company (or "The Paper Store," as most Whiting-Robertsdale residents called it) and applied for a paper route. First I met with the owner, Mr. Chrustowski, who outlined the scope of the job. Shortly afterward, I met the man in charge of the paperboys, Mr. Serafin, whom everyone affectionately called "Dutch."

My application was accepted, and I was assigned afternoon delivery for my street, Cleveland Avenue, Route 6B. With so many customers, it happened to be one of Whiting's highest paying paper routes—$5.90 per week to deliver the *Chicago Daily News*, *Chicago Herald-American*, and *The Hammond Times*. In addition, paperboys collected weekly bills, kept track of customer accounts, and recorded our routes' stop and start times. All told, I had 162 afternoon papers to deliver Monday through Saturday.

During orientation, Mr. Chrustowski and Dutch emphasized the necessity of being on time and placing the paper on the porch, stoop, or steps. If we were delivering newspapers during inclement weather, it was our responsibility to protect them from adverse conditions. Most porches were not enclosed and plastic bags hadn't been invented yet, so we were to place the paper in a container by the front door or in an otherwise sheltered area where the customer could readily retrieve it. We were also cautioned not to toss the paper in bushes, flowerbeds, or on porch roofs. Complaints from unhappy subscribers about poor delivery or misbehavior were grounds for dismissal.

As part of our training, we reported to the back entrance of Whiting News and headed downstairs. A number of tables held stacks of newspapers. Around 1:30 pm, a truck would park on 119th Street and unload the afternoon dailies into a chute accessed from the store's exterior. Bundle after bundle would slide down the chute into the waiting arms of employees who sorted, counted, and stacked papers for the various routes.

One of the most important tasks for every paperboy was to learn how to fold, roll, and twist the paper so it could be tossed on porches without coming apart. Dutch demonstrated the proper paperboy fold, and the older guys working the chute supervised us until we had it down pat.

After a route had been prepared and marked, the assigned paperboy would check it out for delivery. If a paperboy chose not to pick up his papers, they were delivered to his house later in the afternoon. I preferred store pickup because I could have my route done much sooner, usually by 3:00 pm. If I waited for the papers to be delivered to my house, I wouldn't finish until 4:30 pm or so.

To carry papers, we each were provided a canvas pouch with a large shoulder strap. With a bag fully loaded with afternoon editions and slung over one shoulder, a paperboy tilted earth-like, about 23½ degrees off plumb as he walked his route. Paperboys with bicycles would balance their bags over the front fender. In a single motion, while steering the bike with one hand, they'd pull a paper from the sack and toss it right onto the porch.

Because I didn't have a bicycle, my main method of transporting the afternoon news was my wooden Radio Flyer wagon. Filled to capacity with copies of the *Daily News*, the *Herald-American*, and the *Times*, I'd pull it door to door. Some customers on Cleveland Avenue were two-paper homes, but most residents subscribed to just one.

One fringe benefit of being a paperboy was getting to know all the residents on the block. It didn't take long for customers to greet us by name as we delivered their paper. Such friendliness paid dividends when collecting the weekly bill as many customers would add a tip.

My tenure as a paperboy was short-lived, however. When school started in September, my studies and chores at home took precedence. Route 6B went to another paperboy. But in that brief time, I took the initial steps of independence and learned employment lessons that would serve me well.

As boyhood gives way to adolescence, and adolescence to adulthood, additional responsibilities, commitment, and priorities command attention. New strategies and coping skills meet a variety of challenges, whether academic, social, economic, or personal. Being a paperboy taught me organization, time management, responsibility, and respect. That's a pretty good return for a job that paid $5.90 a week.

To the Chrustowski family and Dutch Serafin—thanks!

(2010)

Parting Words

For some reason, we say our most endearing and heartfelt words to one another just before we end a visit or take leave. Hugs, handshakes, smiles, and occasional tears accompany these parting words. These indelible moments of farewell reinforce an awareness we all share: Life is a series of beginnings and goodbyes, and no matter the number of our years, we never quite get used to it. I suspect the social ritual of parting helps lessen feelings of separation and loss while providing an opportunity to convey affection, hopeful intention, and the possibility that we'll meet again.

In June 1998, following 27 years in the classroom, I opted to take the early retirement offered by District 215 in Calumet City, Illinois. Originally hired to teach industrial and vocational education at the district's two high schools, Thornton Fractional North and Thornton Fractional South, I transitioned a number of years later to special education. In August 1995, while on the faculty of T.F. North, I was assigned emotionally disordered (ED) and behaviorally disordered (BD) students.

Suffice it to say, these special needs students are not happy campers. Many come from broken and dysfunctional homes or single-parent, matriarchal households. Although ED and BD students have average or above-average IQ scores, they exhibit low self-esteem, struggle to achieve academic success, and display inappropriate social and personal behavior. Many are angry, recalcitrant, rude, vulgar, and intoxicated with a proclivity for anti-authority mischief. They are urban teenage warriors all too familiar with failure, poverty, neighborhood turf conflicts, street-corner pharmacists, law enforcement officers, and juvenile authorities.

There were eleven culturally and ethnically diverse students in my self-contained, second-floor classroom: two girls and nine boys. Assisting my pedagogical efforts in the classroom was my instructional aide, Ms. G. It didn't take long before my students called me "Mr. Rogers" because I was constantly encouraging them to work and improve.

When an assessment of reading comprehension levels revealed severe deficiencies, I taught them to read. As their reading ability improved, so did their personal and social behavior. Clear, sparkling eyes reflected growing self-confidence, self-esteem, and self-worth. Little by little, millimeter by millimeter, remediation became apparent.

By the time the calendar had turned to 1998, we'd been together for two years and they'd made remarkable progress—academically, socially, and personally. After school resumed following spring vacation, I told them of my plan to retire in June. I wouldn't be here for their senior year.

"Why are you leaving?" they asked.

"Because it's time," I replied. "Life is a series of beginnings and goodbyes, and no matter the number of our years, we never quite get used to it. Change is always unsettling, and at times, difficult." I assured them, however, that everything would be okay.

On Friday, May 22, celebrating their collective achievement of demonstrating year-long appropriate language and behavior, they enjoyed a classroom picnic of White Castle specialties, which perfumed the second floor with the mouthwatering aroma of steam-grilled sliders and onions.

Thursday, June 4, was the last day of school. Just before dismissal, I sent Ms. G ahead to make sure our students' transportation home had arrived. I stood in the hallway just outside the classroom door. As each of my pupils walked out, I thanked them, shook their hand, wished them well, and—disregarding school protocol—hugged them goodbye.

Johnny, a teenager who'd grown up on Chicago's West Side, was the last to leave. I shook his hand and hugged him. He began to walk away, then stopped and turned back.

Looking at me with teary eyes, he spoke his parting words: "Mr. Koch, I wish you were my dad."

He paused for just a moment. Turning away again, he walked to the end of the hall, down the staircase, through the front door, and out of my life.

I went back into my classroom, quietly closed the door, and sat behind my desk for the last time. Looking around the now empty classroom, I tried to understand how 30 years had passed so quickly. My own words came to mind: *"Life is a series of beginnings and goodbyes, and no matter the number of our years, we never quite get used to it."*

Today, Johnny would be in his late thirties. I'd love to talk with him and hear how his life unfolded. Most of all, I'd like to thank him for enriching, nourishing, and capturing my heart with his parting words.

May your parting words enrich, nourish, and engender heartfelt moments of those you love.

(2015)

Pat Pending

Growing up in the 1940s before television gained prominence, home entertainment mostly consisted of listening to the radio or reading books. My earliest memories are of hearing the sounds and voices emanating from the Crosley radio in the kitchen. Listening to World War II updates and national news broadcasts were part of the morning breakfast menu. Then as the day progressed, radio presented a variety of programs to inform or entertain listeners of different ages.

I was four and a half years old when I began to read, though it might come as a surprise that radio was my primary motivation. See, many kids' programs were sponsored by breakfast cereals like Pep (*The Adventures of Superman*), Cheerios (*The Lone Ranger*), Nabisco Shredded Wheat (*Straight Arrow*), Wheaties (*Jack Armstrong, the All-American Boy*), Hot Ralston (*Tom Mix Ralston Straight Shooters*), and Quaker Oats (*Sergeant Preston of the Yukon*). Nearly every program at the time offered a premium for sending in a box top or seal from the sponsor's product, plus a few coins. Thus the origin and focus of my early reading was the cereal box because it provided this premium information, and my favorite cereal box writer was Pat Pending. Let me explain.

Regardless of the cereal brand, the bottom corner of every box always featured the name Pat Pending. Writing thousands of words for cereal makers, this "Shakespeare of breakfast cereals" definitely knew how to get the attention of young consumers. Without question, he was a marketing genius.

Every cereal box with Pat Pending's name presented new words for me to learn. On the side panel, I was introduced to niacin, riboflavin, calcium, and thiamine, just to name a few of the dietary minerals. He listed ingredients like whole grains, cornstarch, sugar, salt, and phosphate as well as vitamins A through D and a lot of stuff I didn't understand. On the back of the box, he included all the important information a kid needed to procure the current premium offer, plus a form to be filled in with name, address, city, and state.

Once the redemption form was cut out and completed, it was placed in an envelope along with the required box top and coinage, then addressed, stamped, and mailed off to one of several cereal-maker meccas, like Battle Creek, Michigan or Checkerboard Square in St. Louis, Missouri.

Like other kids my age, I'd pester my mom to buy a particular cereal because of a special offer or premium. If my radio heroes used a secret decoder, a signal ring, or carried a badge, I wanted one too! Cheerios, for example, offered a model of the Lone Ranger Frontier Town (a total of 71 pieces, spread over 9 different boxes and various mail-in offers), Wheaties had a complete set of miniature state license plates (48 back then), and Quaker Oats even offered a deed to one square inch of the Yukon!

But Nabisco's Shredded Wheat stood out from the pack with a contest to win a real-live palomino pony, tied to the cereal's sponsorship of *Straight Arrow*, a western adventure program. Each entry required just a box top for the chance to saddle up, and I really wanted that pony. But eating Shredded Wheat was like feasting on a whisk broom. I ate so much of it that I was beginning to pass wicker furniture!

Every morning, I'd load up a bowl with my breakfast cereal of choice (based on the premium offered) and chow down. Staring at the cereal box, I read Pat Pending's every word. Besides the colorful graphics and attractive lettering on the outside of the box, occasionally a cartoon booklet was inside, a free bonus for buying the cereal.

Now I hadn't quite mastered spelling yet, so misreading words could cause me considerable embarrassment. One morning, I read on the Post Toasties box that there was a sealed inner cartoon. I ripped off the box top and poured the contents into my mom's large mixing bowl—I wanted the cartoon inside and I wanted it now! Mom came in the kitchen and asked what I was doing. I told her about the free cartoons and pointed to where it said so on the box.

Mom picked up the box and said, "There aren't any cartoons in the box. Cartoon is spelled C-A-R-T-O-O-N. This word is C-A-R-T-O-N.

Carton is another name for box. There's an inner-sealed carton to keep the cereal fresh!"

"Well," she continued, "it looks like you have a whole lot of cereal to eat. Better get started!"

I learned later that Pat Pending was actually an abbreviation for "patent pending," a phrase that indicates legal protection is being pursued for the product in question. Oops! Pat Pending wasn't a person at all. But reading all those cereal boxes still helped me to become a good speller!

(2018)

Plan Period

A teacher's daily schedule typically includes a plan period, a block of time away from classroom instruction and student contact that provides an opportunity to prepare lessons, catch up on paperwork, make phone calls, attend meetings, and work on ancillary tasks. Plan periods are also used to relax and de-stress, socialize and commiserate with colleagues, staff, and school employees, or attend to personal business. And on occasion, plan periods are utilized to engage in some friendly competition.

During my time at Thornton Fractional North High School in Calumet City, Illinois, there were a number of highly talented, athletically skilled individuals who readily accepted a challenge to prove their prowess. Ping-pong was one of the major faculty tournaments for male teachers, taking place in the girls' gym during the lunch hour.

Separate A and B brackets were prepared, and a random drawing paired players in each. Winners remained in bracket A, with losing A players moved to bracket B for a second chance. Round two involved a playoff. Suffer two losses and you were out. The competition culminated with a final match between the champ from each bracket.

Tournament participants included: Ron Armstrong, Bruno Bacys, Bob Bobin, Tom Brow, Brian Cwik, Dick Daugherty, Don Hakes, John Hoese, Mark Hopkins, Jerry Munda, Art Porter, Bob Schneider, Bob Stoeffler, Bob Swingendorf, Fred Washburn, Dave Zahn, John Zelanik, and me. With a plethora of mediocre talent, I was a solid B bracket guy.

Without question, the best ping-pong players I ever competed against were Armstrong, Bacys, Hakes, Porter, and Zahn. The others would let me make a point or two, but these guys shut me down more often than the girls I dated as a teenager. Matches with Ron Armstrong always ended eleven to nothing. He'd rip me—"Eleven, zip! NEXT!" Armstrong really enjoyed the tournament. He'd say, "Save your energy, you won't even need a paddle."

Being left-handed, I thought I had an advantage—opposite ball spin and all that. Then I played Don Hakes, who was generous: He let me score three points. But I rarely saw the ball. My vision picked up a white blur flying past my paddle. I had quite a workout chasing the bouncing celluloid sphere all over the gym.

However, because I have a signed high school diploma, I knew the only way to improve my game was additional practice. The chance to do just that presented itself the night of the "Battle of the Bands" competition at the high school auditorium.

Dave Zahn and I were working security for the event, and Larry St. John, the activities director, had assigned us the hallway behind the auditorium. Before the concert began, Dave and I carried the ping-pong table upstairs from the girls' gym and set it up in the secured zone. While teenage musicians hammered out the latest rock music on stage, we had a battle of the paddles. I recall we each won ten matches, and saved enough energy after those 20 games to carry the table back downstairs.

But the highlight of my ping-pong practice sessions was the afternoon Art Porter and I played during plan period. Art was about seven points away from victory when the door opened. In the doorway stood Richard Kurek, the assistant principal. Porter and I stopped, acknowledged his presence, and then waited.

"Where are you two scheduled?" Mr. Kurek asked.

"We're both on plan," I answered.

"Plan period?" (Kurek had a way with words.) "What are you planning, Mr. Koch?"

"Right now, I'm planning to beat Porter in ping-pong!"

SLAM. The door vibrated with resounding resistance as Kurek left.

Porter and I finished the game and then went about our assigned duties.

The next afternoon, I checked my mailbox in the General Office and quickly exited back into the hall, hoping to avoid Kurek. But as luck would have it, we crossed paths as he was heading to a meeting at the Guidance Office.

Sheepishly, I said, "Good afternoon, Mr. Kurek."

"Afternoon, Mr. Koch."

Side by side, we walked the short distance to the Guidance Office. As I made my move to scurry down the hall toward my classroom in the east wing, Kurek spoke. "By the way, Mr. Koch, how'd that game turn out?"

"Porter won, 21 to 12," I replied.

Without missing a beat, Kurek turned into the Guidance Office with a smile on his face and said, "Porter's very talented. You need more practice."

District 215, Thornton Fractional North Township High School in Calumet City, Illinois—wasn't that a time!

(2013)

Prelude to Winter

The yearly transition from autumn to winter is well underway. Last month's return of Standard Time shifted the arrival of both dawn and evening, affecting the way daylight illuminates the landscape. Shadows of subdued sunlight are filtered between the latticed branches of leafless trees and through gossamer window curtains.

The intensity of summer's solar radiance has yielded to autumn's more agreeable recipe. Now ever-colder temperatures begin to bluster and bully their way to the front of the line, completing the annual cycle of seasons to winter as furnaces, fireplaces, parkas, and down comforters entice us with their manufactured warmth.

At first glance, December isn't the most appealing month. In the absence of celebrating personal milestones like birthdays or anniversaries, the annual prelude to winter presents a dismal meteorological menu of entrées: overcast skies, undisciplined winds, parsimonious sunshine, and cold precipitation (served with or without ice). But ill-tempered weather conditions aside, December's status and importance are truly unmatched.

If the calendar months were a baseball team, December would be the closer. No other month could possibly end a year like December does. During its allotted 31 days of limited sunlight and cold, windy nights (not to mention the occasional snowfall), December ushers in the winter solstice, celebrates the Christmas season, and bids adieu to the old while welcoming in the new via the hats-and-horns party of New Year's Eve.

December's main focus is preparation—winterizing residents, homes, and vehicles alike. In closets, short-sleeve cotton tees, tank tops, and shorts are swapped out for flannel, wool, and easy-layering garments designed for maximum warmth. Snowsuits, boots, and mittens transform children into playful well-insulated bundles of laughter, impervious to cold and snow. Lawn mowers, landscape tools, and garden hoses are stowed for the season, replaced by snow shovels, snow throwers, and windshield scrapers for defense against the onslaught of adverse weather.

In concert with routine duties of preparing hearth and home for winter, December is also the time of year for expectation, excitement, and jubilation. In anticipation of Christmas, ecclesiastical calendars showcase the season of Advent. This time of spiritual renewal and self-preparation enriches the celebration of the birth of Jesus Christ.

Supporting the season of gift giving, retailers accommodate shoppers looking to fulfill wish lists by extending store hours into late evening. Newspapers bulge with increased advertising, sales flyers, and discount coupons. Online and brick-and-mortar stores vie for patrons with special offers. The volume of neighborhood traffic increases as delivery vehicles drop off packages—some to be opened immediately, while others are first festively wrapped to await their eventual recipients.

Seemingly overnight, homes are set aglow with colored lights and illuminated winter scenes, conveying season's greetings to passersby. Normally drawn drapes and curtains are left open to proudly display Christmas trees adorned with lights, ornaments, and other trimmings, while inside, young children secretly hope the story of Santa's visit on Christmas Eve is true.

Radio speakers fill the air with the sounds of holiday music. Christmas specials and classic holiday movies mount their traditional television takeover, including countless airings of *A Christmas Story*, the adventures of Ralphie Parker's family and his personal quest for a Red Ryder BB gun, while a much older chestnut, *It's a Wonderful Life*, starring Jimmy Stewart, takes on the infamous leg lamp with a classic story of a small town not unlike Whiting, Indiana, and its connected residents.

Across the land for a few brief shining hours, thoughts turn kind as churchgoers celebrate the birth of Jesus Christ. At services, Scripture readings of the first Christmas are presented to parishioners amid prayers and hymns with hopefulness for "Peace on earth, good will to men."

Such moments are the gifts of December, another opportunity for humankind to commit to doing better. This month serves as our year-end inventory of how we used the past 12. More than simply the last month of the year or the prelude to winter, December is a gift that welcomes a new season, reviews the recent past, celebrates the arrival of a new year, and commemorates the goodness, kindness, and generosity of humankind bestowed upon all through the gift, love, and blessings of the first Christmas.

Merry Christmas, everyone!

(2016)

GUEST CHECK

TABLE	PERSONS		SERVER
Q	2	46394	S-9

Quality Moments
Quotient of Character

TAX

THANKS FOR VISITING THE MIND CAFETERIA

Quality Moments

I don't remember exactly when episodes of "Quality Moments" became part of my life. What I do know is that these thoughtful pauses can be consciously summoned or, more often, can arrive unexpectedly without prior petition. Only the stars know what specifically activates these mental get-togethers, and they prefer to remain silent. Putting unanswered questions aside as we travel the highways and byways of our lives, these visitations increase in frequency and appreciation.

Quality Moments are a presence of mind consisting of peaceful, easy feelings about experiences and events we've enjoyed in our lifetimes. Occurring at random, they form sanctuaries of tranquility deep within gray-matter neighborhoods. They're a personal visit to the most private places of our inner landscape.

When these gifts of reflective thought come to the forefront of memory, Quality Moments arrive with a poignant precision that embellishes the sweet-sadness of the past. In their wake, they leave an afterglow and yearning to hold onto cherished scenes of once-upon-a-time.

These prized snippets of life are composed of crystalized senses and emotions. Entrées from the meteorological menu often set the stage for receptiveness, working in concert with dawn, sunset, twilight, and star-filled night skies. Each nuance of weather—temperature, precipitation, sunlight, cloud formations, and wind velocity—fulfills a specific role in preparing our cognitive theater for the banquet of remembrance.

Regardless of month or day of the week, these gifts of imagination can be delivered 24/7. In a most pleasing manner, this thoughtful reverie welcomes both past and present while playfully teasing future hopes and dreams.

Folded within the recipe of daydreaming are the sights and soundtrack of our lives. We can be inside or outdoors, engaged in activities, or quietly coasting in our favorite manner. Once the cognitive welcome mat is displayed, it's only a matter of time until a delivery of Quality Moments arrives to dispense gifts to us.

During the season when early darkness and unpleasant weather takes up residence, looking through family photo albums, high school yearbooks, old greeting cards, and personal letters received over the years can spark Quality Moments. Watching videos that recall family gatherings and vacations also serve as an invitation to reawaken remembrance of bygone days and personal treasures. Musing through mementos while relaxing in an overstuffed easy chair, cozily wrapped in a fleece throw, and holding a favorite beverage makes an ideal setting for these movies of the mind.

When seasonal weather turns friendly and daylight lengthens, these conditions beckon us to savor such Quality Moments outside. Before the dawn dissolves darkness and reveals details of the landscape, we can enjoy a first cup of coffee and placidly muse on a porch swing, deck chair, or patio glider as a new day begins to unfold.

Like a trusted companion, thoughts recalling cherished events experienced over a lifetime make the heart smile. Most cognitive keepsakes happened in concert with emerging chronological milestones—marking a coming of age, awareness, enjoyment, or achievement.

Recollection of dreamy teenage romance blends together in the mind as a warm spring drizzle induces caressing, head-to-toe shivers. These emotional rivulets soften the heart and diminish the wistful acceptance of loss. For a few brief moments, weeping willow trees smile and time is suspended, allowing long-ago events to replay with a clarity that refreshes and caresses the soul. Sometimes, we mentally edit such thoughts to lessen regret and imagine a more desirable ending. Such fantasies quickly fade however, leaving us with the unanswered question, "What if?"

Quality Moments are another gift bestowed to all. It matters not if we're a poet, pauper, teacher, or king. These reflective visuals are amenities of our humanness. They're a way to be alone without being lonely, a therapeutic process to enjoy—more than once—the times of our lives.

(2018)

Quotient of Character

In grade school arithmetic, we learned that each mathematical function has its own solution term: addition has a sum, subtraction has a difference, multiplication has a product, and division has a quotient. By definition, a quotient is the result of dividing one quantity by another. A quotient is also a degree or amount of a specified quality or characteristic. It's this second definition that warrants a closer analysis, specifically as applied to our character.

As children, we're schooled on the importance of having good character—the mental and moral qualities distinctive to an individual. Pedagogic emphasis focused on the four essential traits or core values we needed to acquire and nurture throughout life: trust, honor, respect, and responsibility. Although school curriculums never offered a course for character, we were encouraged to observe and model positive, constructive values from parents, teachers, and other adults who touched our lives. We were often asked, "What's your personal plan for goodness?"

The acquisition of good character nourishes self-esteem and strengthens relationships. It's the footing and foundation for a meaningful life. Each day is an opportunity to refine and improve the quality of our nature by thought, word, and deed. Acquiring quality character is a personal contract to pursue and maintain high standards. It demands an elevated level of commitment, and although difficult to attain, the benefits far outweigh any unpleasantness.

Character reflects our personality, attitude, and disposition. Even though personality is an invisible, internal mosaic, we make it visible by our words and deeds. Everyone has the opportunity to choose and decide the content of their character—it's not one-size-fits-all. Loyalty, optimism, dignity, humility, fairness, courageousness, and conscientiousness are a few character traits often referenced. But so much of what we value in each other cannot be easily translated into words. Rather, character is often sensed emotionally as feelings of appreciation for the value people bring to our lives. Our quotient of character can be conveyed verbally ("I give you my word"), by handshake, or by signature.

Try this exercise: List 12 people who are the most influential in your life (use initials if you need to for privacy's sake). These are the people who, in effect, serve as your personal board of directors. Why are these people so valued that you entrust and accept their counsel and mentoring? Consider the qualities that led you to select each of them, and list these qualities alongside their names. After you review their individual qualities, you'll likely find they share quotients of character that celebrate virtue and are all guided by a strong moral compass.

Because we're more alike than different, we share values that enrich and enhance each other. The question is this: If these values are important to you when choosing your personal board of directors, how many people whose lives you've touched would select you to be on theirs?

Our quotient of character is a personal bumper sticker. What image fills the mind at the mention of our name? Does the quality of our character elicit thoughts of integrity and honesty? Do we serve as a positive role model for others? A person's identity should reflect a sincerity and authenticity that displays their true self. It's the core of humanness and forms the wealth of our quotient of character.

(2017 - Previously unpublished)

GUEST CHECK

TABLE	PERSONS	46394	SERVER
R	5		S-9

Random Acts of Kindness
The Rarest Bird
Remembering Mrs. Harmon
A Rising Addiction of the Electronic Kind
The Roller Coaster of Life

TAX

THANKS FOR VISITING THE MIND CAFETERIA

Random Acts of Kindness

Random acts of kindness are expressions of appreciation, little and not-so-little things that enrich another's day, generate smiles, and lift spirits. Tangibly expressed by word or deed, these personal acts of unexpected gratitude are the fringe benefits of living a joyful life.

Once upon a time, all parents taught their children to help one another, share, and take initiative to make things better. These small displays of thankfulness feted family, friends, classmates, and neighbors, and learning to dispense such appreciation spontaneously added quality to their character. Countless times I helped Mom with the dishes.

As we mature, random acts of kindness are evidence of pride in our surroundings and personal demeanor. Respectful behavior, appropriate language, and overall deportment displayed the quality of our character and served as essential building blocks for the foundation of becoming an adult.

Developing self-reliance, independence, a strong work ethic, and a willingness to learn were strengthened by daily random acts of kindness. Before too long, we looked for opportunities to help others, like holding a door for someone, letting a shopper go ahead of us in line, or allowing another driver into traffic from a side street. One of the neatest random acts of kindness is anonymously paying the bill when seeing military personnel or veterans dining out.

A few weeks ago as I waited in the grocery store checkout line, I noticed that a mom with two young children was short a few dollars. A random act of kindness made up the difference so she didn't have to leave items behind. Being kind doesn't have to cost much.

From 1969 to 1971 (long before the existence of cell phones), I was a Curriculum Specialist at the Indiana Department of Public Instruction, working for the Vigo County School Corporation. That meant having an office on the Indiana State University campus in Terre Haute, Indiana, though I was still living in Northwest Indiana at the time. Heading back down to ISU after a weekend home with my family, I was driving along Route 63 when I came upon an elderly couple parked on the shoulder of the road with a flat tire.

I pulled up and asked if I could be of some assistance. The driver was a Baptist pastor at a church northwest of Chicago, and he and his wife were in route to Tennessee for a religious convention. They didn't have a spare tire for their 1970 Buick Electra 225 and asked if I would drive them to Terre Haute so they could get road service.

I was driving a 1970 98 Oldsmobile LS and knew that the two models were very similar, so I volunteered the loan of my spare. In the span of a few minutes, I changed the tire and placed the flat in the Buick's trunk. Giving the couple my name, number, and directions to the service station where they should leave my spare after their flat was repaired, the pastor and his wife were soon on their way.

I'd completely forgotten about the roadside encounter when that service station called a few days later, reminding me to pick up my spare. When I stopped by, an attendant handed me an envelope that contained $20 and a handwritten note of appreciation and blessed thanks. Kindness returned.

One of my favorite locations for a random act of kindness is the Chicago Skyway, the elevated toll-road on I-90 that connects the Indiana Toll Road to the Dan Ryan Expressway on Chicago's South Side. When I go to pay the toll, I always pay for the car behind me, too. Glancing in the rearview mirror, it makes me smile thinking about the occupants trying to figure out if they know the guy who paid their toll. I do the same thing at the drive-thru window when I buy my morning coffee.

The point is this: As we manage busy schedules and pursue daily activities, we seldom pause long enough to give thanks or acknowledge appreciation for life's good moments. To show our collective gratitude, we identify a few special occasions to convey remembrance and celebration to loved ones and friends. We can do better.

A meaningful reminder to dispense random acts of kindness is one I first shared with my high school students in the fall of 1972: "Help

Mom with the dishes." Not a call to wash a sink full of dirty dishes, the expression is meant to inspire and encourage spontaneous gratitude through heartfelt decency. Demonstrated by action, "Help Mom with the dishes" becomes a personal commitment to thoughtfulness, kindness, goodness, and appreciation.

Performing random acts of kindness—alternatively phrased as my reminder to "Help Mom with the dishes"—pays dividends to both the giver and the receiver. These spontaneous gifts of goodness nourish the spirit, gladden the heart, and enrich the soul beyond expectation.

(2013)

The Rarest Bird

What follows is a true story. Now I must warn you that I make up some of my true stories, so you'll have to decide for yourself whether or not any of this is real.

In an almost inaccessible region of the Peruvian rainforest, in a narrow, verdant valley hidden by mountains shrouded in fog, ornithologists, biologists, and native guides have uncovered the first tangible evidence of the world's rarest bird. Until this discovery, information about this feathered creature, thought to herald from the age of dinosaurs, was limited to native legends and folklore passed on by tribal elders from one generation to the next.

Several decades of research employed the latest technological devices—motion-activated cameras and sound-triggered microphones—plus dozens of expeditions into the valley via foot, pack animal, and canoe in search of probable nesting and habitat areas. Countless pictures have been retrieved, though no definitive images of the elusive quarry have been captured, while audio recordings are still being analyzed to determine if mysterious anomalies can be attributed to this avian. But scientists did discover remnants of what they believe to be unique confirmation of the creature's existence: an uncommonly constructed nest on the forest floor.

Made with mud, small plant stems, leaves, and bird saliva, the nest was formed geometrically in the frustum of a cone measuring 2 feet in height and 9 to 10 inches in diameter at the base, topped by a plateaued, circular surface approximately 3 inches across. At the nest's base, biologists found bits of uniquely shaped black and blue eggshell. After considerable examination, discussion, and computerized reconstruction of shell fragments, it appears that this bird lays a 2½-inch square egg!

The egg's geometrically shaped shell prevents it from rolling down the nest's smooth, tapered circumference, offering protection from ground-dwelling predators. Further laboratory analysis of the saliva in the nest's construction revealed molecular enzymes that thwart and repel climbing insects, worms, arachnids, and other enemies from attacking the egg.

Ornithologists from several well-known universities have calculated the physical size and weight of this new species. The electronically generated data suggests the bird produces an egg out of proportion to its size by a ratio of 4:1. But with no actual documentation or other supporting evidence, these conclusions remain pure conjecture. Even so, these learned minds believe their theories and suppositions are fairly accurate.

A few weeks ago, after local natives retrieved recordings from strategically placed microphones near the nesting site, scientists were thrilled to announce they'd captured the first recording of this bird's vocals. They surmise it's not a mating call, but rather the sound made as she strains and struggles to lay the square egg on top of her nest. They ran the tape through several filters to reduce background noise and rainforest chatter in order to isolate the specific outcry of the nesting bird.

With field researchers and laboratory colleagues assembled in the media center, the first broadcast of this cleaned-up audio filled speakers and flooded the room. Barely audible at first, the cry of this unseen nesting avian rose in volume and intensity with increasing crescendo and vociferous ferocity as the sharp-edged, eight-cornered egg was deposited.

"oooooooooooooOOOOOOOOOOOOOOOOOOOOH! AAAAAAAAAAaaaaaaaaaaahhhhh."

Absent definitive anatomical characteristics but awestruck by the creature's intrinsic bird-brained know-how, the assembled group unanimously named it the Oooh-Aaah bird! Scientists are eager to observe the physical gymnastics and facial contortions involved as the Oooh-Aaah bird lays its square eggs, and look forward to studying the new species' other attributes.

For now, however, they'll have to be satisfied with the world's rarest bird announcing, in full-throated splendor, her latest geometric-shaped creation!

(2015)

Remembering Mrs. Harmon

I've always liked Cleveland Avenue in Whiting, Indiana, with its brick roadway and well-kept residences. I'm particularly fond of the 1800 block, as that's where my family resided from 1949 through 1968 and where I lived until I married in 1965. Equally meaningful were the neighbors who helped me along the way. As a kid, I also worked odd jobs for a number of them.

One of my favorite neighbors was Mrs. Harmon, a widow who lived on the northeast corner of 118th Street and Cleveland Avenue in a two-story American Foursquare clad in light green staggered-shake shingles. As an 11-year-old in the spring of 1952, she hired me to cut the grass, trim the edges, pull weeds, and sweep the front and back porches of her home. When winter arrived, I would shovel the driveway in front of her garage (though she didn't own a car) and clear the snow from the sidewalks, walkways, and both porches.

I never knew Mrs. Harmon's first name or anything about her family. Upon completing my work, whether summer or winter, I'd ring the front doorbell. She'd come to the door, hand me a quarter, and say thank you. One especially wintry day, after shoveling several inches of snow from the steps, sidewalk, and driveway, Mrs. Harmon handed me two quarters in appreciation for the additional effort.

Now during the growing season, I cut Mrs. Harmon's lawn every other Saturday. Because my family's house was a short distance away, I brought most of the tools with me—a Craftsman 16-inch push reel mower, a grass-catching bag, a straw broom, and a light lawn rake. Two old bushel baskets Mrs. Harmon had were used to collect the clippings before placing them in her alley garbage can. She also provided scissors to trim the edges of the lawn as well as a small garden shovel that I used with the broom to capture errant clippings from the mower and other debris.

One particular Saturday, I worked from 9:30 am until well past noon. As a lefty, trimming the edges of the lawn with Mrs. Harmon's right-handed scissors meant I was basically using them in reverse. By the time I'd finished trimming the front walk, my left thumb was throbbing and marked by a red ring. Giving my thumb some time to recover, I picked up the broom and swept the two porches and driveway before resuming my trimming duties. Tackling the parkway along the sidewalk and curb was brutal. Today there are power trimmers and edgers that make short work of this task, but back then it was manual labor of the most tedious order. (My left thumb typically resumed normal function by evening.)

Mrs. Harmon must have witnessed me struggling, because when I rang the doorbell after I'd finished, I noticed the front door had been left open. Looking through the closed screen door, I could see the furnishings inside. "Come in," she called. I had never been inside Mrs. Harmon's house before. Immediately, kitchen aromas filled my nose: coffee, fresh bread, and something garlicky. I took two steps inside, stood on the parlor rug, and waited.

Mrs. Harmon came out from the kitchen, wearing an apron and wiping her hands with a dishtowel. "You worked hard today, Albert," she said, reaching inside her apron pocket. "Here's a little treat for you." She handed me a Hershey's chocolate bar alongside my usual twenty-five cent wage.

I couldn't believe it! My first bonus!

"Thank you, Mrs. Harmon."

"You did a nice job today."

Returning outside to gather my tools, I ripped the wrapper off the Hershey's bar and wolfed it down in three bites. Using the upside-down mower as a mobile platform, I balanced the grass catcher, rake, and broom on it with one hand while steering the mower with the other as I walked home. After storing everything in the garage, I entered my house through the back door and went down to the basement to clean up at the laundry tubs. Once upstairs, I eagerly told my mom about the chocolate bar bonus.

"So, where's the Hershey's bar?" she asked.

I told her I ate it.

"You ate it? What about your brothers and sister? I'm sure they would have liked some."

I looked Mom right in the eye and said, "I forgot about them."

Mom looked *me* in the eye and said, "How could you forget about your brothers and sister?"

I didn't have the heart to tell her, but it was *really* easy.

That day, thanks to the kindness of Mrs. Harmon, I learned a lesson that has stayed with me all these years: Keep your chocolate to yourself, be selective about what you tell your parents, and always remember your siblings—*after* you enjoy your chocolate!

(2019)

A Rising Addiction of the Electronic Kind

At times, I'm mystified how quickly we can develop an addiction to things and adopt habits to accommodate our insatiable cravings. The electronic addiction began with Alexander Graham Bell's telephone, grew with radio in the early 1920s, expanded to television by the late 1940s, accelerated in the 1970s with the arrival of video game consoles, and exploded in the 1980s after personal computers arrived on the scene. Today, with several communication technologies now incorporated into a single pocket-sized device, society is rapidly facing a full-fledged electronic dependence of epic proportions.

There was a time when callers' mobility was governed by the length of the cord attached to hard-wired phones. Then cordless phones came along, offering more freedom to roam. We could even step outside the house and stay connected within a certain radius. But today, cell phones offer true total mobility, available to all who have access to wireless technology.

As technology advanced, several electronic interrelationships were established. Telephones, television, video games, computers, calculators, and sundry gadgets formed the internet's mosaic of electrons and silicon circuits. Soon a tsunami of microwave frequencies covered nearly every nook and cranny of planet Earth. Everyone, it seems, wished to peek through Microsoft's Windows or take a bite of the newest computerized Apple.

With the acceleration of technology, we can be in touch anywhere, anytime. With the right device, we can watch movies, read books, check email, play games, plan schedules, list appointments, and listen to music, talk, or text. If we're so inclined, pictures and videos can be transmitted instantaneously recording the present, moments before it becomes the past. As long as power is available, we've got access to the world's information at our fingertips, whether via desktop, laptop, or pocket device.

But like most advances, this one comes with a price. Aided by chips and circuitry, we've ushered in an age of electronic isolation, eroding face-to-face contact. In the years BC (Before Computers), folks would visit with each other in person.

As wonderful as the telephone is, and as long as it's been a part of life, many calls were but a prelude to an actual get-together where human interaction was experienced through body language, eye contact, and touch, in addition to the words spoken. But there's really no electronic replacement for the kind of connections transmitted to our senses via such emotional immediacy.

Radio, unlike telephones or most television programming, gives us the freedom to listen and do other things. Housewives in the 1930s and 1940s could listen to radio programs while completing domestic chores. Old-time radio was user-friendly, with favorite shows providing hands-free imagination as household duties continued uninterrupted. And when radios became portable, listeners could enjoy these same programs or music wherever they chose. The distraction or loss of focus while listening to the radio was minimal.

With the advent of television, however, we soon discovered that ears are far superior at multi-tasking than eyes. As television sets appeared in more and more homes, further changes entered the American scene. The dinner hour either accommodated an additional guest at the dining room table or now took place in the living room where supper was served on TV trays. Family conversation was curtailed as watching television took priority over talking. Requiring a captive audience, television would later further separate family members as additional TV sets were purchased to accommodate individual viewing habits.

Nevertheless, America has continued to embrace members of the electronic family and their offspring. The main limitation of radio and television is that they're typically a one-way dispenser of information (call-in shows offer one exception). But computers came along and made instant interfacing possible, often to points far removed from our own.

Now with portable, pocket-sized electronic devices, too many people believe they can multitask with their eyes while staying focused on primary activities. Drivers talk on the phone and get so involved in the conversation that they lose concentration, jeopardizing others in traffic. Some, with thumbs flashing across keypads, text as they drive or walk down the street, even as they navigate crosswalks. Videos have flooded the web featuring electronic addicts walking into walls, falling into fountains, and damaging vehicles, all because they're too focused on their phones.

And what about other public spaces? Is it not possible to dine out without taking a call? Why share private conversations with the entire restaurant? Is it too much to turn off cell phones during church services? Likewise, a phone not set to silent during a wake service at a funeral home signals extreme insensitivity. And at sporting events, shopping malls, schools, and even public restrooms, texting is rampant. Is everything that important, or worse still, are we that lonely that we feel the need to be in constant contact?

There's a time and a place for everything, as the saying goes, but to curb this rising addiction of the electronic kind we must recognize that better self-discipline, wiser decision-making, and a willingness to use our devices more responsibly is required.

(2011)

The Roller Coaster of Life

Growing up in Whiting, Indiana, a trip to Chicago's Riverview Park was on everyone's to-do list. Located on the Northwest Side at Western and Belmont Avenues, the amusement park had been the place to "Laugh your troubles away!" since opening day in 1904.

By turns classy, scruffy, glitzy, and garish, Riverview Park featured a variety of attractions and thrill rides, including three roller coasters ready to test teenage bravado: The Comet, The Silver Flash, and the epitome of courageous daring, The Bobs—a wooden roller coaster that was almost 90 feet high and reached speeds of 50 miles per hour, considered by many to be the greatest coaster ever built.

Riverview Park sold its last ticket in September 1967 (the expansive grounds are now home to the Riverview Plaza shopping center, DeVry University, and a police station, among other things), but roller coasters continue to draw crowds to amusement parks and theme parks around the world. Some are home to a whole host of coasters designed to challenge patrons' courage. Built with the latest technology, engineering, and design, these thrill rides feature towering heights, steep-angle drops, body-wrenching twists, heart-pounding curves, inside loops, DNA-like helixes, and head-down suspended cars rocketing along the rails at more than a mile a minute.

In the queue prior to boarding, eager guests (and those persuaded by the enthusiasm of others in their company) are screened by age and physical size, and they're also cautioned that having certain health issues may result in adverse effects. Loaded into coaster cars and locked into position by restraining bars or special harnesses (or some combination thereof), riders soon experience an emotional rush of terror, excitement, and breath-taking thrills. Then, after just a handful of breath-holding minutes, they're returned to the starting point to regain their composure and sensory stability.

Such intense rides are not for everyone. But even if we never step foot in an amusement park or theme park, there's no avoiding the roller coaster of life. And it's best to buckle up, because this ride is a one-size-fits-all operation—not to mention a mandatory one! From the moment of birth we're faced with ups and downs, twists and turns, straightaways, emotionally wrenching twists, heart-pounding events, and unexpected challenges that test our courage, resolve, intelligence, abilities, beliefs, and faith.

Of course, our awareness of life's roller coaster isn't immediate. But at some point in our younger years we come to understand that we're on a journey. We begin to appreciate the ability to review the past to help both facilitate the present and face an unknown future. Making tenuous plans, our hope is easily eroded by events not under our control as well as uncertainty, fear, and our own fragility.

By interacting with family members and others in close proximity, we assess how they've fared on life's roller coaster thus far—physically, emotionally, academically, socially, and personally. These role models serve as our initial companions on our own ride. As we advance in years, we welcome teachers, classmates, coworkers, colleagues, friends, and a few strangers too. These folks might influence us and even occasionally come along, but it still remains our ride—we're in the front seat alone with little control!

It's a startling statement, but that's just life's hands-on, learn-by-doing, trial-and-error course of study. Having to fly solo is really the only way we develop the cognitive strategies and coping skills necessary to conquer the challenges we'll encounter.

Boarding life's roller coaster at birth, we start a slow, typically pleasant climb to a level called the age of reason. Beginning in kindergarten (or for some, preschool), we mark our progress forward through each grade level, all the while experiencing a series of escalations and downward traverses— gains and losses.

First, we reach the uppermost level of grade school only to travel to the bottom of middle school. Then we struggle to reach the top of middle school, but as soon as we've conquered that summit, we're plunged to the ground floor of high school. Four years later, we're handed diplomas as graduating seniors, but just as we're proudly savoring our conquest of adolescence, we dive at dizzying speed toward the base of adulthood. In the blink of an eye, once more we're rookies, novices, and neophytes, now striving to gain status in the upward movement of the adult world.

Regardless of whether we've entered college or university, the vocational or corporate world, or military or municipal service, we discover the requirements and effort to get to the top are more complex, challenging, demanding, and stressful. Living even the most mundane life taxes our physical and emotional stamina, depleting and draining our energy more than anything ever has before. Instead of slowing down, life's roller coaster only seems to speed up in intensity—teaching, testing, and toughening every fiber of our body. As obligations and responsibilities increase, we're bounced and jounced around, getting bumped and bruised along the way.

Zipping along the track throughout our adult life, we're presented with windows of opportunity that open and close. We're confronted with choices, selections, and options that demand thoughtful consideration. And at random intervals, we're called upon to make decisions that have life-changing consequences. At times, personal tolerance and limits are breached and the ride becomes too stressful, causing us to jump the rails—physically, emotionally, and spiritually.

Thankfully, most of us will complete our ride on life's roller coaster and celebrate with appreciation, gratitude, and satisfaction for the journey we had. Its duration and the challenges we'll encounter are known only to the stars. For now, they prefer to remain silent. Enjoy the ride.

(2018)

GUEST CHECK

TABLE	PERSONS	46394	SERVER
S	13		S-9

School's Out for the Summer!
Seasonal Shadows
Season of Peace
The Sense of It All
Sheet Metal Romance
Shortcuts
Soon It Will Be Christmas
Standard Oil Company
Stepping Stones and Milestones
Stieglitz Park
Still Can't Say Goodbye
The Summer of '55
Summers of a Lifetime

TAX

School's Out for
the Summer!

Lately, there's been a discussion about whether school systems should eliminate summer vacation and institute year-round instruction. Students would still attend the mandated 180 days, but those days would be spread out over the year. Perhaps year-round school is an idea whose time has come.

When I was in grade school in the 1950s, I couldn't wait for summer vacation, partly because I wouldn't have to worry about getting biffed by Sister Bruiser for a while, partly because I'd have all-day recess, and partly because I wasn't too thrilled with school itself.

When the final bell sounded for the school year, we lined up two-by-two and marched out of school like a pint-sized parochial platoon preparing for maneuvers. Master Sergeant Sister Bruiser gave the moving columns of potential apostles a final inspection before discharging us to the outside world. As soon as we cleared school property, we broke ranks and assumed normal kid conduct: pushing, shoving, swinging book bags, and general rowdiness.

At the end of fourth and fifth grades, I recall several boys beginning to sing this end-of-school anthem:

"School's out, school's out,
Teacher let the monkeys out.
Some jumped in, some jumped out,
And one jumped in the teacher's mouth!

School's out, school's out,
Teacher let the monkeys out.

No more lessons, no more books,
No more teacher's dirty looks!"

By the second "School's out," all of the student parolees had joined in. These were the days before school buses, so neighborhood residents heard several dozen rounds before the pupil-herd dispersed to individual homebound routes.

This was also the pre-uniform, pre-permanent press, pre-automatic washer/dryer era in parochial education. A few years earlier, Sister Superior wanted to require that boys wear white shirts and ties to school. A number of angry mothers quickly banded together and stormed the convent en masse, swinging Sunbeam irons and throwing Argo starch on the front steps. Luckily, the parish monsignor arrived in the nick of time to quell the uprising. The issue of boys wearing white shirts and ties to school was never mentioned again.

Back then, summer vacation seemed like forever. A kid had from June all the way to September before they had to worry about school. A few days after we were let out, the nuns packed up and left for summer training camp at their motherhouse somewhere down south. This meant we could play softball on the empty lot next to the convent without the intimidation of watchful nuns behind curtained glass. This had to be what Thomas Jefferson and the other Founding Fathers meant when they talked about freedom!

Not only had we been released from our scholastic prison, the jailers had left town too. For three delicious months, kids didn't have to worry about raising their hand before speaking, and they could use the restroom anytime they wanted—without hurrying. In school, Sister always monitored the boys on their restroom break. She stood just outside the washroom door holding a stopwatch while her charges made their personal porcelain novena. If a kid didn't come out within a pre-set time, the wayward boy came face to face with a scowling representative of the salvation police.

Sister's appearance usually generated considerable fear and panic, and many frantic boys suffered zipper-inflicted injuries. The sight of an ecclesiastical penguin standing at the threshold of the comfort station while in the process of purging unwanted fluids is definitely one of life's major challenges. We either learned how to multitask or suffered the consequences. Most grade school boys had trousers with rusty zippers!

Besides summer vacation, the next most important thing was our report card—not necessarily the grades, but the comments Sister wrote. In those days, if we passed everything, she would write at the bottom of the card, "Promoted to Grade [X]." This made it official that we'd survived and were moving up the ladder of scholastic salvation.

At the end of the fifth grade, my promotion to sixth grade must have been in doubt, because on my card Sister wrote, "Watch this space!" Academically, I was not a star. I excelled in only two areas: recess and prayer. I figured as bad as my grades were, I needed all the help I could get. Eventually, with Heaven's intervention (likely a phone call from my mom), I'd passed all my classes and was promoted.

I wasn't the worst student, however. There was one other kid who didn't pass anything except the time he ate six Twinkies and passed gas. Unfortunately, that particular offering wasn't part of the curriculum, so instead of extra credit, Sister gave him a penance. She also banned Twinkies from the classroom!

As years accumulate, we notice changes. One is that summers get shorter. Time really zips by—school is barely dismissed in June before kids start returning in mid-August. Other things have changed too. Report cards are no longer handwritten but computer generated. Like a favorite snack from long ago, Mrs. Klein's Potato Chips, report cards today are "Untouched by human hands."

Today, many students ride buses to and from school, but singing "School's out, school's out..." on a bus just isn't the same. Also most parochial schools, as well as some public schools, now require students to wear uniforms. As soon as uniforms became mandatory, nuns started dressing like civilians. Many parochial schools now have no nuns at all, which just goes to show that breaking a habit has become more uniform than anyone anticipated. On the other hand, Twinkies are once again allowed in school. School officials must figure that the way education is going today, every child should have the chance to pass something!

School's out for the summer! Enjoy.

(2008)

Seasonal Shadows

During the autumn season, before all the leaves of summer abandon their boughs to carpet landscapes or sail away on muscular gusts of wind, November arrives to take control for the second half of the fall season. November displays early darkness, cloudy gray skies, and an almost colorless palette. Against parsimonious daylight, branches of leafless deciduous trees resemble the latticework of ragged-edged doilies, swayed by rambunctious, discourteous winds.

All living things know it's time to bundle up, hunker down, and find places of safety, warmth, and comfort. It's a time of preparation. With a sense of urgency, the pace of daily routines quicken in order to compensate for the time change, a limited amount of daylight, lower temperatures, winter-like weather and the unwelcome arrival of seasonal shadows. In the Northern Hemisphere, November, like asparagus and kohlrabi, is an acquired taste.

To be fair, seasonal shadows are not November's fault. We learn early that what happens to us as a child stays with us all of our days—good or bad, happy or sad, pleasant or painful. With limited life experience, we encounter words and events that leave indelible marks on our heart, mind, and emotions. When memories of uncomfortable sadness, anxiety, fearfulness, foreboding, and guilt accumulate, they overpower joyfulness and cloak our mindset with shadows and emotional turmoil. Healthcare professionals often refer to this malaise as Seasonal Affective Disorder (SAD).

For me, the arrival of seasonal depression begins with the onset of early darkness. Simply changing clocks from daylight saving time to standard triggers unease. Beginning around Halloween through New Year's Eve, personal effort and strategies are employed to stave off feeling down in the dumps and help maintain a positive attitude. For many years, I avoided holiday celebrations or muted my participation to reduce levels of anxiety and debilitating loneliness. Today, the best way I've found to ward off these autumnal blues has been to keep physically and mentally active, like having a to-do list that necessitates being out and about.

Making priorities that focus on others is also essential for keeping seasonal doldrums at bay. Being alone is to be avoided or lessened. But engaging in solitary activities like reading, watching movies, listening to favorite music, or working on household and craft projects do help to keep both mind and body active, as does staying in touch with friends and family via phone calls and visits. Still, the battle of seasonal shadows fatigues mind, heart, and spirit.

As we mature and accumulate life lessons, we learn how to cope, adjust, and manage difficult days by changing negatives to positives, problems to adventures, and joyless moments to giggles and grins. Encounters with unsettling remembrances and unfriendly memories are addressed through personal acceptance, honest analysis, and understanding of causation and circumstance. Quiet repose, prayerful intercession, tranquil meditation, and peaceful reflection all contribute to dispelling foreboding shadows—transforming them to lighthearted thoughts of thanksgiving, appreciation, laughter, and love.

Today, seasonal shadows are like an unwelcome relative—still part of the family but closely monitored and interactions controlled. I know these feelings will never be totally conquered. They're a permanent part of who I am. The best I can do is to reduce their potency to disrupt and disturb life's good moments.

Each of us has the power to let bygones be bygones. What's needed to render seasonal shadows ineffective is to pardon ourselves and also forgive those who delivered mistreatment. But some will refuse to forgive, continuing to carry emotional baggage that hinders their personal enjoyment of life. They prefer victim to victory. Over the years, I've learned that the triumph over sadness isn't easy. It requires an unflinching belief in the goodness of people, a positive sense of humor, and a little faith and reverence for things we cannot see.

November makes a delivery of 1,440 minutes every 24 hours, yielding after 30 days to December. Every November 13, I take time to remember my father's birthday. He was born in 1903, in the house his father built on Oliver Street in Whiting, Indiana.

My father passed away in September 1965. He been gone more than 50 years, and I still miss him. Thinking about him enriches treasured memories of once-upon-a-time. If he were here today, he'd be pleased to know that seasonal shadows no longer have dominion over his youngest son's spirit.

(2014)

Season of Peace

With all the unrest and turmoil here and abroad, it may seem wrong to refer to this time of year as the "Season of Peace." As the economy continues to struggle, demonstrators clog public thoroughfares while elected officials fail in their responsibilities to serve their constituents. Hollow words, weak leadership, and abuse of power and authority have enabled corruption, greed, and reckless spending to erode the founding principles of America.

Decisions that are counter-productive to business, economic growth, and the well-being of United States citizens are made with abandon in order to appease self-serving agendas, narrow-minded visions of ideology, and curry favor with special interests. This gives rise to frustration, mistrust, and anger. In extreme cases, personal discouragement and resentment crowd out feelings of goodness, appreciation, and peace.

Perhaps similar factors led Jill Jackson-Miller and Sy Miller to write the hymnal classic "Let There Be Peace on Earth." Recorded by a number of artists and sung at countless worship services, the words set forth a challenge for each of us to choose peace over discontent. During the year, news outlets cover efforts worldwide to achieve peace. But all too often these reports are accompanied by images of destruction, violence, and chaos. Peace seems so elusive—but why?

Of all the people we know and come in contact with—family, coworkers, colleagues, friends, acquaintances, and complete strangers—we can only change ourselves for the better. As much as we'd like to believe otherwise, we control only one person.

Even though there are different genders, races, sexual orientations, religions, creeds, cultures, ages, and stations in life, we are the same. We also want the same things. We want to be appreciated, to be valued, and to belong. We want to feel successful, important, necessary, honored, and respected. We want someone to love—and if we're very fortunate—have someone love us in return.

We want an abundance of blue skies, green lights, tranquil days, and peaceful nights. We want our heart filled with happiness and joy and our spirit to soar, overflowing with charity, kindness, goodness, thoughtfulness, and faith. We want peace of mind, body, and soul. We want a full measure of God's blessings.

For a few brief shining hours every year, we set aside differences and thoughts turn kind. Throughout the world, people celebrate the one perfect birth of this earth, giving serious consideration to "Peace on earth, good will to men." Seasonal songs and hymns of Christmas fill airwaves, houses of worship, shopping malls, and all places where peace can find residence. Again and again, familiar melodies and lyrics announce the season of seasons, beckoning everyone to bestow peace on one another.

Think about the magnitude of that challenge: Peace on earth begins with each of us. We're responsible for making the world a more peaceful place. Like gifts, the blessings of Christmas—faith, hope, and charity—are presented each and every day. We have to willingly share all that's good, decent, kind, and pure of heart. During the 1,440 minutes of each day, we must freely dispense goodness, kindness, care, concern, and compassion for all who have touched our life, sharing and bestowing these acts as gifts of peace.

Another Christmas provides an opportunity to put into practice the true meaning of human kindness through prayerful thoughts, words, and deeds. This holy day enables us to share the blessings and gifts of the first Christmas with all—loved ones and total strangers, adversaries and friends, and rich and poor. Most importantly, Christmas allows each of us to contribute to one of humankind's most sought after and treasured desires: "Peace on earth, good will to men."

Merry Christmas, everyone!

(2011)

The Sense of It All

Each time we activate one of our senses, we broaden our inventory of awareness and add to its category: sight, hearing, smell, touch, and taste. We employ our senses every day of our lives, automatically identifying the past or present. Either we've previously experienced the same or similar stimuli or we're adding new references to our inventory of humanness. Most often we compare and contrast what was and what is—past to present. The past is our compass to the present, and the present is our guide to the future.

Rarely do we employ a single sense to gather information. Our senses are part of a team that works together to help the brain sort, distinguish, embellish, and display thoughts and images. Try and use only one sense when savoring a slice of just-baked apple pie or determining the freshness of brewed coffee. Using a single sense is like trying to sneeze with our eyes open—it's impossible!

Which sense dominates? That depends on the moment, circumstance, condition, and need. In the event that one sense is damaged or limited, other senses will compensate and become more acutely tuned to take in necessary information. But if all sensory function is normal, our senses work in concert, amplifying, identifying, sorting, and transmitting information to necessary neurons. Together, they make humanness absolutely delicious!

What are your favorite sights, sounds, smells, textures, and tastes? Many take us back to the impressionable days of childhood, adolescence, and early adulthood. They trigger comfort, melancholy, remembrance, uncertainty, anxiety, laughter, smiles, and images of once-upon-a-time. Recollection of these sensory experiences arrives randomly, cutting across time and place, age and circumstance, and satisfaction and regret.

Some of my favorite sensory experiences are popcorn, baking bread, sunrise and sunset, early morning fog, spring rain, and screen doors applauding as they clap for children going outdoors to play. Steam locomotive whistles, factory whistles, and church bells all signal moments of importance to me.

Also meriting mention: little kids pajama-ready for bedtime, children's laughter, a loving hug, sleigh bells, the feel of clean terrycloth, the sound of a baseball being sent skyward, ducks and geese displaying their "V" for victory in the cool autumn sky, the perfume of conifers, freshly shampooed hair, and a smiling face.

So many flavors tease and tantalize the senses, like chocolate, fried chicken, corn on the cob, and homemade lemonade on a hot summer afternoon. The sounds of nature in the wee small hours of summertime paint portraits for the ears, and wildflowers bathing in warm sunshine make music for the eyes. Our senses are truly part of the human symphony that enriches, enhances, and nourishes the spirit.

Despite hectic lifestyles and schedules, sensory awareness is always in full operating mode as we go through daily routines, fulfilling obligations and keeping appointments. Multitasking is the norm, as technology, basic needs, and personal priorities vie for attention. In microseconds, our senses relate both internal and external conditions, temperament, emotion, safety, and security as we make our way through each day.

Of course, our "sixth sense"—common sense—operates at full bore as the overseer, governor, and guide for the other five. In the twinkling of an eye, common sense tells us to draw back or move ahead and increase or reduce the involvement of physical or cognitive actions. But even with this safeguard, common sense is often shunned aside, disregarded, and ignored. When emotions gang up on common sense, clearheaded thinking is diminished, often with uncomfortable consequences and painfully learned lessons.

We're taught as children to use our senses to expand our awareness and quality of life and the world in which we live. We learn that there are tangible and intangible senses to help direct us along the way. How well we pay attention to our senses and to what degree we let common sense guide us as we make decisions will determine the quality of our days.

The most formidable task is making sense of it all.

(2010)

Sheet Metal Romance

My family didn't own a car when I was growing up, so I always looked forward to mid-September when automobile dealerships would buzz with anticipation and excitement for the newest models making their debut. With considerable fanfare and drama, advertising campaigns on radio, television, and in print invited the public to visit local showrooms and feast on the latest automotive eye candy.

An all-American industry, the major automakers of the 1950s and 1960s included General Motors, Ford, Chrysler, American Motors, and Studebaker-Packard. Since the end of World War II, consumer demand had escalated for the latest automobile technology, design, and comfort. Competition among manufacturers was fierce, as innovations were irresistibly brought together to entice buyers to open their wallets and welcome months of payments. By the mid-1950s, cars had become a status symbol—a personal statement of means, identity, and image. Driveways and garages showcased these glistening urban chariots of innovative form and function.

You probably already know this, but guys love cars! This sheet-metal romance begins early in life. Focusing on fender skirts, canted tail fins, gracefully formed hoods, trunk lids, and roof lines, guys are swept into a dreamland full of piston-driven engines, stick-shift transmissions, dual exhausts, hardtops, convertibles, sleek-looking interiors, and push-button radios.

For teenage boys, talking about cars is one of three major conversational topics. In the fall of 1956, the new 1957 models arrived in dealers' showrooms. As a 15-year-old high school junior whose family never owned a car, checking them out at Ciesar's Chrysler-Plymouth, Swarthout Chevrolet, and France Ford in Whiting, Indiana, was like visiting

Fantasyland. New-car scent filled the dealerships. Lacquer and enamel finishes dazzled the eye, reflecting light from highly polished Blue Coral wax, as did the glistening chrome details buffed to their highest luster.

Running a hand over the sculpted hoods and fenders of these automotive masterpieces elicited a sense of awe. Examining dashboards, gauges, levers, and accessory controls was enough to take our breath away, not to mention the mixture of cloth, vinyl, and leather materials used for interiors and floor mats. Whitewall tires, hood ornaments, and manufacturer logos set against vibrant colors completed this sheet-metal symphony of the senses. These machines were magnificent!

Maybe it's because adolescents are easily impressionable, or perhaps it's a matter of being in such close proximity to an unattainable desire, but seeing these 1957 models left an indelible impression on me. Without question, 1957 was a banner year for American automakers. Many models became classics and remain sought-after to this day. Recalling the majesty of those cars makes me smile. Some favorites:

➤ **Ford's 1957 Thunderbird:** Two tops—a standard convertible folding roof or a removable glass-fiber hardtop with porthole window. Powered by a 285-horsepower V8 engine with an automatic or 3-speed manual transmission. Produced to rival General Motors' Chevrolet Corvette, it was priced at $3,408. Cool, daddy-o!

➤ **General Motors' 1957 Pontiac Bonneville:** Making its debut, the Bonneville was available only as a fuel-injected convertible. The expensive sticker price of $5,782 included every available option except air conditioning and external continental kit. The over 300-horsepower, fuel-injected V8 engine had a top speed of 101.6 mph—the fastest Pontiac ever produced. Spectacular!

➤ **Chrysler's 1957 300C Convertible:** Equipped with a 375-horsepower Hemi V8 engine, dual quad carburetors, solid valve lifters, and full-race camshaft. The fastest car in America in 1957. Priced at $4,055, its split egg-crate chrome grill dominated the frontal view. Stylish vestigial fins flowed into vertical tail lights. Awesome!

➤ **Ford's 1957 Mercury Turnpike Cruiser:** 1957's Car of the Year, according to the nationally syndicated *This Week* magazine. Available in 2-door or 4-door hardtop models with power everything standard. For $4,103, it had a 290-horsepower V8 engine, Holley 4-barrel carburetor, and Merc-O-Matic drive transmission. This car's most striking feature was the electric-powered vertical rear window. Slick!

➤ **General Motors' 1957 Oldsmobile Super 88 J-2:** Offered as a 2-door hardtop, three 2-barrel carburetors fed the 300-horsepower V8 engine. Available with brocade interior, this vehicle was elegance personified for $3,200. So fine!

➤ **Chrysler's 1957 Plymouth Fury:** Available only as a 2-door hardtop in off-white with gold spear-shaped trim for $2,658. Powered by a 290-horsepower, fuel-injected engine. Classy!

➤ **General Motors' 1957 Chevrolet Bel Air:** Whether 2-door hardtop, 4-door hardtop, or convertible, the Bel Air is perhaps the most recognizable classic car ever produced. With a front grill of gold anodized aluminum, a hood featuring twin rocket air intakes, and distinctive blade fins with ribbed aluminum panels, the Bel Air defined the 1950s more succinctly than any other automobile. Equipped with a 283-horsepower V8 engine, the Bel Air was simply the best! Sticker price for the hardtop was $2,757. Outta sight!

In the years that followed, I enjoyed several other sheet-metal romances, including a 1960 Oldsmobile 98 white-topped ebony convertible and a muscled 1962 Oldsmobile Starfire Coupe. But the cars of 1957 will always hold a very special place in my memory—youthful, less-complicated, friendship-filled moments.

In a personal relationship, guys search for their one true love. But when it comes to cars, most would opt for a harem!

(2011)

Shortcuts

As youngsters, we often took shortcuts. In Whiting-Robertsdale, Indiana, it didn't take long for a kid to figure out ways to get from one place to another as quickly as possible. Sometimes we took conventional routes and traveled streets. Other times, we used a combination of streets and alleys to get to our destination. As we grew older and more experienced with hometown geography, we added routes through neighborhood yards and empty lots, between buildings, across railroad tracks, and over fences.

Youthful energy and exuberance fueled our desire to use the quickest way to get from here to there. We were occasionally scolded for not using the sidewalk, leaving a neighbor's gate unlatched, stepping on someone's lawn, scaling fences, or for trespassing on a stranger's property, but most of the time these shortcuts served as uninterrupted passages through youth.

The vast majority of kids who used shortcuts knew the practice was a temporary means to an end. We realized that as we grew older, shortcuts would be frowned upon and viewed as a character flaw—an unwillingness to invest the necessary energy, effort, and commitment to properly complete a task. Today we seem to be moving in a direction away from responsibility. At times, it resembles a stampede.

The evidence is everywhere, particularly in the workplace. Business tycoons, corporate leaders, senior management, and white- and blue-collar employees search for, invent, and go out of their way to find shortcuts to fulfill personal desires. Financial shenanigans like stealing, scamming, and misusing investment funds are just a few of the fraudulent practices (and criminal acts) employed by greedy individuals taking a self-serving shortcut to the good life. Honorable, dedicated employees are left with next to nothing after investing their working years in companies that later turn their backs on the very people who helped them profit.

Too many politicians and government officials discard public trust and fill their pockets and personal coffers with taxpayer dollars. What's not skimmed off is often wasted on pet projects, kickbacks, and earmarks meant to embellish their image, bolster their power, and increase their political pull as they shortcut their way through public life. They so enjoy feeding at the public trough that their primary focus is not public service but getting reelected.

Look at our elected officials and political leaders, and ask these questions: Have they improved their constituents' quality of life? Have they been honorable stewards of taxpayer money? Have they improved the promise of America? Can we see and feel the goodness of their public service? Or is their time in office an accumulation of shortcuts to taxpayers' pockets?

Social institutions, government organizations, and businesses once revered as the bedrocks of American society are now ridiculed, weakened like rain-soaked cardboard castles. We've become conditioned to accept violence, corruption, and second-rate standards of behavior, personal conduct, and performance. Too many people no longer challenge vulgarity, sleazy media, slip-shod work, or immoral conduct. Good people are often mocked and derided as being out of touch. Recalling the common phrase "Going to hell in a handbasket," it seems many Americans have found the shortcut, and traffic is heavy.

How many parents and children spend quality time together as a family—conversing at the dinner table, participating in daily activities, or attending religious services? Who is there to teach children by word, deed, and example? How are the children of fragmented families compensated for absent parents and a dearth of role models? Where do kids go for guidance, comfort, direction, belonging, and love? Who is there to teach children the sacredness of being alive? Shortcuts.

How many children arrive at the schoolhouse door unable to read or write, ill-behaved, underfed, neglected, and unloved? Far too many parents take the shortcut to childrearing, leaving schools to pick up the slack. How many children come to classrooms unprepared for class, sleep deprived, angry, upset, and in some cases, overmedicated? How many children end their day without nightly prayers, bedtime stories, and warm hugs and kisses? Shortcuts.

The sad thing about all of this is that once conditioned to such a mindset, people will seek shortcuts throughout life. In our modern world, we see evidence of shortcuts across the board, and all too often, our cleverness does us in. Americans want honest and effective government, financial success, economic well-being, security, and freedom, but we're too busy to study the issues, contact our elected representatives, make our voices heard, and exercise our duty as citizens. Our complaints and excuses are many, but ballots cast are few. Shortcuts.

When you think about it, so many want so much using a shortcut, whether it's success, celebrity, respect, trust, honor, friendship, commitment, or love. And what about the ultimate arrogance: Those who want a shortcut to Heaven, but are unwilling to follow the Word and pay the price.

We're all on a similar journey, headed for the same destination. Once upon a time, taking a shortcut was cool. Today, maybe we should find a better way.

(2008)

Soon It Will Be Christmas

A Letter to My Children

To Christine, Kevin, John, and Dan:

Soon it will be Christmas: another opportunity for thoughts to turn kind and display goodness, thoughtfulness, and love. Hopefully, our attempt is a continuation of the past year and serves as icing on the cake.

Like most years, these 12 months have been a mixed bag of triumphs and disappointments, sunshine and cloudy days, success and give-me-another-chance, and laughter and tears. Each new year, we're filled with renewed idealism, bursting with hopes and dreams. By year's end, reality has taken over and a number of those hopes and dreams await renewed opportunity to be fulfilled. Such is life.

As I approach my sixty-seventh trip around the sun, I've been reflecting on previous orbits and the accumulation of time, events, purpose, and memorable moments. Most of my life has been focused on chalk dust and classrooms.

When I entered first grade in September 1946 at Sacred Heart School in Whiting, Indiana, I was terrified. I was uncertain that I could learn and please Sister Perpetua (aka Sister Bruiser), deal with physical maladies, tolerate teasing from less-than-kind individuals, and overcome flaws and fears learned through family. I was a trial-and-error kid who struggled mentally and physically. Somehow, from some unknown source, I learned how to deal with adversity, make my own sunshine, and become a survivor.

My final two years at Sacred Heart were filled with conflict. I was fed up with autocratic rules and regulations designed to control and diminish the spirit. Education at Sacred Heart was not about learning—we were trained. Granted, there were islands of salvation in which to take refuge, like serving Mass for Father Daniels and classmates who bonded over a shared anti-authority, "break-the-habit" attitude that carried us through graduation. When I entered Whiting High School in September 1954, it was a new beginning.

High school opened new windows of opportunity, and I took advantage of the course offerings, especially machine shop. Even so, I didn't do very well academically because I was more interested in fun and foolery than homework and exams. With additional schooling out of the question, I was glad to find a job in the steel mill. Four years later, I earned my Machinist Journeyman card.

Then, through the advice and counsel of my high school machine shop teacher, Mr. George McClure, the idea to become a teacher took root, as did a more positive mindset. A college education now seemed possible. Beginning undergraduate studies at age 23 challenged my abilities, emotions, and resolve, but the rest, as they say, is history.

Along the way, I was fortunate to find someone who supported and believed in my dreams. Your mother taught me how to see with my heart, and the four of you have enriched and enhanced my life immeasurably. There is not a day that I do not offer prayers of thankfulness. You all made out the best when my favorite carhop became your mother.

Life unfolds in unexpected ways, and we're all forced to play the hand we're dealt at birth. We can't change cards, but if we play them intelligently, life offers rewards and benefits.

Today as grown-ups, we go about our lives as we see fit. That is as it should be. Each of you has the right to sing your life song your way. As your father, I know in my heart that your mom and I didn't give you the gift of life.

Life gave us the gift of you. I appreciate all you are, all you've accomplished, and treasure the value and importance you give to my life.

I wish you all the very, very best. Thank you for being you. Merry Christmas!

Always with love,

Dad

(2006)

Standard Oil Company

Anyone who grew up in Whiting, Indiana, from the turn of the 20th century to the 1960s knew it was the city that the Standard Oil Company built. Refining crude oil and processing petroleum into commodities and products—heavy and light lubricating oils, gasoline, kerosene, asphalt, and by-products that nourished other businesses—the company provided economic stability to the municipality.

So intertwined was the company with Whiting's fortunes—serving as the primary employer for residents and responsible for the majority of the city's tax revenues—that students who attended Whiting High School, the city's only high school, were called the Oilers. (The nickname was also a nod to the railroad crews that had maintained the tracks and equipment for "Pop Whiting's Siding" in the community's earliest days.)

For years, male students received three things upon graduating: a diploma, a metal lunch box, and a bicycle. The diploma was displayed or placed in a drawer, while the lunch box and bicycle traveled with them every day to the Standard Oil refinery. Countless young women also began employment there as well, working as stenographers. The pay was good and the location convenient, with tenure usually determined by marriage and motherhood.

Generations of Whiting residents worked and supported their families with the economic bounty earned from the refinery—grandparents, fathers, mothers, sons, and daughters. Blue-collar employees operated pipelines and cat-crackers and toiled on assembly lines and in warehouses, while white-collar colleagues worked in research laboratories and offices. Taking pride in their work, all celebrated their contribution to America's growing transportation and technology networks.

In the 1890s, my grandfather, Peter Koch, moved north from St. John, Indiana, to Whiting, and soon took a job at the newly built Standard Oil refinery. In 1918 and 1922, immediately following graduation from Whiting High School, my uncle Ray and my father Albert began careers at Standard Oil. My brothers, Norman and Ronald, would also work there.

I was the first member of the family to forgo employment at the refinery. Instead I opted for a machinist apprenticeship at Inland Steel's Indiana Harbor Works in East Chicago, Indiana. I exchanged riding a bicycle to work with a metal lunch box slung over the handlebars for a Shoreline bus and a brown-bag lunch. Nevertheless, I still referred to myself as the "Permalube Kid," after a popular brand of motor oil produced at Standard Oil.

Traveling on Indianapolis Boulevard from the Illinois state line to Whiting's city limits or along Calumet Avenue from Five Points to 129th Street, we'd encounter over a half dozen Standard Oil service stations along the way. The familiar Standard Oil torch and oval logo, along with the company's Red and Gold Crown trademarks, adorned gas pumps, storage tanks, and billboards throughout the community.

The Standard Oil Company not only constructed a refinery in Whiting, it forged strong civic ties and created traditions. The baseball and softball fields adjacent to the refinery's barrel house were named Standard Diamonds. Throughout the year, Standard Oil sponsored events ranging from beauty contests to Christmas parties. Labor Day weekend was an annual end-of-summer highlight as the company transformed Whiting Park into a carnival with amusement rides, games of chance, sideshows, and food vendors, and also hosted playground activities, picnics, and other special highlights.

At Christmastime, holiday candles from Standard Oil's candle factory adorned homes throughout the city (wax was a byproduct of a processing procedure, igniting another revenue stream for the company). Even the city's most prominent building, the Whiting Community Center—officially the Whiting Memorial Community House, dedicated to those who'd served in World War II—was built and presented to the city by the founders of Standard Oil, the Rockefellers.

Standard Oil became a vital part of the history and lore of Whiting, Indiana. It was a model of how to transform a little-used railroad siding and barren lakeshore property into a thriving municipality and industrial base.

But as with any corporate benefactor, a price was exacted. Long before pollution laws existed, and decades before the Environmental Protection Agency (EPA) provided government oversight and authority, Whiting's residents endured atmospheric discomforts in exchange for the benefits rendered by processing liquid black gold. There were days when the air was heavy with petroleum byproducts, challenging the respiratory systems of the young and not-so-young. Malodorous industrial perfume scented the air and caused olfactory openings and sinuses to rebel.

Man and beast were equally affected. For years I believed there were giant bluebirds in Whiting, only to learn that they were actually asthmatic pigeons gasping for breath. On particularly difficult days, one could hear the resident birds coughing as they tried to fly through clouds of particulates suspended in the atmosphere.

Legend has it that one Friday night, following kickoff at Whiting High School's football field ("Oiler Stadium," as it had been unofficially named), the air was so thick with pollutants from the refinery that the football got stuck. The game was delayed until a gust of wind loosened the ball and the game continued. Talk about hang time!

But the one event most remembered by longtime Whiting residents is the Standard Oil fire that nearly took out the town.

The explosion of the refinery's hydroformer on an early Saturday morning in August 1955 fueled 18 acres of fires, leaving an indelible mark on the minds and hearts of all who called Whiting home. It took eight days for the fire to be controlled and contained, and the aftermath forever changed the demographics of the city. Entire neighborhoods were vacated, purchased, and absorbed by the refinery. "The Little City by the Lake" received a wake-up call that Saturday morning, and things were never the same.

A number of years later, the Standard Oil Company was sold to the American Oil Company. Although the familiar torch logo remained, the change was obvious. As residents adopted new shorthand, replacing SOCO with AMOCO, we knew that an era had ended. When the company's chicken coop-like candle factory along Indianapolis Boulevard came down, it was another sign of change and further things to come.

Whiting residents eventually witnessed the extinguishing of the trademark torch and oval in 1998 when AMOCO was purchased by British Petroleum (BP). By 2001, AMOCO's red, white, and blue color combo had been replaced by BP's green-and-yellow palette featuring a stylized sunflower. The transition from SOCO to AMOCO to BP was now complete, though the Whiting refinery itself continues to be a well-oiled operation.

In its heyday, Standard Oil was truly the best. It really was the standard of excellence!

(2007)

EDITOR'S NOTE: In 2017, BP announced the reintroduction of the AMOCO brand, operating stations alongside BP in some U.S. cities.

Stepping Stones
and Milestones

September is one of my favorite months. Like cask-aged fine wine, September fills our glasses with an abundance of ambrosia, including celebrations and milestones. This ninth page of the calendar showcases both summer's highlights and fall's preview. With its celestial crossing of the equator, September's solar splendor proudly displays a balance of day and night in celebration of the equinox. For zodiac birthdays, Virgo and Libra offer a contrast of reserved shyness and active imagination.

One of my favorite songs is "It Was a Very Good Year," most famously recorded by Frank Sinatra for his 1966 album, *September of My Years*. Listening to it always prompts memories of treasured days. Visions of the stepping stones and milestones of my life make me smile as I recollect my own very good years.

When I turned 17, I was a senior in high school.
My world was limited to small town experiences,
Teenage desires, and working through adolescent emotions.
Birthdays in January are frozen gifts that melt one's fears.
It was the first time I ever held hands and opened my heart
To a young lady who captured my affection.
We walked together beneath stars that knew the answer but kept silent,
When I was 17.

My parents were married on the last day of September 1933, a Saturday. Twenty-seven years later, on September 24, 1960, I had a first date with a young lady who would become my soulmate. Since marked on the calendar as Magic Day, my bride always receives a single football mum as a reminder of her senior homecoming game where we shared moments to remember.

September is also a transition month. Summer's last hurrah gives way to the arrival of the sweet-sad season of autumn. Using daylight-shortened hours, leaves begin their colorful transition in preparation for their dismissal and delivery from branches to ground. Shuffling through nature's botanical cornflakes awash in September's moonlight conjures heartfelt emotions.

At 21, my life was steel mills and machines.
It was a time for commitments, promises, and dreams to reveal
About sharing a journey, building a life, and happily ever after.
When I looked into her eyes, I saw the rest of my life
And made forever plans,
When I was 21.

September goes its own way, thriving on mathematical oddities. No other month in the same year ends on the same day of the week. September also always begins on the same day of the week as June the following year. December, however, is an impatient copycat, always beginning on the same day of the week as September.

Turning 35 was a milestone of sweet sadness,
With little ones, obligations, and passion that pulled apart the heart.
Sleepless nights and long hours, keeping promises made when love was new.
On the island of me, alone but never lonely, I captured the dream.
The cost to mind and heart was painful and
enduring, but the price was paid.
Appreciative words concealed the tears and hid the losses in shadows,
When I was 35.

Traditionally, September signals the return to school, with classrooms opening for business the day after Labor Day. That first Monday of the month always brought mixed emotions—the end of summer vacation, the first day back with classmates, plus new teachers, new students, and sometimes a new school. Parochial or public, grammar school, junior high, or high school, on the Tuesday following the holiday, it was game on.

> *These days, routine and sameness have replaced the new.*
> *The seasons march to a faster cadence and time double-steps to keep up.*
> *We try to keep pace and struggle to conserve energy and stamina.*
> *Now that it's autumn, we live more on remembrance than anticipation.*
> *Life is viewed as a tapestry almost complete,*
> *With contentment, satisfaction, and hopefully few regrets.*
> *Regardless of the number of our years,*
> *There is need for tranquility, appreciation, and wine-like sweetness*
> *For the way we've spent our days.*

What's special about this September is that my brother Norman celebrates his 84th birthday. Born September 4, 1934, he has enjoyed 83 orbits around the sun and over 30,295 days. Norman is currently enjoying retirement in Arizona, following a 42-year career in Engineering Research with Standard Oil/AMOCO/BP both here in Whiting, Indiana, and Naperville, Illinois. He is a 1952 graduate of Whiting High School and a U.S. Army veteran.

Over the course of his career, Norman travelled throughout the United States and visited several foreign countries. From border to border, shore to shore, my oldest brother always enriched and enhanced the life of the people he worked with and befriended. He's a good and decent man whose example guided me along the way. Although seven years his junior, Norman's footsteps and shadow nurtured and directed the pathways of my early adult life.

My brother is an amazing, knowledgeable, insightful, creative, and fun-to-talk-with guy. Our weekly telephone conversations are rich with past and present topics as well as future adventures we've got planned.

One of Norman's favorite songs is Frank Sinatra's "My Way." Truly this song describes his self-reliance, independence, acceptance, and ownership of who he is and what he has accomplished over his lifetime. It's his personal anthem of stepping stones and milestones.

"My Way" is one of my favorite songs, too. And so, Norman, with love beyond words, I wish you a very good year. Happy birthday!

(2018)

Stieglitz Park

Stieglitz Park. Just reading those two words triggers images and memories of a place held dear by longtime residents of Whiting-Robertsdale, Indiana.

Created upon the City of Whiting's founding to provide homes for employees of the Standard Oil Company, the development was originally named Rockefeller Park. But when Standard Oil's founder and chairman John D. Rockefeller heard about this unauthorized use of his name, the area was renamed Stieglitz Park after its developer and builder, Gustav Stieglitz.

Stieglitz Park formed the southernmost portion of Whiting (or to be precise: Section 17, T 37 N.R. 9 West of 2nd P.M.). It was bounded on the north by 129th Street and on the south by 131st Street. Indianapolis Boulevard divided Stieglitz Park east to Forsythe Avenue and west to Louise Avenue. Residents east of Indianapolis Boulevard had home addresses on Forsythe Avenue, George Avenue, and Indianapolis Boulevard. Residents west of Indianapolis Boulevard had home addresses on Louise Avenue, Berry Avenue, May Street, 130th Street, Alice Street, and Indianapolis Boulevard. (Louise, Berry, May, and Alice were Mr. Stieglitz's children.)

A total of 346 parcels became available for homeowners and business proprietors. House lots ranged between 25- and 30-foot frontages, and alleys were about 20 feet wide. Streets and avenues, with the notable exception of Indianapolis Boulevard, had a 30-foot width for vehicular traffic. Suffice it to say, it was a close-to-your-neighbor subdivision.

Stieglitz Park became blue-collar headquarters for Standard Oil workers. Like a peninsula border-fenced by pipelines, storage tanks, and petroleum-refining units, this section of Whiting became legendary, home to hardworking, God-fearing, family-oriented Oilers. Though residents ventured into town to attend church, school, and transact necessary business, Stieglitz Park was also home to its own spots for libations, groceries, and gatherings.

The neighborhood set the norm for territorial imperative. Everyone who lived in Stieglitz Park knew everyone else who lived there, and visiting outsiders were thoroughly scrutinized. Stieglitz Park even had its own designated patrolman. Most kids walked to their respective parochial or public school. Limited vehicular ownership meant many adults walked where they needed to go, too, though some Standard Oil employees still preferred biking to work.

Stieglitz Park thrived until August 27, 1955, when a gigantic explosion and fire at the refinery largely destroyed the neighborhood. No residents returned to live there, and Standard Oil bought out all of the property owners, save one holdout who remained for a number of years before finally accepting the company's original offer. In the end, the formerly tight-knit Stieglitz Park neighborhood became a tank field.

Though Mayberry, the idyllic North Carolina town from television's *The Andy Griffith Show*, is a fictional place, viewers came to cherish it as a wonderful place to work and live. The show's residents enjoyed routine days that came gift-wrapped like holiday presents, and whatever problems arose were handily resolved by knowledgeable, family-centric townspeople. Years later, recalling Sheriff Andy, his son Opie, Aunt Bee, Deputy Barney, and the other denizens of Mayberry still brightens the minds and hearts of all who watched the series, longing for those once-upon-a-time moments.

I often refer to Whiting as my industrial Mayberry. Neighborhoods like Stieglitz Park, Goose Island, South Side, and the area home to the "119th Northsiders" added to the folklore, aura, and urban legends of its citizens. For anyone who grew up and lived in Whiting-Robertsdale in the 1940s, 1950s, and 1960s, no further explanation is necessary. In those days, Whiting-Robertsdale was a self-reliant, full-service community. Dominated by the Standard Oil refinery, "The Little City by the Lake" offered a complete menu of amenities, businesses, and services that sated the needs of residents and visitors alike.

Although Whiting and Hammond are separate cities, the latter's Robertsdale neighborhood had the good fortune to be geographically adjacent to Whiting. So connected are these two communities that they share the same zip code (46394) and telephone prefix (659). Every day, local residents cross streets and avenues to shop, work, worship, and share in municipal activities and celebrations. Free-range neighborhood kids traverse both communities, visiting the Whiting Community Center and using playgrounds, parks, beaches, and lakes to engage in shared interests while forging and cementing friendships.

As a kid, I had no knowledge of Mayberry—*The Andy Griffith Show* didn't premiere until October 1960. But those unfamiliar with the charms of Whiting-Robertsdale would often ask, "Why live there?" How can one be at home amid petroleum storage tanks, refinery pipelines, cat-crackers, and a hydroformer? Breathing air mixed with smokestack emissions from steel mills, a corn processing plant, a soap producer, a roofing manufacturer, and nearby refineries did present its challenges. Depending on which way the wind was blowing, there were days when the sky changed both color and viscosity, causing birds to cough and aggravating Whiting-Robertsdale residents' pulmonary maladies.

One only had to look beyond the surface to discover a community with deep connections. Today, these long-ago moments are shared treasures of a gentler, less-complicated time. Struggles and difficulties (because there were those too) became badges of honor as we endured through the ready support of family, friends, and neighbors.

Regardless of change and the passage of years, Stieglitz Park, like Mayberry, continues to kindle fond remembrance of a very special place.

(2016)

Still Can't Say Goodbye

November has always been a difficult month for me. Seasonal shadows, reduced daylight, unfriendly weather, and sundry unsettling feelings gnaw at my mind, providing a challenge to maintain a positive attitude and appreciation for the calendar's gift of 30 cloudy and gray indoor days. To help stave off this unwanted, disheartening sufferance, I listen to favorite songs that capture the essence and treasure of important life moments.

Once background to romanticized high school moments, these songs later served as a buffer to hectic, difficult days filled with family obligations, work responsibilities, and personal doubt. Today, such well-marinated melodies are emotional pharmaceuticals that soothe, comfort, and console. Hearing familiar oldies and Top 40 one-hit wonders initiates cognitive time travel back to moments I hoped would never end. Revisiting these thoughts releases an internal emanation of pleasurable reflection.

Music is an indelible part of the soundtrack of life. Throughout our days, lyrics and melodies form emotional connections with important events and experiences. Often songs are inspirational and exuberant even in spiritual or patriotic contexts. On other occasions, music is pensive and poignant.

These melodies and lyrics, written by total strangers, touch us in unimagined, quite personal ways. We remember songs from radio, movies, high-school sock hops, *American Bandstand*, special occasions, and holidays. Hearing them floods the senses with memories. Many offer wistful moments from yesteryear: friendships, separation, romantic togetherness, struggle, and uncertainty. Others convey feelings of comfort and fulfillment or longing for idyllic moments that never quite became reality.

In some wonderfully unexplainable way, hearing a favorite song brings instantaneous clarity to past moments. Detailed recollection of specific events arrives with IMAX-like clarity to the mind. In stereophonic sound, images and senses fill your personal auditorium with total recall. Long dormant emotions awaken feelings from yesteryear, releasing heartfelt yearning for once-upon-a-time.

One of my favorite songs is Chet Atkins' "I Still Can't Say Goodbye," about a man remembering his late dad and the moments they enjoyed together. My father's birthday is November 13, and although I never shared times with my dad like the boy in the song, I nevertheless remember my father thoughtfully and prayerfully on his birthday. If you've never heard this song, search for it on YouTube or wherever you stream music online.

So much of childhood is wishful thinking, starry-eyed dreaming, and pure fantasy. Growing up, we absorb countless emotional challenges, good times and disappointments, and laughter and tears. Most of what confronts a child is not their doing, with adults having total dominion over them. But our insight increases as we mature, and we come to understand what should be valued and treasured and what should be discarded. We also learn the need for making our own sunshine to dispel seasonal shadows amid the joyless cloudy and gray days of November.

My dad died in September 1965, two months before his 62nd birthday. He's been gone 50 years now, and I still miss him. Like the song says, I still can't say goodbye.

(2015)

The Summer of '55

In August 1955, I eagerly awaited the start of the new school year at Whiting High School. As a 14-year-old sophomore, I was preparing for registration, selecting courses, and rejoining classmates in pursuit of my high school diploma.

It had been a productive summer: daily household chores, neighborhood odd jobs that generated spending money, and hanging out with friends at the Community Center, Whiting Park, Nick's Pool Room, the Hoosier Theatre, and various corners on 119th Street. At home, our 17-inch black & white television provided entertainment and family togetherness. Overall, things were relatively mundane. The mid-1950s were rather docile, and nothing much out of the ordinary ever happened in Whiting, Indiana.

Since the late 1890s, we were a Whiting and Standard Oil family. In 1949, my family moved to the 1800 block of Cleveland Avenue, allowing for convenient walks to work, grocery stores, church, schools, businesses, parks, playgrounds, friends' homes, and the Shoreline bus stops. The fact that my family never owned a car was added incentive for walking. But due to diligent and persistent alley scavenging as a grade-schooler, I'd found enough discarded parts to construct a rideable bicycle by the time I was in eighth grade. So I also had wheels!

On Sunday, August 21, my older brother Ron had left for camp at Lake Wawasee in Syracuse, Indiana. He would begin his senior year at Whiting High School upon returning at the end of August. My oldest brother, Norman, was in the army, stationed in New Hampshire. At home, along with my parents was my 10-year-old sister, Barbara. Our hometown of Whiting was tranquil, comfortable, and safe. However, in the early morning hours of Saturday, August 27, the mundane became chaotic, dangerous, and frightening as events unfolded that severely tested the spirit and strength of residents throughout "The Little City by the Lake."

Without warning, Standard Oil's Fluid Hydroformer Unit 700 exploded at 6:12 am. Shrapnel and debris from the blast rained over a quarter mile of the city. Metal pieces driven by the explosion became deadly projectiles over residential neighborhoods and adjacent refinery units, damaging homes and causing loss of life. Massive flames erupted immediately after the initial explosion. The fire and searing heat set off additional explosions that accelerated the gigantic, out-of-control firestorm.

As early risers, my family was just beginning this latest Saturday. Hearing the explosive, thunderous roar that shattered the silence and rolled uncontrollably through the air, Mom assumed it was a prelude to rain and told me to close the attic windows normally left open overnight for ventilation. I did so dutifully, but noticed the morning sky to the west was a cloudless bright blue. This thunder had nothing to do with rain.

My dad, a veteran Standard Oil employee, went to the front room and looked toward the refinery. One glance told the story. "Standard Oil just blew up!" he exclaimed.

In a flash, I was fully dressed and on my bike riding to 119th Street and Indianapolis Boulevard. Pedaling toward Ciesar's Chrysler-Plymouth, I noticed shattered glass from the dealership's windows covering the roadway. Wary of flat tires, I peeled around and backtracked to 119th Street and then headed east.

Startled residents had come outside and were milling about, trying to assess what happened. I rode past both Woolworth's and J.J. Newberry's 5 & 10, again noticing broken glass covering the sidewalk. I took New York Avenue, making it as far as the Standard Oil research buildings. Thick black smoke, laced with frightening flames, churned upward. Heat from the fire was now evident as the number of sirens increased with emergency responders headed to the refinery. I was scared—I had seen enough. Quickly, I turned around and pedaled home.

Mom believed the best way to reduce anxiety and deflect fearfulness was to keep busy, so she decided to do laundry. As the fire raged and uncertainty about residents' safety mounted, my sister and I clothes-pinned newly laundered garments to the wash lines in the backyard. Dad headed to the Community Center, now headquarters for city officials monitoring the disaster.

It took eight days for the fire to be fully extinguished. Sixty-seven storage tanks, Hydroformer Unit 700, and Whiting's Stieglitz Park and Goose Island neighborhoods were damaged or destroyed entirely, forever changing residents' lives and the geography of the city. The death of a 3-year old boy, who was pinned by a 10-foot steel pipe that tore through the roof of his family's home, only added more sorrow to this terrible tragedy.

Today, only memories of the fire remain. The City of Whiting is vibrant, thriving, and in the midst of a renaissance. Such resilience showcases the leadership, spirit, strength, and character of this Mayberry of the Midwest, a very special hometown.

(2014)

Summers of a Lifetime

Summer has a magic all its own. Just the sound of the word sets off remembrances of summers past: the people, places, and times of our life. Days of endless recess from school, idyllic hours at the park, crowded beaches, and boisterous sandlots—plus daily domestic chores that interrupted youthful adventures—flip across the mind like entries in a scrapbook whose dog-eared pages have faded with age.

I recall blue skies from countless Junes and think back to warm July rains that foreshortened displays of baseball skills and newly waxed automobiles. And I think back to hot August nights that pulsed with the soundtrack of youthful voices, while September announced summer's last call for sunscreen and sunglasses.

All summer long, hot rods and roadsters jockeyed for position at the drive-in restaurants in Indiana's Calumet Region (Art's, Blue Top, Fat Boy, Kelly's, Pow-Wow, Sammy's, Serenade, and Son's). Under a rainbow of pulsing neon lights, promenading street sleds showed off their highly buffed lacquer, intensely polished chrome, and purring lakes pipes. Piloted by urban Casanovas vying nightly for the title of top chick wagon, these asphalt chariots challenged hardtop vs. convertible, chopped vs. channeled, stick shift vs. automatic, V6 vs. V8 engines, 2 barrel vs. 4 barrel carburetors, single vs. dual exhaust, Naugahyde vs. leather, and speed vs. style.

Cool cats sporting shades after sundown worked push-button dashboard radios, finding disc jockey banter hyping the latest one-hit-wonder to invade the Top 40. Romantic couples parked under starry skies at Robertsdale's Bobby Beach and checked out the submarine races or headed to the Hammond 41 Outdoor Drive-In, where movies took second billing to more desirable activities.

Memories ricochet from season to season, age to age. In one scene, a 4-year-old boy plays aimlessly on the driveway of his Lincoln Avenue garage-flat home, poking at ants with a twig, then examines multicolored pebbles, studying variations of color, shape, and texture. In another, schoolrooms dominate summers with remedial reading and math instruction in the Whiting Primary and McGregor School buildings. Temporarily sheltered from summer's menu of sunshine, blue skies, and fresh air, Miss Stewart and Mr. Snap taught struggling scholars the fundamentals of language and calculation.

Many of my life's summers are categorized: the summer of Little League, the summer of Inland Steel, and the summer of 1957 (the prelude to my senior year at Whiting High School). Activities and obligations, duties and responsibilities, and objectives and goals filled days and nights under sunshine and stars, all part of life's recipe. There were the warm sunny days spent serving on Mom's backyard laundry detail, tying clotheslines and raising clothespoles to dry items in the sun. And there were spontaneous fishing excursions at Wolf Lake with neighborhood buddies, armed with bamboo poles, bobbers, and a coffee can full of earthworms.

How many grounders, fly balls, and line drives did my Rawlings baseball glove capture on Whiting-Robertsdale's sandlots and diamonds? How many hours were spent on the beach at Whiting Park or on the swings near the pavilion? Various Fourth of July celebrations cross my mind, recalling my personal parade of seasons. I think back to being a high school teen, when warm summer evenings drew friends like magnets to the corners of 119th Street and over to the Whiting Community Center, gathering to share friendship, Top 40 tunes, soft drinks, and adolescent concerns.

A number of my summers are defined by a single event: the end of World War II, my first Major League Baseball game at Comiskey Park, the Standard Oil fire, high school graduation, the Fourth of July when ownership of a new 1960 Oldsmobile 98 convertible ushered in days of top-down good times, receiving my draft notice for the military, the moon landing, a June marriage, and graduation from college. These were all important turning points in my life that left indelible marks on mind and memory.

But all the other days that fill the mosaic of my summers are no less significant. How to organize and catalog 68 years of summer, a total of 6,120 days of solstice celebration tucked within the months of June, July, August, and September? From June 21 to September 21, the playboy of the seasons teases and tantalizes, challenges and cons, energizes and exhausts, and possesses and bestows the delectable banquet of living. Each of us confronts this season with our own unique mindset, developing strategies to meet change as years accumulate.

With the arrival of another summer, there's time for reflection and remembrance. Summer vacation from the classroom, summer work in the steel mill, sharing summer with family and friends—bits and pieces of hours and days gone by at the speed of life. Today, the pace is a little slower. Each day is viewed as a gift. The 1,440 minutes of each 24 hours are precious and valued. Time is to be used and moments savored in such a way they leave a pleasant afterglow in the mind.

As before, duties warrant attention. Flowers need moisture, the lawn awaits mowing, and sundry tasks pop up like pesky weeds that warrant constant attention. But with all of summer's demands, there's the exhilarating sense of belonging, of partaking in Heaven's plan to give a good account of our days of earthly stewardship in order to enjoy the banquet prepared from the harvest of our lives. Such are the summers of a lifetime.

(2009)

GUEST CHECK

TABLE	PERSONS		SERVER
T	10	46394	S-9

Thanksgiving Blessings
Thoughts
Time Does Things
To Be a Teacher
To Measure What We've Lost
Traditions: Endangered or Lost?
Treasured Freedom
A Tree for Christmas
Turning 67: Observations, Musings, and Opinions
The 28th Amendment: A Proposal

TAX

THANKS FOR VISITING THE MIND CAFETERIA

Thanksgiving Blessings

Looking along the table
At the family gathered there,
I think of all the living
That it took to bring us here.

Built with courage, passion, and toil,
And tempered by faith, laughter, and tears,
We savor all those jeweled moments
That now connect the years.

With bowed heads and folded hands,
We render thanks through prayerful words in private ways.
Gratitude and appreciation is piously conveyed,
Without regard to how each prays.

There is bounty on the table and peace fills the heart
As family celebrates together, joined by those who live apart.
To those who traveled to share goodness on this day,
A special note is added in recognition for their stay.

Past seasons echo with the voices of our kids,
Who enriched each banquet with the antics they did.
Spontaneous, joyful laughter made bellies quiver and shake,
Flooding eyes with happy tears and creating sidesplitting aches.

Because youth is wasted on the young,
Seats at the table are now occupied by much older ones.
Formal names have replaced monikers once familiar to call,
But still, there's unity beseeching: "God bless us all."

And pausing for just a whisper, a tiny snippet of time,
I think of those who've touched my life and now reside divine.
Far beyond the stars or wherever they may be,
God bless them all for helping me—and peace eternally.

The blessings of Thanksgiving are Heaven's gift sublime,
Poignant thoughts of yesteryear and once-upon-a-time.
They fill my mind with treasured moments on Thanksgiving Day,
Like casks of fine aged wine.

(2018)

Thoughts

One of the wonderfully delicious mysteries of being human is the gift of thinking. While thinking refers to the process of producing thoughts, there's no scientific consensus as to what thought is or how it's created. We know that thoughts are electrochemical reactions within the brain, but because of the complex nature and number of these reactions among the over 100 billion nerve cells—interconnected by trillions of electrical junctions called synapses—understanding this cognitive production remains elusive.

But what are thoughts? Loosely defined, thoughts are arrangements of ideas that result from the process of thinking. Within each of us, there's this almost mystical cognitive triangle: thinking, thoughts, and ideas. Together they allow us to make sense of our world. During our waking hours, we constantly and continuously decode, interpret, predict, and experience the world and the environment in which we live.

When asleep, the cognitive triangle goes on recess to express its proclivity for mischief within the playground of our mind. We commonly call this phenomenon dreaming. Random adventures, episodes, situations, and events flood the mind. The dream state can be pleasant or terrifying, enjoyable or stressful, mundane or bizarre. An entire field of scientific scholarship is dedicated to the genesis, interpretation, study, and analysis of dreams.

Humans are sensory-driven by nature. We use sight, sound, smell, taste, and feel to identify and understand our world. The problem with thinking, ideas, and thoughts is that they're all intangible—they have no physical properties!

What is the shape and size of a thought? How much does a thought or idea weigh? Even though we "see" in our mind the product of our thinking, can retrieve past thoughts and ideas, and are able to inventory bygone experiences, the results are abstract—a gossamer entity without tangible components. How do we fulfill a request to "Hold that thought" or "Hang on to that idea" when thoughts and ideas travel along invisible pathways and dance among neurons with unrestricted freedom? It's like trying to grab smoke or hug a shadow.

One of our main tasks in life is to pass along knowledge learned about living to our contemporaries and those who follow after us. We accomplish this through words, actions, and deeds. As a gift to those who touch our lives, we communicate information in a variety of ways, and in doing so, convert intangible thinking, ideas, and thoughts into tangible erudition.

Maybe that's the way it should be, because over time so much of what we learn in life becomes outdated and unusable. The present becomes the past and serves only as a reference to what was, helping to gauge progress. Does anyone today need to know how to repair a bicycle inner tube, a Bendix brake, or a vacuum-tube radio or television? Would anyone today need to make window screens for their car to keep mosquitos at bay while enjoying the outdoor movie theater? I think not. Even once-essential household chores like starching and ironing clothes, waxing floors, changing storm windows, and stoking the coal-burning furnace are now only archaic reminders of yesteryear.

As one matures, there's a troubling realization that the total inventory of the mind—thoughts, ideas, personal knowledge, and life experiences—will remain captive, inaccessible to others, and thus lost. I wish everything positive we learn could be shared and appreciated. Who knows, maybe some future historian will read about the use of car window screens at outdoor movie theaters and learn how that protective netting enriched togetherness.

In the meantime, we should talk, listen, and be good to one another by celebrating, appreciating, and sharing the personal gifts that live as thoughts within our hearts and minds.

(2018)

Time Does Things

Usually we think of time in terms of past and present. We're able to reflect on events that happened long ago or moments just passed. We can also live in the moment as each minute unfolds and presents a plethora of possibilities. Since we can't spend time in the future to glimpse what will be, we must be satisfied with the present or past.

Time does things. Moments do not freeze, lock in, or otherwise immobilize life happenings—we experience a constant flow of present to past. Changes can be miniscule or major, focused or broad-based, personal or universal, subtle or pronounced. Simultaneously, the effects of time are both random and predictable.

No two individuals are affected by time in exactly the same way, even when both parties witness the very same event. Experiences are recorded in our mind in harmony with our personality, genetics, environment, and previous occurrences. Each snippet of time-based information can be positive, negative, or neutral. We subconsciously file words, symbols, images, and other sensory information for ready access if and when they're needed. We also store emotion-based events from various times of our lives, a full spectrum of memories that ranges from joy, pride, and satisfaction to pain, sorrow, and regret.

Is time the causation of change or is change the result of a maturing cognitive awareness, stimulated by expanded knowledge, curiosity, imagination, and conscious choice? Regardless of origin, we all notice how the passage of time makes things different.

Often these changes are anticipated, welcomed, and celebrated. Other occasions, not so much. There can be reluctance to confront circumstances that disrupt the status quo, threaten elimination of familiar markers that have been part of our lives, and challenge memories of once-upon-a-time. While progress is necessary, it can also be somewhat unsettling.

Time is treasured. There's a natural emotional yearning to hold onto moments that define who we are. Countless books, songs, poems, and movies about time convey our attachment to feelings, events, and defining life experiences. And time takes on even more importance as we age.

Too often, especially during our formative years, time is taken for granted. Operating as if there's an unending supply, any misuse of time goes nearly unnoticed. But as the years accumulate and we reflect on past moments, we realize how precious and limited time really is. So a gnawing question remains: Are past taken-for-granted days unfulfilled tomorrows or wasted yesterdays?

There are times we'd all have liked a do-over, revising a choice or decision we made or revisiting a certain opportunity or moment, not realizing at the time how meaningful and important it would become. Unfortunately there's no preparation, rehearsal, or rewind button for life. With every passing second, the present becomes the past—time is unchangeable.

Each of us must take total ownership of our thoughts, words, and actions. Perhaps that's why humans acquired understanding, forgiveness, charity, faith, and love. These all help soothe and heal emotional discomfort, regret, pain, and sorrow. The therapeutic value of such cognitive pharmaceuticals increases with age—a fringe benefit of the geriatric experience.

As children, the use of our time doesn't carry the kind of importance or value it does as adults. Some necessary life lessons only time can teach. Each enriches, strengthens, and increases our resolve to willingly accept without regret what was, to cherish and celebrate what is, and prayerfully petition for courage and acceptance for what is yet to come.

Time is both sunshine and shadow. Each second, minute, hour, and day is reflected in the manner in which we choose to live our lives. We fully understand and accept the reality that time does things. Hopefully the milestones from our personal journey become badges of honor.

So many moments to treasure, so many memories to savor. What time is it? The time is now!

(2016)

To Be a Teacher

As a former high school teacher for more than four decades and having also served as a university teacher-trainer imparting wisdom gained from real-life classroom experience, pedagogical fundamentals have long been emphasized as the essential foundation for those preparing to become secondary teachers.

In concert with their major area of expertise, instructional preparation was directed toward the Affective Domain and the modalities necessary for effective pupil learning (what's known as "teachable moments"). This approach helps students develop beneficial strategies for using their values, attitudes, beliefs, emotions, and feelings to deal with a multitude of academic and personal challenges.

Two essential questions are submitted for these teachers-in-training to consider: (1) If this student were my child, how would I want them taught? (2) If this student were my child, how would I want them treated?

The connective maxim conveyed is this: "Don't ever forget what it felt like to be a teenager." Additionally, I shared this advice born from my own experience: "Refrain from bringing your personal baggage into the classroom. Teaching is fundamentally a rather straightforward objective—to make a positive, constructive difference in the lives you touch." In essence, teachers preserve the past, reveal the present, and create the future.

My road to becoming a teacher was not an easy one. I graduated from Whiting High School in 1958 at age 17, and spent the next six years at Inland Steel's Indiana Harbor Works in East Chicago, Indiana, as an apprentice and journeyman machinist. At 23, I answered the Selective Service draft, and though classified 1-A, I was never called to serve.

Uncertain about my future, I spoke with my Whiting High School machine shop teacher, George McClure. He encouraged me to become a teacher, guiding me through the process of registration at Indiana State University. He continued this support and counsel well into his retirement. Other former WHS teachers provided similar guidance and encouragement: Jessie Allen, Tom Faulkner, Alex Kompier, Jack Taylor, and James Ulrich. They willingly shared their classroom expertise with a 20-something novice educator and, in doing so, changed my life.

From September 1964 to January 1967, undergraduate studies consumed my time. Monday through Friday, I was on the ISU campus, returning home on weekends to work at Inland Steel in the sewers of the 24" Bar Mill to help pay education costs. I'd leave home on Mondays at 2:00 am, drive down to Terre Haute, and arrive on campus in time for my 8:00 am class. On Fridays, I was on the road back home by 2:30 pm.

Such was my schedule for the next three and a half years. In my mission to become a teacher, I took 20-plus credit hours per semester, read more than 400 pages of material a week, and slept just 3½ to 4 hours each night. Heaven's benevolence was most generous and I completed my undergraduate Bachelor of Science degree in January 1967. A year after that, I earned a master's degree—emblematic of my continual quest to learn, and grow, and live.

My rookie year as a middle school Industrial Arts teacher in 1967 was a blur. Scrambling to create meaningful lesson plans, organize classrooms, maintain equipment, detail inventory, procure supplies, and keep accurate grade books—plus fulfilling all the ancillary duties assigned to me—devoured days, evenings, and nights well into the wee hours of the morning.

Being a teacher taxes both physical and mental energy, stamina, and emotional strength. Unfortunately, teaching is a profession that's often criticized, derided, and disrespected. But teaching is also a most wonderful way to spend a life nurturing, guiding, and mentoring. Teachers are the guardians at the gate, essential technicians in society's scholastic fix-it shops. Teachers wear many hats, providing opportunities for students to become better versions of themselves academically, socially, and personally. It's exhilarating to watch a weed become a rose!

There's considerable personal pride to being a high school teacher. Watching the transition from child to adolescent is almost magical. High school freshman arrive as old children and graduate four years later as young adults. To be a key part of this transformation is absolutely priceless, the treasured profits of being a teacher.

Accumulated classroom experience increases a teacher's self-confidence and self-assurance, which in turn fortifies body, mind, and spirit. Over the course of my teaching career, I taught middle school students, high school students, and college students. Subsequent certifications enabled me to teach those with special needs, to be a teacher-trainer, and to serve as the dean of students. I also had the honor of sponsoring extra-curricular clubs, organizing various school activities, planning field trips, and monitoring a myriad of athletic and social events. And in ways I never expected, students taught me so much in return.

Yet I can't quite fathom the sum total of 44 years spent teaching. It seemed like 44 minutes! Time went by at the speed of life. I learned no one grows up in a straight line. It's a series of advances and retreats. We all need someone to celebrate our triumphs and also be supportive when things don't go so well.

For everyone who touched my life and helped me become a better person, I offer prayerful words and heartfelt appreciation. They made it possible for me to be a teacher.

(2017)

To Measure What We've Lost

How do we measure what we've lost? Some losses are easy to document. There are sundry devices to indicate changes in level, quantity, intensity or amount in both relative and precise degrees. Tangibles like weight, temperature, consumption, calories, blood pressure, distance, and time are easily measured. But how are intangibles measured? How do we gauge life-affecting elements that have no physical properties? How should the loss of a loved one be measured? Or personal sadness, sorrow, joy, or happiness?

What instruments are available to evaluate the emotional devastation and damage that occurs within us? How do we measure spiritual apathy or the erosion of moral standards? What grading system notes the quantity and quality of personal character—the levels of trust, honor, respect, and responsibility present at any given time? If we're a "quart low" on trust, where do we go for replenishment? How do we know when our moral filter needs cleaning or replacement?

As a nation, we've let so much slip away over the years that we now struggle to understand meaning, purpose, and direction. Consider the civic carnage: loss of allegiance to democratic ideals, the deterioration of the American work ethic, the absence of attention to detail, a flippant attitude toward commitment, a disregard for the sacredness of life, and a cavalier dedication to duty.

How do we estimate the loss of missed opportunities to be kinder, more thoughtful, generous, understanding, and charitable? How do we measure the degree of damage done to neglected and abused children? In the arena of political, social, religious, and civic endeavors, we tacitly accept, tolerate, and justify shoddy performance at all levels. If we could definitively calculate these detrimental elements, we might demand more accountability and employ immediate remedies. Right now, the loss seems so final.

How do we calculate the loss of childhood innocence and wonder? How is the erosion of imagination, inquisitiveness, and exploration measured? We must know the severity in order to take the appropriate corrective action.

How do we assess the loss of security and safety at home, school, work, and play? How do we gauge the impact of violence in our daily lives? What magnitude of fear causes people to withdraw, retreat, and give up?

How do we justify the loss of faith in our politicians, clergy, government, and ourselves? What scale of loss determines the damage of corruption? What definitive instrument is there to assess rampant greed, selfishness, immorality, and evil? What criterion is there that clearly shows the wear and tear on the human spirit?

Many go about their daily routines insulated from such concerns as if they don't exist. Others justify their ambivalence because specific circumstances don't apply to them or directly affect their lives. This kind of selective blindness and deafness is easy to embrace, preventing the cognitive intrusion of uncomfortable feelings. But time is running out.

The ideals, values, and agencies that serve as the bedrocks of the United States—represented by family, church, school, and government—are being challenged and threatened. There's so much that needs to be done and the work must begin with each of us. Now is not the time to shrink from responsibility. Now is the time to become involved, measuring what we've lost, and begin remediating the deficit.

(2008)

Traditions: Endangered or Lost?

Traditions are customs, practices, doctrines, and knowledge transferred from one generation to the next. What follows is a review of traditions that once upon a time defined our society, the American way of life, and our personal character. Some have disappeared completely, while others are endangered and are fading away. Still others have been shoved aside for reasons not fully understood. Are we better off with or without these traditions? You decide.

Traditionally, people took pride in their social and personal behavior: appropriate language, attire, grooming, demeanor, deportment, faithfulness, commitment, courtesy, kindness, respect, trust, honesty, responsibility, thoughtfulness, and moral conduct.

Endangered or lost?

Traditionally, schools were a safe place for students.

Endangered or lost?

Traditionally, family, church, and school formed the bedrocks of society. Each agency worked for the betterment of individuals' lives and shared many of the same objectives and goals. A hallmark of this societal triad was their mutual support for their respective roles in everyday life.

Endangered or lost?

Traditionally, we applauded academic success, athletic prowess, and achievement. Upon graduation, each student was expected to have acquired an appropriate quantity, understanding, and quality of citizenship, self-reliance, language arts skills, creativity, social skills, and cognitive ability.

Endangered or lost?

Traditionally, parents taught their children common sense, nurtured self-esteem, assigned household chores, promoted family-centered values, demonstrated an honorable work ethic, propagated religious doctrine, and prepared a solid foundation for self-reliance, personal character, and the challenges of adult life.

Endangered or lost?

Traditionally, we took pride in personal letter writing. Today it's email or text messaging—electronic scribbling that often shuns the proper use of the English language.

Endangered or lost?

Traditionally, parents and schools emphasized reading comprehension and mathematics. Today, many children are deficient in mastering these essential skills.

Endangered or lost?

Traditionally, parents and schools emphasized accurate spelling and legible penmanship. Today, spelling and handwriting seem to be of less importance.

Endangered or lost?

Traditionally, families ate dinner together, parents reviewed homework, read bedtime stories, and said nightly prayers with their children.

Endangered or lost?

Traditionally, courtship, engagement, marriage, and having children—in that order—was the personal, social, and religious norm for standard moral behavior.

Endangered or lost?

Traditionally, the school year began the day after Labor Day. Today, it's typically the middle of August, while a number of states have year-round schooling.

Endangered or lost?

Traditionally, schools went on Christmas vacation and Easter vacation. Today, they're called winter break and spring break.

Endangered or lost?

Traditionally, Christmas shopping season began the day after Thanksgiving. Today, it's the week before Halloween.

Endangered or lost?

Traditionally, store employees offered shoppers greetings of "Merry Christmas!" Today, it's "Happy Holidays!"

Endangered or lost?

Traditionally, phone calls made to U.S. numbers were answered in English. Today, they're often directed to call centers in foreign countries, and we have to press 1 for English.

Endangered or lost?

Traditionally, a highlight of autumn was the perfume of burning leaves, a scent synonymous with the magic and tranquility of the last warm days of the sweet-sad season. Today, homeowners who burn leaves risk being ticketed or fined.

Endangered or lost?

Traditions are often lost due to an erosion of significance, allegiance, and importance brought about by change and the passage of time. Often we only do what is personally valued and meaningful to our life. We make choices and decisions by setting priorities and assigning them the appropriate emotional currency before proceeding.

In the final analysis, we each must become our own personal historian, the keeper of our life treasures. We must each decide what is endangered or lost.

(2008)

Treasured Freedom

Another Independence Day has come and gone, and we've resumed our non-holiday activities. Even so, I wanted to take a few moments to consider the meaning of the Fourth of July.

A few days ago, our local paper, *The Times*, conducted curbside interviews, asking, "What is your most valuable freedom?" Responses touched on basic freedoms—speech, religion, etc. Reading these ordinary citizens expressing their thoughts about freedom, I thought about the question and the events that led to the birth of the United States.

The decision to form this nation—the United States of America, a democratic republic—was the first time in history that men declared their independence and their allegiance to an idea: "And for the support of this Declaration, with a firm reliance on the protection of divine Providence, we mutually pledge to each other our Lives, our Fortunes and our sacred Honor." The Founding Fathers' intent was to bestow, guarantee, and defend the individual sovereignty of every citizen.

Sovereignty. Think about the meaning of that word: "To possess absolute jurisdiction and authority." Every citizen has the right to govern their own life as they wish, making decisions and living according to their beliefs.

As a nation, we take these liberties for granted. We need to be reminded that freedom means responsibility—allegiance to an idea! Think about what this means. A democracy is the most difficult way for people to live together. It's an invitation for disagreements, arguments, discord, unfairness, and conflicting points of view. But a democracy also provides opportunities for achievement, goodness, kindness, compassion, and mutual cooperation.

Yes, a democracy may be the most difficult way for people to live together, but it's the best way! This system of government means that we must all do our part to make things better, not only for us and our loved ones, but for the generations not yet born.

Democracy is a commitment, a chance to do better. We've all been around long enough to know that the price for our way of life—the sovereignty of America and each American citizen—is a costly one. History books, graveyards, monuments, and daily newscasts painfully report the price of our freedom. As Americans, we proudly support our troops and mourn the loss of young lives defending our ideals. Even so, our system of government is not perfect.

Dissenting voices are quick to point out our nation's weaknesses and flaws. They question motives and challenge intent, focusing on contradictions, unfairness, and tarnished ideals. But we must remind naysayers and proponents alike that democracy is a permanent work in progress. Even with all its problems, America is still the very best place on this earth to live. Every year, thousands of individuals risk everything to come here. Few leave. This is humanity's Promised Land. America is truly blessed.

It's been 229 years since our Founding Fathers agreed to the principles expressed in the Declaration of Independence, written by Thomas Jefferson. Over the next months, they set their signatures to the document that created our country, setting off a firestorm that changed history and brought ruin to many of their lives. Who were these 56 men who signed the Declaration of Independence? What price did they pay for pledging their allegiance to an idea?

Five were captured by the British, labeled traitors, and tortured before they died. A dozen had their homes and possessions ransacked and burned. Nine of the signers fought in the Revolutionary War and died from disease or wounds. Two lost sons serving in that same war, while two others had sons who were captured by the British and were never heard from again. This was part of the price for sovereignty, freedom, and allegiance to an idea!

Here are the names of the signers of the Declaration of Independence: John Hancock (President of the Continental Congress), John Adams,

Samuel Adams, Josiah Bartlett, Carter Braxton, Charles Carroll (of Carrollton), Samuel Chase, Abraham Clark, George Clymer, William Ellery, William Floyd, Benjamin Franklin, Elbridge Gerry, Button Gwinnett, Lyman Hall, Benjamin Harrison, John Hart, Joseph Hewes, Thomas Heyward, Jr., William Hooper, Stephen Hopkins, Francis Hopkinson, Samuel Huntington, Thomas Jefferson, Francis Lightfoot Lee, Richard Henry Lee, Francis Lewis, Philip Livingston, Thomas Lynch, Jr., Thomas McKean, Arthur Middleton, Lewis Morris, Robert Morris, John Morton, Thomas Nelson, Jr., William Paca, Robert Treat Paine, John Penn, George Read, Caesar Rodney, George Ross, Benjamin Rush, Edward Rutledge, Roger Sherman, James Smith, Richard Stockton, Thomas Stone, George Taylor, Matthew Thornton, George Walton, William Whipple, William Williams, James Wilson, John Witherspoon, Oliver Wolcott, and George Wythe.

The signers of the Declaration of Independence were, for the most part, ordinary men who became extraordinary patriots—nine were farmers and landowners, 11 were merchants, and 24 were lawyers and judges. Wanting to make things better, these men believed that freedom and sovereignty were more valuable than property and their very lives.

When we study the history of this period, we understand that the Founding Fathers were not wild-eyed, uneducated malcontents but well-respected, learned individuals. They could have sat back, accepted British dominance, and declined becoming involved in nation-building with misguided colonists. These men had security, yet valued liberty more. They stood up for what they believed in, and individually and collectively paid the price for us.

Throughout our country's history, there are accounts of the price paid for defending our freedom, liberty, security, and sovereignty. Every July 4, we commemorate and celebrate the events that formed the United States of America. Officially, it's Independence Day, when citizens throughout this land proudly proclaim their patriotism and allegiance to the USA.

Along the way, in the midst of all the parades, fireworks, and celebrations, let's silently thank those who've made this day possible. Remember the Founding Fathers, military veterans, and all who have helped guard our liberties and freedoms these past 229 years. Remember, too, those who continue to make the Fourth of July possible—American military service personnel stationed abroad, some in harm's way, and their families and loved ones.

Happy (belated) birthday to us! God bless America!

(2005)

A Tree for Christmas

It was less than a week before Christmas and still there was no tree. The front rooms of other homes in the neighborhood all glistened with brightly decorated spruces and pines, but his family's parlor was dark. Trees were selling for 75 cents up to $3 but they simply did not have the money. Raising a family of six in 1948 on the salary of a payroll clerk allowed for the basics—food, housing, clothes—and little else.

As a 7-year-old boy, he quietly wanted a tree, wished for a tree, and needed a tree to make it Christmas. But knowing that money was scarce, he kept these thoughts to himself. Wearing mended mittens and hand-me-downs from his older brothers didn't matter much. He accepted that. But he ached for a tree, a real Christmas tree, the kind they had in the office building where his father worked. It was the tallest and greenest evergreen tree he'd ever seen. A rainbow of lights flickered and danced against the many ornaments, and the tinsel shimmered with every movement of air. That was the kind of tree he wanted, the kind he dreamed about, and at night during prayers, the kind he asked God for.

It was at supper the next evening, while the six of them savored homemade chicken noodle soup, that the miracle happened. His dad had just remarked that it was the shortest day of the year and starting tomorrow, the days would begin to get a little longer as the earth spun its way through winter. Once this mini science lesson had finished, his mom smiled and told them how she'd managed to save 75 cents by taking in some laundry, and that they could use the money to buy a Christmas tree.

So after dinner, he and his father headed out into the bitterly cold night. Christmas trees were being sold by Condes' Grocery in a lot on the southwest corner of 119th and Atchison, two doors east of the store, a seasonal extension of the family business. The little boy walked quickly alongside his father, using his long topcoat as a partial windbreaker and keeping his balance on the icy sidewalk by quickly stepping in and out of frozen boot prints.

The little boy daydreamed excitedly about the tree they were soon to buy, imagining it in all its regal splendor. He heard his father shiver. His dad had never liked the cold, and as far back as he could remember, had always been afraid of the dark.

The father thought about the tree too, quietly fingering the coins in his pocket. He thought about his family and Christmas. And he thought about his youngest son walking beside him. The little guy believed in Santa Claus, he really believed that wishes come true. He also wondered how he'd explain the ragtag tree he'd have to buy with the small amount of change in his pocket. He continued to shiver.

Though the walk to Condes' Grocery was almost six blocks from home, few words were exchanged. They entered the tree lot, which was illuminated by three or four bare light bulbs hanging from a post. There were trees of all sizes, each tagged with its type and price. A fire burning inside a barrel kept Pete Condes warm between sales.

The boy's father had known Pete for a long time, having traded at Condes' Grocery for over a decade. He always had a friendly smile and a warm greeting for his customers. Pete would offer little kids a cookie and ask them to be good in exchange for it. Nodding yes, they eagerly took the free treat.

Pete went to a corner of the lot and returned with the most beautiful tree the little boy had ever seen. It was taller than the boy's father and bushier than the big tree on display at his dad's office. The tag turned slowly in the bare-bulb light. It read $3.

In a soft voice, the kind the little boy hadn't heard him use since his grandmother's funeral, his father explained to Pete that he had only 75 cents to spend. The young boy watched his father closely. He thought he saw him draw back away from the tree lot ever so slightly, like he was getting ready to turn around and walk back home. As this slight movement caught the light in his father's eyes, the boy had a sad feeling that his dad might cry. But before he could say something, move toward him, or do anything, Pete's voice took over his ears.

"Look here," Pete said, "I've had a tough time selling this big tree. Most folks want the small ones, so here's what I want to do."

The little boy's eyes were riveted on Pete's face and he thought it was then that Pete winked at him.

"You take this tree off my hands as a favor to me, you know, to help me out, and I'll make it a Christmas special for 75 cents."

The two men shook hands slowly and exchanged words the boy couldn't hear. Then Pete helped his father get a balanced grip on the tree and the two of them headed home with it.

Breaking the silence that had once again taken hold, the young boy looked up at his father and said, "You know, Dad, this is going to be a good Christmas."

His father glanced over at his youngest bobbing up and down, and smiled.

"I think so too, Doc. I think so too."

"One more thing," his father added. "You be sure and say a prayer for Pete tonight before you go to sleep. Understand?"

"I understand," the boy answered, as the cold night wind softly hummed through the needled branches of the Christmas tree.

Turning down Oliver Street toward home, the father adjusted his grasp on the tree with his left hand. His right hand was warmed in his coat pocket as he fingered the coins—three silver quarters. He smiled to himself. The little guy was right. It was going to be a good Christmas.

(1990)

Turning 67: Observations, Musings, and Opinions

Asking for help isn't a sign of weakness. Rather, it's a *sign* of strength.

Attitude is 90 percent of living.

People who are afraid to die are also afraid to live.

Self-worth is beneficial to our well-being. Self-importance can become self-destructive.

Everyone has greatness within. We have to figure out what that greatness is and give our gift to others.

If we spend the majority of our time trying to be happy, we'll never be happy. If we spend our time making others happy, we'll always be happy.

Laughter is necessary for good health. Laugh often *with* others and always *at* yourself.

The gifts of kindness and thoughtfulness are always returned more abundantly.

Love cannot be bought. Love must be given freely and unconditionally—always.

Women are smarter than men—always have been, always will be.

Women never forget. Men can't remember!

Seeing the face of a newborn child is the closest we ever get to see God while on this earth.

Not believing in God is like asking me to believe that the dictionary resulted from an explosion in a print shop!

All children do not learn the same way.

Celebrate difference. Like snowflakes, no two people are alike.

Regardless of age, we can all learn something new each day.

We only do what is important to us.

For some things in life, the price is too high.

Time is more precious than money.

Our health is priceless.

I love the Whiting High School Class of 1958. Their friendship has become a life treasure.

So many seemingly simple tasks become a struggle, and worthwhile ventures are often elusive.

Promises made should be kept.

Commitments are contracts within us. They bind together heart, mind, spirit, and soul.

Always read the fine print.

Education is the key to economic strength, effective government, and the lifeblood of democracy.

Next to unconditional love, sovereignty is the greatest gift we can give another.

There are many different kinds of love.

Appreciation engenders love.

Everyone needs a reason to get up in the morning.

Everyone wants to feel valued, necessary, and successful.

Everyone wants to be loved and have someone to love in return.

Some people are dumb as a shovel.

Everyone who supports abortion rights has already been born: the arrogance of selfishness.

Hard times and personal struggle build self-reliance and independence, strengthening and fortifying character.

You may give up on America, but America will never give up on you. The United States offers unlimited opportunity—that's why the word American ends with "I can."

The two most important jobs in life, citizen and parent, are entrusted to amateurs.

It doesn't matter what's happened to us. The important thing is what we do about it!

Everyone has a story. Tell someone yours.

Two questions to ask yourself in front of the mirror: "Am I satisfied with my life?" "Am I joyful?"

As teenagers, on our first date, I looked into Suzanne's eyes and saw the rest of my life. As my soulmate, she taught me how to see with my heart.

Share your sunshine, give away your smiles, and pray for an endless supply.

I cannot remember the last time I was angry.

I can always remember the last time I laughed.

Never be so bold and ask God to make life easy. Be humble enough and pray that He makes things possible.

God always answers our prayers. We have to listen carefully because at times he says no.

As a high school graduate, all I ever wanted was a chance to do better!

Always say thank you.

What happens to us as a child stays with us all our days.

Schools have become society's fix-it shops.

So many of today's kids have everything, but they have nothing. We had next to nothing, but had everything!

We have to believe in sunshine, especially on cloudy days.

Only 10 percent of what we worry about ever happens.

Every day should be an adventure. Discover your passion and pursue it unceasingly!

Teaching is magic!

Growing old is sometimes scary.

Babies are like the dawn. The elderly are God's human sunsets.

Whether you believe in God isn't nearly as important as whether God believes in you.

We don't like to eat our own words, say we're sorry, or admit wrongdoing. We prefer to delegate blame and spin our way out of responsibility.

We are all teachers. We learn from each other.

Holdings hands is sign language from the heart.

Respect is never given. It's earned through decency and love over a lifetime.

The days you don't read are the days you don't eat.

Work each day as if you're paying your own salary.

Have faith in your own dreams. Be true to yourself.

Hug someone today.

Say a prayer for someone today.

Savor the past, celebrate the present, and embrace the future.

(2008)

The 28th Amendment: A Proposal

On July 4, 2017, the United States of America will mark its 241st anniversary as an independent, sovereign nation. The Declaration of Independence was adopted on July 4, 1776, and 11 years later, in 1787, the states and Founding Fathers ratified what has been called the greatest human document ever produced: the United States Constitution.

Since its adoption, the Constitution has been amended 27 times. Each amendment reflects a need to right wrongs or to advance the effectiveness and betterment of the country under the rule of law. With that history in mind, a proposed 28th Amendment warrants serious consideration today.

The executive and legislative branches appear hindered by a system that demands elected officials spend an inordinate amount of time and expense preparing for and sustaining re-election to another term. While officeholders once considered themselves public servants, politicians today think of it as a career. Historical records reflect both pros and cons regarding this service vs. career argument.

Political entrenchment in office encourages a mindset of entitlement, power, and control. Longevity, seniority, and associated perks affect government efficiency and entice erosion of quality service to voters and taxpayers. There's also the matter of judicial appointments to the U.S. Supreme Court, which are lifetime positions. Is this the best way to ensure and provide "Equal Justice Under Law"? Consider the amount of time, energy, and money that could be better utilized serving the people rather than campaigning for office or maintaining entrenched power.

The proposal for a 28th Amendment to the Constitution would modify provisions of the 22nd Amendment, while reflecting the structure of the First Amendment of the Bill of Rights by bundling and addressing separate provisions of the Constitution. Briefly put, the 28th Amendment would set term limits for the three branches of the government—executive, legislative and judicial—and mandate that "Congress shall equally abide by all laws imposed on the American people." No tenure, no exceptions.

In addition, though all existing congressional pensions would be honored, senators and congresspeople elected to office after ratification of the 28th Amendment would be required to follow the same retirement and health programs offered by the Federal Government to the American people. Pay raises for elected officials would be determined by the consumer price index (CPI) or capped at 3 percent annually, whichever is lower.

Term limits under the 28th Amendment would be defined as follows:

President:	*One 6-year term.*
	Line-item veto powers for budget legislation.
Senator:	*Two 6-year terms, a maximum of 12 years.*
Representative:	*Three 4-year terms, a maximum of 12 years.*
Judges:	*Mandatory retirement at age 75 for all federal judges, including Supreme Court justices.*

Enacting such term limits will restore the Founding Fathers' intention, namely that serving as an elected official in the executive, legislative, and judicial branches of government is a privilege, not a career.

Critics contend that amending the Constitution is a difficult and tedious process, and that such an amendment will likely never become reality. But consider this: The 26th Amendment, granting the right to vote for 18-year-olds, took only three months and eight days to be ratified. Why? The American people demanded it! And this was in 1971, years before computers became part of everyday life, and well before cell phones and social media. Also, reviewing the 27 amendments to the Constitution, seven of them took just one year or less to become the law of the land. Again, when the American people made these changes a priority, their voices were heard.

French writer Victor Hugo once said, "Nothing is as powerful as an idea whose time has come." It's time to give the proposed 28th Amendment some serious consideration.

(2017)

GUEST CHECK

TABLE	PERSONS	46394	SERVER
U	2		S-9

Unforced Errors
University of Inland Steel

TAX

Unforced Errors

I first heard the term "unforced error" while watching a televised tennis match. As defined, an unforced error is a missed shot or lost point that's entirely the result of a player's own blunder and not because of their opponent's skill or effort. Applied to politics, an unforced error is making a foolish statement or poor decision that provides opponents an easy opening. In everyday life, unforced errors are more widely known as mistakes, caused by poor decision-making, lack of preparation, or pure boneheadedness (commonly referred to as stupidity).

As we inventory our actions over a lifetime, separating the plusses from the minuses, there are a number of events that generate concern, embarrassment, and consequence due to unforced errors. At the core of these misdeeds is usually ignorance or lack of preparation. We often engage in tasks that require a degree of thought, planning, and organization. Even though we willingly partake in such ventures, we often do so without the proper mindset necessary for success.

Many times we fall victim to our own personal frailties: immaturity, insufficient self-discipline, lack of commitment, inadequate focus, and disingenuous dedication to reaching a desired goal. We also have a tendency to settle for less than achieving our best, like accepting a lower grade as "good enough" rather than really striving for an A. It's no wonder that such ambivalence often results in mediocre accomplishment. In school, work, relationships, and competitive activities, we rarely sustain a level of commitment that reflects a priority of importance.

As humans, we only do what's important to us. We get complacent or fall into a routine and decide the reward isn't worth the effort. The price is too high, or it would involve too much time and energy. By devaluing the currency of importance, we can avoid doing things that might make us uncomfortable. Suffice it to say, we lack the passion to succeed. Like annual New Year's resolutions announced with much bravado, we allow other factors to erode our stated promises and don't follow through as originally planned, assigning so-called resolutions to our cognitive pending file.

There are two types of unforced errors: those that can be quickly corrected or remedied and those that cannot. The latter are the kind of unforced errors that gnaw at our spirit. Locked in the past without any chance of modification, these life mistakes are reminders of choices, decisions, and actions made in haste without the benefit of preparation, precaution, mature thinking, or consideration of consequences.

Included in this category are the most haunting kind of unforced errors: those caused by hurtful words conveyed during episodes of undisciplined emotions. When recalled, these incidents make the mind wince and invite uncomfortable feelings, leaving the cold realization of permanence in their wake. Just as we can't un-ring a bell or put toothpaste back in the tube, we can't simply take back injurious speech. Some unforced errors bear bitter fruit and lasting remorse.

When we were kids, people around us often overlooked inappropriate behavior because of our age and lack of maturity. But once we became teenagers, we'd crossed the threshold of responsibility and excuses lost their currency. No longer could we simply take our stupid back—there were real consequences. We were held accountable for our actions, choices, and behaviors, and had to take full ownership of everything we did or said.

Unforced errors cast long shadows within us that trigger uncomfortable feelings. Fortunately, most unforced errors are minor infractions and can be remedied without much embarrassment or lasting remorse. Such missteps in life quickly fade from remembrance like insignificant whispers. Even so, regardless of how innocuous these errors might have been, some still have permanence, returning periodically like a renegade asteroid. They zip through our memory if only to remind us that these snippets of life also retain meaningful importance and enduring value.

Hopefully, the vast majority of our unforced errors are viewed as badges of honor, the cost of living an active, engaged life enhanced with adventurous escapades. After all, unforced errors cannot be avoided, only reduced. They're the price we all pay for participating in life, and the way we learn necessary life lessons.

(2018)

University of Inland Steel

My plan after graduating high school in June 1958 was to enter the four-year machinist apprenticeship program at Inland Steel's Indiana Harbor Works in East Chicago, Indiana, and become a journeyman machinist. A college education wasn't initially a consideration, so my intention was to work in the steel industry until retirement.

As the premier steel manufacturer in the U.S., Inland Steel's training programs were coveted by all seeking skilled trade careers in the industry. I began apprentice training in August 1958, and upon successfully completing 8,000 hours of on-the-job industrial training and 435 hours of related technical classroom instruction, I earned my Machinist Journeyman card in July 1962. I was granted Machinist Standard a year after that.

What I didn't realize back then was that Inland Steel was more than a steel manufacturer. It was also a campus for learning indispensable life skills. In a wonderfully unexpected way, the four plants, dozens of departments, and a myriad of employment opportunities transformed the industrial blast furnaces, open-hearths, bar mills, steel-producing divisions, and offices into an educational facility I now fondly refer to as the University of Inland Steel.

At the time, Inland Steel had 25,000 employees at the Indiana Harbor Works. Payroll was truly a cross section of American society, made up of different ages (17 to 64), genders, ethnicities, races, education, skills, political viewpoints, and religious beliefs, as well as veterans from both World War II and the Korean War. Inland Steel represented diversity at its finest!

The four separate plants at Inland Steel featured dozens of specialized departments. Although I was assigned to the Main Machine Shop in

Plant 1's Mechanical Department, my apprenticeship afforded me the opportunity to work in several other plants and departments. The variety and versatility of these experiences served as both footing and foundation for lifelong learning. In essence, the steel mill became my societal classroom, blending an industrial city and teaching campus together, and making a lastingly positive difference in my life.

Progressing through the machinist apprenticeship program and associated work assignments within various divisions (North Balcony, South Balcony, Fitting Floor, Main Machine Floor, Machine Repair, and others) allowed me and my peers to expand our mechanical, cognitive, and social skills. Primarily on station to fabricate, maintain, and service machinery and mill equipment, we faced a variety of conventional and specialized tasks that continually challenged our capabilities and tested our versatility. In doing so, we enriched our proficiency in task analysis, gained problem-solving expertise, and increased our inventory of life lessons.

As is true at colleges and universities, the most valuable source of information for us novice mill apprentices came from on-the-job interactions with coworkers. With over 200 employees, the Plant 1 Machine Shop boasted some of the most highly trained, intelligent, life-experienced, and creative individuals anywhere. These industrial blue-collar scholars were outstanding! (See Appendix C.)

Six years to the day I was hired, I "graduated" from Inland Steel, departing the Indiana Harbor campus for a downstate university where I would earn a teaching degree. Still, I returned to Inland for "post-graduate" learning, working weekends and summers as a general laborer for the next three years. In total, my resume boasts work experience in all four plants at Inland Steel as well as the research department.

That same resume includes attendance at seven different colleges and universities, having earned a bachelor's degree, four master's degrees, several administrative licenses, and multiple certifications for both secondary education and college teaching. But of all my achievements, the one I treasure most of all is still the Machinist Journeyman card from the University of Inland Steel at their Indiana Harbor campus.

Inland Steel's course of study was a reality-based, life-lesson curriculum that taught trust, honor, respect, and responsibility. When I "enrolled" there in 1958, the minimum wage was $1.95 an hour. That sum might seem woefully inadequate today, but the education I received in return remains priceless!

To everyone at Inland Steel who helped me along the way—blue-collar or white-collar, hourly or salaried—I am indebted to you for teaching me important life lessons, the manipulative and cognitive skills to be a machinist, and most treasured, your personal gift of friendship.

(2018)

GUEST CHECK

TABLE	PERSONS	46394	SERVER
V	2		S-9

Veggie and Fruit Talk
A Very Good Year

TAX

THANKS FOR VISITING THE MIND CAFETERIA

Veggie and Fruit Talk

Since childhood, we've been reminded to get our daily servings of fruits and vegetables. Cooked or raw, these foods are healthy and delicious. Now, the conventional way to ensure regular consumption of fruits and vegetables is to include them in meals or as snacks. But produce can also be served verbally.

The English language is chock-full of fruit- and vegetable-inspired idioms and colloquialisms. Some offer a creative way to define emotions, behaviors, and actions, while others colorfully describe people, places, and things. Enjoy this representative cornucopia of veggie and fruit talk.

They are two *peas* in a pod ... He is the *apple* of her eye ... He went *bananas* when he found out working is not *peaches* and cream ... That car is a *lemon* ... That guy is *pea*-brained ... She's as cool as a *cucumber* ... He's got *cauliflower* ears ... Those jokes are really *corny* ... That guy is full of *beans* ... That classic car is in *cherry* condition ... Just dangle a *carrot* in front of him ... That subject is a hot *potato* ... She is *plum* good looking ... His face turned *beet* red ... His physique is *pear* shaped.

They're both in a *pickle* now! ... He has *garlic* breath ... That cute boy has *apple* cheeks ... He's no baseball player, he couldn't hit a *watermelon* with a 2x4! ... Why do they call her *carrot* top? ... Understanding men and women is like comparing *apples* and *oranges* ... He won't go, he's a couch *potato* ... Newlyweds like to enjoy a honeymoon salad: *Lettuce* alone ... He was in the water so long he looks like a *prune* ... They couldn't go, so they're having sour *grapes* ... How do you like them *apples*?

The cold turned her nose *cherry* red ... He has a head like *cabbage*, eyes like a *potato*, and ears like *corn* ... He looks as American as *apple* pie ... She thinks life is a bowl of *cherries* ... Getting the full story was like peeling an *onion* ... Concerned? They don't give a *fig* ... After he upsets the *apple* cart, he'll try to extend an *olive* branch ... It may seem like small *potatoes* to you ... She's quite a *tomato* ... He's got his *pumpkin* face on ... Remember the *salad* days of youth?

That's using the 'ol *bean* to figure it out ... He's out of his *gourd* ... He got a *strawberry* sliding into second base ... That's a *peach* of an idea ... He acts like he just fell off the *turnip* truck ... She heard it through the *grapevine* ... He wants to be top *banana* ... She was able to *cherry* pick her choices, so she got a *plum* assignment ... He got two bites at the *apple* and still failed ... He's so tall and skinny, they call him *string bean*.

There are also a number of non-specific fruit idioms, some of which have seemingly been around for eons. Recall that in the Bible, Adam ate of the forbidden fruit in the Garden of Eden, taking a bite of the apple after he'd been expressly warned against it. Or consider a related expression, "Stolen fruit is the sweetest." Tell someone they can't have or do something, and they might still continue the pursuit because stolen pleasures can be the most satisfying.

In court proceedings, evidence that's gathered illegally or unconstitutionally is generally disallowed or inadmissible as it's "fruit of the poisonous tree." In marriage, government, and other situations, certain outcomes are described as the "fruit of the union." The results of hard work are referred to as the "fruits of one's labor," while "bitter fruits" refers to undesired outcomes, and "low-hanging fruit" implies minimal effort. Of course, we'd all like our efforts throughout life to bear fruit, but things aren't always so peachy keen!

That's enough veggie and fruit talk for now. I'm going to the grocery store to pick up some fresh produce. But before I head out, here's a joke off the top of my melon:

"Knock, knock."
"Who's there?"
"Cantaloupe."
"Cantaloupe who?"
"Cantaloupe tonight, Dad has the car!"

(2018 - Previously unpublished)

A Very Good Year

One of my favorite songs is Frank Sinatra's "It Was a Very Good Year." Always near my birthday in the last half of January, I recall the opening lyrics and savor memories of being 17 and in my senior year at Whiting High School in Whiting, Indiana, in 1958.

From the outset of the new year and subsequent months, events unfolded that shaped my life and left indelible impressions and imprints upon my mind, heart, and spirit. During that year, there were exhilarating experiences as well as sorrowful occasions. It was a time of beginnings and goodbyes. And it was a time to continue the process of emerging from adolescent to young adult, from dependence to self-reliance, and from student to factory worker.

As a sophomore, lacking spending money and not yet old enough to work, I had to forego the purchase of a class ring. But on my 16th birthday in January of my junior year, I was hired as a pinboy at the Whiting Community Center's bowling alley. Night after night, setting double alleys and occasionally a double match, I gathered up felled pins, slid them into the rack, returned the ball, and cleared out in time for the next collision between rubber and wood. Pinboys were paid a dime a line or $3 per match.

My goal at the start of senior year was to earn enough money to purchase my first suit at Lewin-Wolf, a premier men's clothier on 119th Street, Whiting's main business district. A white Van Heusen shirt, a yellow knit tie, and argyle socks were also on my list, completing an outfit I intended to wear to Class Night and graduation. And of course, there were other expenses to cover as a high school senior too.

So with the support of Andy Yanas, who managed the Community Center and supervised the pinboys, and Hardy Keilman, who managed the bowling alley, I took advantage of every opportunity to set pins. I was always on time and never complained. Even on nights when I wasn't scheduled, I'd still go to the Community Center in case someone didn't show or got sick.

The year began with an affair of the heart. Call it infatuation or teenage romance, but I had developed a degree of affection for a girl in my class. However, I struggled with a mix of awkwardness and apprehension about conveying my feelings to her. Though Tuesdays were league bowling nights (good money), I wasn't scheduled to work this particular Tuesday, January 21, which was also the evening of my seventeenth birthday. For some reason, the young lady who was the object of my affection came by the Community Center to visit with classmates and friends. We met and exchanged small talk.

Somehow I summoned the courage to take action, accompanying her on an errand. We walked together down 119th Street through the melting snow and slush, laughing and talking about school and other events of the day. Eventually our path ended at her house. Briefly speaking together on the open front porch, the look in her eyes, the scent of her perfume, and easy laughter conveyed feelings unlike any others I'd had before.

Returning to the Community Center around 8:00 pm, Andy said a pinboy had taken ill and asked if I'd set the late match in alleys 9 and 10. Though my least favorite pair of alleys, feeling energized and euphoric with my mind on adolescent ardor, I agreed. And so it was that the night of my seventeenth birthday while setting pins, I savored moments only a teenager understands.

Even with a steady job, folding money rarely resided in my wallet for long. Since the suit purchase was my priority, I'd decided that the senior prom in May was expendable. However, a few of my classmates came to the rescue—purchasing the $8 ticket, arranging for flowers and a tux, and providing transportation—so I was able to cover the remaining expenses, including souvenir pictures and the after-prom dinner. The same young lady I mentioned earlier agreed to share that evening with me. Elegantly attired in formal wear, we danced alongside our classmates to the music of Johnny Kay and his orchestra at Madura's Danceland. Later, we enjoyed our meal at Club Waikiki in Chicago.

As senior year drew to a close, our class mirrored the friendship and unity from four years of sharing, belonging, and mutual respect. Shortly after the traditional Bum's Day assembly showcasing senior nonsense, one classmate—my best friend—died of a heart attack. With less than a week before graduation, we attended his funeral and tried to understand why this fine young man was taken in the spring of his life. Senior week activities were muted, and Class Night and graduation were subdued. Privately, I promised always to remember him in prayer and treasure the friendship of my classmates.

Immediately after commencement, we all went our separate ways. A number of my fellow graduates joined the military and several dozen enrolled in college, but the majority searched for employment in neighboring businesses, refineries, and mills. In mid-August, through Heaven's kindness, I found work at Inland Steel's Indiana Harbor Works in East Chicago, Indiana, as a machinist apprentice.

So beginning in September after Labor Day, I was back in a classroom for apprentice school every Monday from 5:00 pm to 9:00 pm. Shift work at Inland Steel was part of the schedule, with weeks alternating between working the day shift (Monday to Friday, 7:30 am to 4:00 pm) or the night shift (Tuesday to Saturday, 4:00 pm to midnight). Making the transition to full-time employee in the working world was anything but glamorous. Every day there were new skills to learn, technology to understand, and coursework to complete. Slowly, and at times unsteadily, I progressed.

By year's end, I had settled into the routine and regimen of a blue-collar worker. Life was unfolding according to a plan not always understood.

Looking back almost 50 years later, those times seem surreal. Without question, those moments served their purpose. And I have to admit, Ol' Blue Eyes got it exactly right: It was a very good year.

(2006)

GUEST CHECK

TABLE	PERSONS	46394	SERVER
W	10		S-9

What Do You Stand For?
What Else Do You See?
What Happened to Christmas?
What If...
What's Important?
When I Wore a Younger Man's Clothes
The Wonderful World of English
Work Ethic
Working in the Fields
Wrinkle-Free Spirit

TAX

THANKS FOR VISITING THE MIND CAFETERIA

What Do You Stand For?

At a meeting I attended the other day, someone asked, "What do you stand for?" The inquiry was not about opinions, like Ford vs. Chevy, Cubs vs. Sox, paper vs. plastic, or any of the mundane things that are typical subjects of casual conversation. Rather, this question targeted a person's core beliefs, questioning the very foundation of their character and the elements of which it's made.

We don't usually give much conscious thought to how we became the person we are. Occasionally we'll find ourselves saying, "Well, that's just the way I am," without ever considering why. From the moment we're born, we're influenced by family, friends, religion, school, career, technology, the workplace, the environment, current events, and day-to-day interaction with others.

Our character and resulting behavior are formed from personal experience, print and electronic media, solitary study, thoughtful meditation, and social relationships. Consciously and subconsciously, we collect bits and pieces of information fed to our brain by sensory organs. We constantly sort, accept, reject, refine, adjust, catalog, and store this information for future use. When the time comes, we retrieve what's needed and act accordingly.

The challenge is that what we stand for doesn't remain static. What's important to us as a child changes as we mature. As young adults, unforeseen circumstances exert influence and cause us to reconsider what's important. Such transitions continue throughout life. When we're asked, "What do you stand for?" at age 20, our response is much different than at age 50.

Think about what was important to us growing up and what's important to us today. As children, primary concerns were of fun and frolic: seemingly limitless days of playing, eating, resting, sleeping, and discovering the newness around us. Personal safety, security, and well-being were assigned to others. We had reduced responsibilities, a benefit of serving the apprenticeship of youth.

Now think about the challenges we face as adults, dealing with family, parenting, illness, finances, earning a living, aging, and all the everyday occurrences that demand our attention, energy, and effort to persevere. Whether experienced individually or in some combination, these challenges can have both a positive and negative effect on our behavior, mindset, and perspective. Every experience tests and tempers our mettle.

As youngsters, we were taught elements of good character—trust, honor, respect and responsibility—and cautioned to display appropriate behavior and manners because others would judge us by what we said and did. Without a full understanding or appreciation, we were taught how reputation is formed, and also learned that reputation can be juxtaposed with character. Stated succinctly, reputation is who people think we are, but character is who we really are. All too often, we're not judged as who we are, but as who we've led others to believe we are.

As a teacher, in addition to course material, I emphasized those four elements of good character, challenging students to make them part of their person. Bonding these elements together are qualities of goodness, thoughtfulness, kindness, faith, compassion, forgiveness, appreciation, charity, and love. Today these qualities seem in such short supply, and examples of flawed character more prevalent. A few times during the year, we identify opportunities for our thoughts, words, and deeds to turn kind. But why not live each day demonstrating who we really are?

Another new year has begun, celebrated with get-togethers amid "Auld Lang Syne" and awash with promises of improvement, resolution, and renewal. What will we accomplish? What will we learn? What problems will be solved? What challenges will be overcome? Will our faith in each other be increased or diminished?

The new year affords us reflective moments to inventory our character—to compare and contrast our progress over past years, to measure what we've learned versus what we know, and to examine who people think we are versus who we really are.

Everyone should stand for something. What do you stand for?

(2014)

What Else Do You See?

Eyesight is one of our more valuable senses. Visualization of our world enables us to make choices, determinations, and judgments, enjoying the richness and fullness of each day. But eyesight alone is not sufficient to take in and process all the tangible and intangible information being viewed. We look but do not always see.

Too often we assume that only our eyes are used for sight. But we also learn how to see tactilely, cognitively, and with our heart. There are people who have 20/20 vision but remain blind beyond their field of vision. Some consciously avoid seeing other conditions, emotions, and circumstances. They turn a blind eye to reality in order to deny unsettling factors that contradict their assumptions and understandings. Such shortsightedness is rooted in fear, anger, anxiety, and ignorance.

When confronted by conflicting images, children shy away from asking questions because of a reluctance to hear answers at odds with their knowledge. During adolescence, when issues challenge beliefs, mindset, personal prejudice, and bias, many teens become argumentative and recalcitrant rather than approaching these troubling circumstances with clear, analytical thought. Instead of being open to alternative explanations, they stubbornly guard against an invasion of unsettling counter viewpoints. The internal pressure is formidable.

As we mature and become more seasoned, the quality of our eyesight is reduced. We turn to eyeglasses, contacts, or surgery to provide better clarity. Still, a number of people continue to look away, close their eyes, and focus on less-stressful scenes—out of sight, out of mind.

Not all individuals are comfortable with change. Not everyone wants long-held traditions discarded in favor of new ways. In government, business, industry, education, society and religion, things change—some for the better, others not so much. Laws, government regulations, business practices, industrial technocracy, educational philosophy, social mores, and religious tenets are constantly being scrutinized, reviewed, and questioned. Principles that went unchallenged for years are now threatened with voices crying out for review, modification, and change.

In order to get a clearer picture, we must open our eyes and our heart. What else do we see? What also needs to be considered? Living in an age of instant communication, points of view—pro and con—are presented on screens of every type and size, from computers to tablets and cell phones. Television is a 24/7 font of information, and newspapers, talk radio, magazines, and books of every genre provide additional sources of viewpoints, philosophies, and agendas.

Teaching in the classroom, I'd have my students look at their cleared desks and ask, "What do you see?"

"A desk," they'd quickly answer.

"What else?" I countered.

Befuddled, they'd fall silent, trying to figure out the trick or twist to my question.

After a lengthy pause, I'd tell them. In addition to seeing a desk, one can also see structure, mathematics, physics, chemistry, metallurgy, creativity, design, engineering, machining, and human ingenuity.

The basic image is but a single piece of the mosaic. Also visible are essential abstract elements. Seeing becomes an act of appreciation for imagination, knowledge, application, skill, creativity, and ability. Such insight is available when viewing people, places, and things. Seeing with open eyes, an open heart, and an inquisitive mind embellishes, enriches, and elevates human sight and awareness to extraordinary levels, filling the spirit with riches beyond measure.

The words of poet Edna St. Vincent Millay capture the essence of human vision: *"The world stands out on either side, no wider than the heart is wide. Above the earth is stretched the sky, no higher than the soul is high."*

When we see someone, do we consciously appreciate the beauty and wonder of humanness, the uniqueness of individuality? Most of the time we take so much for granted. In daily person-to-person contact, do we appreciate the smile, voice, touch, and personality of those who share this journey?

We're so quick to judge and categorize those we see but truly do not know. We make assessments garnered from information and images. We form opinions based on fact and fiction, hearsay and gossip, and sundry sources.

When you look at someone, who and what do you see? Is it just a casual glance, or do you take time to absorb and savor the goodness, thoughtfulness, kindness, unique humanness, and exceptionality of their person? We receive countless gifts through our eyes, from the mundane to the majestic. Look carefully: What else do you see?

(2012)

What Happened to Christmas?

I've just about had enough. I'm realistic and of sufficient age to understand how power, money, and greed can impact our society, but we've arrived at a point that boggles the mind. Before Halloween had even arrived, stores were stocking shelves with Christmas merchandise!

In years past, the traditional first day of the Christmas shopping season has been the day after Thanksgiving, with thousands of shoppers heading to Chicago's Loop or to suburban malls to begin filling their gift lists. Now Thanksgiving is being run over by merchants and marketers who smell money in them-there pine needles of the yuletide tree. But that's just one indicator of how far we've regressed as a nation.

Many of the same retailers who salivate at luring consumers into their establishments, separating shoppers' money from purses and wallets, make it a policy for their employees not to greet customers with "Merry Christmas." Instead, they instruct them to say "Happy Holidays," lest anyone be offended by the reference to a Christian holy day.

As a high school student in the late 1950s, things were different. Our time away from school in late December was called Christmas vacation. Today, it's called winter break. As I recall, we had an all-school Christmas assembly the last day of classes before early dismissal at 2:00 pm. At Whiting High School, a public school, the choral groups sang traditional Christmas songs and carols. The closing song was "Silent Night," with the entire student body joining in with the onstage chorus.

Today, public schools rarely present traditional Christmas assemblies, and many student choirs aren't heard singing religious Christmas carols lest someone take offense or feel disenfranchised because they have a different religious identity (or no religious beliefs at all).

Within the last few years, even the traditional Christmas tree has come under attack. Various groups—unhappy with the mention of any God-referencing activity, event, or occasion—tried to relegate the yuletide conifer to a "holiday tree," encouraging businesses, media, and big-box retailers to "de-Christmastize" this time of year in favor of a secular approach.

In 1870, President Ulysses S. Grant signed a law making Christmas a federal holiday. Imagine if such a bill was debated in Congress today. Some of our current elected officials want to eliminate "In God, We Trust" on our currency and "Under God" from the Pledge of Allegiance. What are they afraid of? The United States of America was founded on a firm belief in divine providence and Judeo-Christian values. America's Founding Fathers readily petitioned for God's help, strength, guidance, and blessing as they formed the United States of America.

From the outset, government buildings showcased sacred phrases and words of Scripture, with religious paintings and sculptures also on display. Religious traditions have always been an integral part of the American social fabric. Today, secular anti-God groups are doing their utmost to rip and shred our nation's spiritual fabric, removing references to a supreme being, lest it challenge their concept of righteousness and generate thoughts about our purpose in life.

It's amazing that Santa Claus hasn't taken a hit. After all, "Santa" means saint. Good 'ol St. Nick is sneaking around right under the noses of these anti-God secularists. How embarrassing it must be for some of these Christmas bashers to condone kindness, generosity, and joy. Ho-ho-ho, Santa says the joke's on them!

The American people had better wake up and get involved. As citizens, there's much we can do. Individually, we can send emails and write letters to elected officials at all levels, and make it known we'd like to retain the traditions of Christmas.

More immediate and direct is that each of us, at every opportunity, should convey our greetings and wishes for a "Merry Christmas" to everyone with whom we have contact. After purchasing the morning paper, coffee, baked goods, groceries, or other merchandise, end your transaction by saying "Merry Christmas" to store employees. And give whatever gratuity you feel appropriate.

Take a few moments from your day and share the essence of the Christmas season. Remember the gift presented to all humankind on the first Christmas. Then willingly share this present with family, friends, and strangers alike.

Have a merry and most blessed Christmas, everyone!

(2006)

What If...

With the beginning of a new year just around the corner, we tend to follow age-old tradition and make resolutions, most of which are forgotten by the end of January. Some commitments that are meant to correct bad habits might last a little longer, until they too become cumbersome and are also discarded.

All of this is okay because resolutions are informal agreements with ourselves, not iron-clad contracts. Many resolutions involve improving our physical well-being, like eating or drinking less, exercising more, or quitting smoking. But these require behavioral modifications, and that's no easy task.

Suppose, however, that this year we try something different. Instead of making a list of personal resolutions, we decide to confront problems that face us all by asking, "What if?" and using every available resource to solve them. For instance, what if...

> We said enough is enough to violence—on television, in movies, in music, and on our streets.

> We decided to end child abuse.

> Parents focused on teaching their children positive, constructive values.

> Every child was able to read proficiently at their grade level.

> Every child was able to solve math problems at their grade level without a calculator.

We demanded that our elected officials serve their constituents with integrity, honor, and responsibility, rather than bowing to special interest groups.

We decided to make children our most important everything!

America got fed up with being politically correct.

We took common sense off the endangered list.

All the deadbeat parents paid what is owed to their children.

Every child came to school adequately fed, properly clothed, feeling loved, and ready to learn.

Schools charged parents for the food their children throw away in the cafeteria.

We found an effective way to teach children that sex and love aren't the same thing.

We discovered a way to sustain the Christmas spirit throughout the year.

We found a way to sell education as effectively as we sell burgers, beer, and automobiles.

The family was made whole again.

Society followed the Ten Commandments on a regular basis, more or less.

Motorists heeded stop signs, speed limits, and handicapped parking zones, and always fastened their seat belts and used car seats for little kids.

Every child was taught the sacredness of being alive, their innate value, and their potential for greatness.

There was an epidemic of kindness, goodness, and decency.

Every tax dollar was spent wisely.

"Homeless in America" became an extinct phrase.

Students believed that school is something done *for* them and not *to* them.

We spent as much time reading as we do eating.

A license was required to be a parent. Perhaps the number of unwanted, neglected, and abused children would diminish.

We decided to respect and protect life—born and unborn.

We were held accountable for our actions.

We had to renew our citizenship, being evaluated on what we've done to make our community and country better.

We made being a better person a priority.

We look forward to the start of a new year with much anticipation. It's a fresh start, a clean slate, and a new beginning. But the new year also ushers in another chapter of our continuing journey, and it's how we use this latest allotment of days that the value of our time will be judged.

Once again, we'll review our personal inventory of goals to be accomplished. And on January 1, we'll post resolutions on refrigerator doors and bathroom mirrors. How successfully we meet these challenges depends nearly entirely on us. Could we increase the odds of success by asking, "What if...?"

I hope the new year brings us all an abundance of laughter, love, good health, and good fortune. Happy New Year, everyone!

(2005)

What's Important?

We spend so much time deciding what's important. Every year, we adjust our inventory of importance, adding new items and discarding old ones. We elevate some priorities in our lives while lowering others, a ranking that reflects our current station and age.

Just as some flowers are perennials and others are annuals, a growing process of maturation is required until the full value of certain items of importance is revealed. Some are things and others are matters of the heart, but regardless of form or function, we guard, cultivate, and nurture what's important to add substance and meaning to our days.

Along the way, some matters of importance emerge unexpectedly, demanding immediate mindfulness and total focus. Other unforeseen arrivals of importance intrude, commanding attention like a broken tooth. These intrusions rob one of time, effort, and emotional energy as the accompanying stress and anxiety challenge our inner resolve. But whatever the form, magnitude, or origin, all matters of importance tap into our physical, moral, and spiritual strength.

If we carefully review what was important to us as a child through the hindsight of adult perspective, the remembrance of those items generates feelings of melancholy, naiveté, selfishness, and some degree of embarrassment. Viewed through retrospective glasses tempered by age, things once considered so critical no longer have the same intensity or urgency they did at the time they were part of our lives. We wonder, at this point in life, how such trivial items ever warranted concern at all.

Throughout life, a number of individuals volunteer to tell us what's important. Some are well-intentioned, but others attempt to involve us in their personal agenda. Some back up their authoritative-sounding "Most

Important" list with documentation, drawing upon historical records, past precedent, written words, and personal experience.

Various methods are used to convey the necessity to adopt life's important edicts: fear, violence, food, counseling, guidance, concern, and love. Parents, teachers, and others in positions of authority have their retorts for what's important: "Do this or else!" "Because I said so!" "If you don't, you'll be punished!" "Because it's what's best for you!" "Because I love you!"

Of course, sometimes this authoritarian posture is rendered ineffective. Thus the approach shifts to negotiation: "If you do this, you can have that," offering a treat or bribe in exchange for cooperation. Occasionally, an assigned task is not completed as scheduled. Such negligence usually results in a reprimand and a stern reminder of how important compliance is.

The answer to the question of importance is within each of us. Whatever makes our personal list of what's important must be tempered with common sense. Whatever we do needs to be presented with goodness, understanding, joy, and kindness. Importance should reflect integrity without strings attached.

Keep in mind that what's important to us may not be as important to others. We advertise to others what matters to us by our words, actions, and demeanor. And we validate what's important by our thoughts, attitude, and comportment.

Find a quiet moment and ask yourself what's important—to you and others. Check to see that there's sufficient goodness, kindness, laughter, and love. And ensure that each item of importance is shared and presented with trust, honor, respect, and responsibility.

Over a lifetime, so many things seem important, but in reality few really are. Because of their rarity, they become the real gifts of life. What's important to you?

(2009)

When I Wore a Younger Man's Clothes

More than outward trappings of clothes, jewelry, and accessories that enhance our physical appearance, fashions also define and govern personal perspectives, attitudes, priorities, and actions. Fashions serve to present an image cultivated over time to define who and what we are. At times, cosmetics are used to artificially enhance and complement natural features. Applied improperly or to excess, makeup becomes counterproductive, diminishing desired attributes. But applied with artistic skill, the same cosmetics can mask or mitigate characteristics and features deemed undesirable.

As years accumulate, our personal concept of fashion changes. What seemed crucial to us as youngsters no longer carries the same degree of importance. Lifestyle, environment, personal habits, genetics, and experiences all play a part in adjusting our fashions—outwardly and inwardly.

Similarly, as we age, flaws and blemishes are accepted as badges of honor. Battle-tested evidence of living a life rich with challenges, concerns, and responsibilities, they're further confirmation that we've been schooled in life lessons that have tested our core values.

When I wore a younger man's clothes, life was a competition. Today, I view it as a journey. When I wore a younger man's clothes, things were most important. I've since learned that the most important things in life are not things at all. We get so wrapped up in our toys, gadgets, and conveniences. Materially, we believe we have everything, but in reality we have very little.

When I wore a younger man's clothes, I was impatient and impulsive. I was prone to act without thinking about consequences or how my actions might affect others. Now, as a seasoned citizen, there's careful consideration, analysis, and respectful, reflective contemplation prior to commitment.

When I wore a younger man's clothes, I was an island—independent and unconnected. The arrogance of youth, coupled with a mindset of invincibility, left me awash in false confidence and a reluctance to accept counseling and advice. The supply of days seemed limitless, so I spent each one with carefree abandon.

Today, as an aging human unit, the motion and movement of my personal tectonic plates now connect me to the mainland of common sense, based in reality and secured by foundations of faith, trust, respect, and love. Each dawn signals a dwindling number of remaining days. Every one of the 1,440 minutes in those 24 hours is treasured like a collection of fine gemstones—fringe benefits of the Geriatric Adventure.

When I wore a younger man's clothes, most everything was a contest. I expended so much energy, effort, and desire to be first. Today, every day is viewed as a generous, benevolent gift. Being number one isn't all it's cracked up to be.

As a kid, I ate Wheaties, buying into the cereal's advertising slogan, "Breakfast of Champions." I also feasted on bowls of Quaker Puffed Wheat & Rice, cereal "Shot from guns!" At this point in time, achieving champion status is not my aim. I'm more than satisfied being in the second division. And instead of being "Shot from guns!" I'm content with my cereal being gently stirred.

It's satisfying finding comfort in a less hectic, stressful pursuit of each day. Complexities are now simplified, and ease has overcome frenzy. Trying to prove something with every venture no longer holds the glamour it once did. As the seasons accumulate and we change within and without, our fashions vary. When I wore a younger man's clothes, everything was about self—sometimes to the point of selfishness. Now blessed with over six decades of dawns and sunsets, selfishness has faded, replaced by service to others.

Instead of focusing on personal self-importance, my core priorities have become shared kindness, goodness, thoughtfulness, and helpfulness to others in need. I've also learned that kindness begets kindness, goodness begets goodness, and thoughtfulness begets thoughtfulness. These are not new lessons—they're as ancient as Ecclesiastes. They were taught to me when I wore a younger man's clothes.

It might have taken a while, but those lessons were learned. Although I no longer wear a younger man's clothes, I'm still fashionable because now I understand.

(2008)

The Wonderful World of English

Without giving it much thought, most of us come to awareness hearing and speaking English. Modeled by parents and family members, we begin to gain usage of words and develop our ability to communicate. Adding body language, facial expressions, and tone of voice, our language skills expand. Reading, the cognitive process of decoding and deriving meaning from words formed through the selection, order, and arrangement of the 26 alphabetical letters, is one of the most highly valued and prized skills we can acquire.

In school, we spend the first three formal years of education learning to read. From fourth grade on, we read to learn! We don't spend much time inquiring about the origin or history of English, but learn the language to improve our lives. Does anyone particularly care that the earliest forms of English date to the year 700 AD? Or that the roots of English extend back to 3500 BC and a prehistoric language called Indio-Hitte? But we do care about the vast choice of words available to convey what's on our mind.

English is a language for all occasions and all facets of life. Specific disciplines have their own dictionaries: law, medicine, science, technology, and engineering, to name just a few. These special lexicons add richness and depth to both the written and spoken word. But whether we're a poet, pauper, teacher, or king, the English language provides avenues for writers of every persuasion to display their literary prowess.

Today, modern American English reflects the vitality, creativity, and versatility of America herself. Every year, expressions, catchphrases, and colloquialisms vie for acceptance in dictionaries and speech. From subtle to profound, an unlimited source of words, different shades of meaning, degree of description, and precise application afford new opportunities for all who write and speak English. This intellectual banquet continually adds alphabetical flavor to the menu for the benefit of all who partake.

Thus, English is a living language. At present, with over a million-plus words, multiple definitions, and diverse, distinctive applications for writing and speaking, English continues to evolve, expand, and increase our ability to express human thought and knowledge. After mastering the 44 sounds of short and long vowels, consonants, digraphs, and controlled vowels, the eight parts of speech, and a working knowledge of expressing complete sentences—we're good to go. Countless words can be adapted for various meanings, parts of speech, and application.

Years ago, the word "party" was solely a noun: *"I'm going to a birthday party."* Today, party is a verb: *"Let's party!"* At one time, the mouse was a despised rodent. Then Walt Disney created a mouse named Mickey, who became a beloved character via film and television appearances. Later, personal computers brought an indispensable electronic mouse into every home. Same word, different meanings. That's the magic of English.

The most important thing we learn about the English language is that words are powerful and permanent! And their impact on our lives is long-lasting. Words can make us happy or sad, joyful or depressed. There's no more powerful force than the written or spoken word.

The use of language can lead to our success or our demise. Words can raise or crush our spirit, build us up or tear us down, encourage us or discourage us, heal us or hurt us, save us or destroy us. How many times have our feelings been hurt by unkind words? How often have our eyes filled with tears because of heartfelt words of comfort and love? How many times have words made us laugh, smile, or our heart soar?

Words touch every emotional fiber. Think about this: When we learn how to select and arrange alphabetical letters into words—and use the right word, at the right time, and in the right way—we reap rewards beyond our dreams.

We use English every moment of our day. We listen, speak, read, text, email, and react to the wonderful world of English. And we're constantly adding new words and modifying, changing, adapting, manipulating, and creatively using English to express our thoughts and ideas effectively.

When combined with body language, facial expressions, tone, and emotions, English becomes even more potent, passionate, poignant, and purposeful.

Aside from love, the most valuable gift we can give to someone else is the gift of words—teaching them to read, understand, communicate, and appreciate the greatest of all languages, English.

(2013)

Work Ethic

Early on, my parents taught my siblings and me the importance and value of work. There wasn't a formal application process or anything like that. One day we simply found ourselves using a dust cloth, scrubbing floors, vacuuming rugs, washing dishes, scrubbing pots and pans, cooking, baking, assisting with laundry, and sanitizing the porcelain lifesaver in the family's comfort station.

On other occasions, we were introduced to the cleansing power of vinegar on dirty window glass, Climaline detergent on concrete basement floors, and Johnson's Paste Wax on wood furniture. As part of our domestic apprenticeship, we became intimately acquainted with products like Fels Naptha, Kitchen Klenzer, Lysol, American Family Flakes, Beacon Wax, Duz, Rinso, Lava, and Linco Bleach. My family never owned a car, but if we had, there would have been a bumper sticker saying, "SEARCH FOR DIRT!"

Before the age of reason, we were instructed in the fine art of chicken feather removal. Standing on a crate in front of a laundry tub filled with hot water, I learned how to pluck feathers from the latest unlucky guest to join our dinner table. The scent memory of poultry perfume from soaking chicken feathers has lingered a lifetime.

By age 10, we were quite skilled at using dish rags, dish towels, washing machines, irons, ironing boards, brooms, mops, buckets, vacuum cleaners, push reel lawn mowers, garden hoses, rakes, shovels, and garbage pails. By the time I was in sixth grade, my work ethic was well honed, the result of a hard lesson a couple of years earlier when I'd used the wrong word while talking to my mom.

It was my ninth birthday—January 21, 1950, a cold and gloomy Saturday morning—and I was complaining there was nothing to do. After all, shouldn't a birthday be filled with fun activities? But at our house, Saturdays were dedicated to housework: dusting woodwork and furniture, vacuuming rugs, scrubbing bathrooms, and wiping floors. Cleanliness was king, even on birthdays.

Moping and mumbling in the midst of my personal pity party, I walked into the kitchen where my mom was washing dishes, expecting to hear "Happy birthday!" Instead she looked up from the sink and asked, "What's your problem?"

Not considering my answer first, I blurted out, "I'm bored! There's nothing to do!"

"Bored, are you?" she replied. "Well, I have something for you to do. This floor needs a good scrubbing. Get the pail, scrub rags, scrub brush, and Fels Naptha. You won't be bored scrubbing the floor."

So there I was, Mr. Birthday Boy, on my hands and knees removing scuff marks and soil from the well-worn kitchen linoleum. I knew, though, my work had just begun—Mom was great with add-ons. After the kitchen floor was done, she said, "Well, as long as you have the scrub brush and rags, you may as well clean the dining room floor too." Then, noticing I was nearly finished there too, she added, "Wipe down the back stairway to the basement. It looks like it needs it." Annie's two-room scrub always turned into a three-chore trifecta.

One good thing came from all of this: I never used the word "bored" again!

A few years later, during my freshman year in high school, I foolishly tested Mom's authority once more. Monday evening was laundry time. After the freshly laundered clothes were hung on the wash line strung throughout the basement, it was my job to wipe up the concrete floor. Elbow deep in Climaline detergent, I complained about what I believed to be a borderline unnecessary chore.

"Mom, did you ever read about how Lincoln freed the slaves?"

Her reply was quick and needle-sharp.

"Yes, I did, but Lincoln doesn't live in this house, so keep working!"

Now household chores weren't rewarded with an allowance. Rather, in return for compulsory domestic labor, my siblings and I reaped the benefits of clean clothes, meals, and comfortable accommodations. So in order to earn spending money, I did odd jobs around the neighborhood.

In winter, there were snow covered porches and walkways to clear, and in summer, an abundance of lawns to cut and weeds to pull—truly minimum wage affairs. My highest pay, 25 cents weekly, came from cutting Mrs. Harmon's lawn on the corner of 118th Street and Cleveland Avenue. Besides mowing the lawn, I had to trim the edges and sweep the sidewalk, driveway, and both front and back porches.

Then opportunity knocked in the summer of 1952, and the job of paperboy arrived. Route 6B, Cleveland Avenue from 119th Street to the railroad tracks, was available weekday afternoons: The *Chicago Daily News*, the *Chicago Herald American*, and *The Hammond Times* had to be delivered. I'd also be responsible for collecting biweekly payments from customers. Following a brief interview with Mr. Chrustowski and Dutch Serafin at the Whiting News Company, I was given a shoulder-strap canvas sack, a route book with customers' names, and the newspapers ordered. The job paid $5.90 a week.

My tenure as a paperboy was brief, lasting only until school began. Deciding to become an independent contractor, I collected old newspapers instead of delivering them. Scrap paper was worth a penny per pound, so I'd go door-to-door asking for old newspapers and magazines. All through the autumn, winter, and following spring, I collected papers and tied them in 25-pound bundles.

The $43 check from Hammond's Lake Iron & Metal more than paid for my baseball glove and spiked shoes from Neal Price's in time for Little League season. I also bought a new baseball bat from Whiting News. The rest was saved for ancillary expenses.

In addition to work-ethic training, I learned how to organize, manage, plan, and accomplish goals. At home, I regularly demonstrated my proficiency at scrubbing, laundry, and other housekeeping tasks as I continued to help Mom with the dishes. To this day, I believe I was the only Whiting Little Leaguer with dishpan hands!

(2009)

Working in the Fields

Winter's early darkness and snowfall driven by rambunctious winds encourage well-seasoned residents to hunker down inside our homes. Snugly covered with down comforters, we're situated close to heat registers and sip honey-laced tea. In the hours east of midnight, classic black-and-white movies on television keep company with restless geriatrics who struggle with erratic sleep. On one such night, a movie strikes a chord within us, awakening thoughts and images interlaced over a lifetime, energizing our spirit and dispelling feelings of loneliness.

It's really mysterious how long-dormant memories are triggered in the mind. Like a cognitive hiccup, a sensory-based catalyst disrupts our normal routine and calls attention to the importance of realities once experienced matter-of-factly. In an instant, we're reminded of life's pace and how challenging it is to process the torrent of information fed into our gray matter.

Often preoccupied by personal duties and obligations, we fail to realize the quickness of each passing day. There's an agenda to be followed, and the ramifications of tasks, labors, and interactions—interconnected with one another, minute by minute—go unnoticed. Our awareness is usually directed toward objectives or goals, hoping to achieve desired outcomes, rather than focusing on any sort of introspective thought. No matter the task at hand, we need to pace ourselves so that we fully appreciate the lesson being taught.

Regardless of age or station in life, each of us spends our days according to our means, capabilities, skills, and interests. Subconsciously, we allocate a quantity of energy, effort, and time to maintain our personal comfort zone. Hectic schedules and random distractions are inevitable, which cause us to become sidetracked or lose focus, requiring redirection as we toil in the fields.

How many activities and duties performed over a lifetime are viewed as insignificant, monotonous, unglamorous, or unimportant? Like a tenant farmer sowing the fields, we follow routines of sameness. We trudge along well-worn paths as we live out the hours of each day.

When do we realize that every moment in life is precious and burgeoning with treasure? Once recognized, these moment-gifts must be accepted and embraced. What does it take to change inconvenience to opportunity, disruption to welcome, misery to joy, and work to love? At what point in our lives does the transition take place that changes shadow to sunshine, sorrow to happiness, vengeance to forgiveness, and selfishness to charity? What's necessary to transform the meaningless to meaningful?

From our earliest years, we're encouraged to count our blessings. If we're fortunate, we find ourselves humbled by ordinary moments that become extraordinary memories. As we labor in the field, we must pull unwanted weeds in order to cultivate good growth.

Scripture recorded over thousands of years conveys necessary lessons to ensure a bountiful harvest. How many times in life have we witnessed a weed become a rose or an unwanted event become a treasured remembrance? Often these moments arrive disguised as a painful experience or personal tragedy, but in their aftermath they leave us renewed strength and fervent faith. What's the magic and mystery of working in the fields, day after day, struggling to meet obligations, duties, responsibilities, and commitments? From what source is the spirit replenished when fatigue, despair, loneliness, and illness challenge our will to continue?

We find solace and take comfort in unexpected places that had previously gone unnoticed. Strangers thrown together in similar situations quickly develop common bonds and help one another. They become friends through small acts of kindness—giving without an expectation of receiving. Some lend a helping hand in moments of crisis and need, listening to those who are alone and have no one else. And others take time and share conversation with those in distress who are seeking support, comfort, and reassurance. Like cultivating and caring for a garden, each snippet of human interaction nurtures the heart and strengthens the spirit.

Throughout life we carefully tend the fields, hoping our efforts will bear the fulfillment of dreams and reward us with Heaven's bounty as promised ages ago. Like children, we're filled with anticipation and excitement, eager to savor the bountiful harvest from our endeavors someday.

After many years, we learn that some weeds—initially unwanted—are worthy of care because they, too, have importance. Rather than rushing to judgment, we must understand that everyone has gifts in need of nurturing, encouragement, and opportunities to flourish. With proper care, some weeds can become roses in our lives. We also learn that growing among the weeds are elegant lilies of the field, jewels that tease sunshine from the sky above and within ourselves.

The richness of our lives is a mosaic of diversity: work, play, rest, prayer, and belief in all that is good. Our wealth is measured in the accumulation of purposeful actions, thoughtful consideration of others, moments of conveyed appreciation, and kind words. This is the abundant bounty harvested from working in the fields.

(2009)

Wrinkle-Free Spirit

What happens to us when we're young stays with us all of our life. In 1950, I was a fourth-grader at Sacred Heart School in Whiting, Indiana. Fourth grade is one of those uniquely formative years that most people prefer to erase from memory or put so far back in the cognitive files it never sees daylight again. But every now and then, remembrances pop up like crocus, and we can't help but revisit moments that make us wince.

As I said, the year was 1950. Pope Pius XII, in his encyclical, had proclaimed the dogma of the Assumption of Mary, Mother of God. Special devotions and prayers to Mary were prepared and offered for indulgences and intentions throughout the Catholic Church. Parochial schoolchildren, too, shared in these prayers and activities.

The local Catholic diocesan paper, *Our Sunday Visitor*, sponsored an essay contest about the Virgin Mary for children in Grades 4 through 8. One essay from each grade at each school would be selected and sent to the diocesan office for judging. The winning essay would be printed in the *Sunday Visitor* alongside a profile of the author and their school. As fourth-graders preparing for sainthood, we eagerly went about writing our entries. The classroom monarch would select the best one.

Sister Mary Applesauce (her real name withheld to protect bingo privileges) took a no-nonsense approach to learning. Very serious about this project, she encouraged us to put our thinking caps on and excel. At the time, my behavior and scholastic performance in the class were less than stellar. I figured this was a chance to elevate my status with her. Even as a fourth-grade parochial school kid, I knew enough to try and get back in Sister's good graces.

To impress everyone with my knowledge of cutting-edge technology and current events, I titled my essay, "The M-Bomb." The hydrogen bomb had just been tested and accounts of its terrible, destructive force filled newspapers daily. My thesis focused on the power of praying to the Virgin Mary, Mother of God, a force more powerful and effective than the H-Bomb. I penciled my 250-word essay on loose-leaf paper and handed it in.

Imagine my surprise when Sister declared that my essay was the best! She called me up to the front of the room to read it to the class. With shaking hands and nervous voice, I read my work, handed it back, and returned to my desk. Then Sister held up my essay and said, "Although this is the best content, Albert's handwriting is too difficult to read."

Crumpling up my essay on her desk, she announced the second-place winner's essay would instead be sent to the diocesan office. (The girl who finished second had beautiful cursive handwriting.)

A short time later, we went outside for recess. Upon returning to the classroom, I noticed my crumpled essay was nowhere to be seen. I didn't have to courage to ask Sister, but I suspected the wastebasket had received a loose-leaf paper snack.

The lesson is this: At times, people will try to wrinkle and crumple our spirit. For whatever reason, they will say or do things that hurt us. We can choose to wallow in sadness and tears or find the strength and resolve to overcome their thoughtlessness.

Over the years, I experienced a number of failures. My benchmark, however, is the first-place award I never won. It taught me to work harder, be more thorough and precise, and try again. Seeing my written thoughts crinkled and discarded helped make me a survivor. I learned the triumph over sadness is not easy. To forgive, offer kindness, and laugh away hurt requires an inner strength and faith in goodness. Once captured, these qualities enrich and enhance the human spirit.

Looking back, I was ahead of the times—I developed self-esteem with permanent press. Those who try to crumple dreams or crease hopes are ultimately unsuccessful. That's the magic of a wrinkle-free spirit!

(2007)

GUEST CHECK

TABLE	PERSONS	46394	SERVER
X	2		S-9

X Marks the Spot
X-Rays for Fun and Profit

TAX

THANKS FOR VISITING THE MIND CAFETERIA

X Marks the Spot

A close inspection of the duties assigned to the letters of the alphabet reveals some interesting facts. E is essentially everywhere, used most often in words. S serves as the start to more words in the English language than any other letter. Four letters, Q, R, V, and Y, are never quiet, refusing to yield in vocabulary. Some members of the alphabet, like H, attach themselves to a companion to make noise (think TH or SH), while others are known to align as a silent partner (see GN, KN, PN, and PS).

Speaking of duos, QU is quintessentially inseparable, always appearing together. The purpose of this permanent partnership may be to quash the role of the letter K, which shares a similar sound. On the other end, the quartet that ends hundreds of words, TION, holds a superior position to the trio of ING and duo of LY—so little respect for gerunds and adverbs, sadly.

Top marks must be awarded to the first four letters of the alphabet—A, B, C, and D—for their longstanding tradition of representing achievement, progress, and quality. Following on—ignoring the curious exclusion of E—the letter F is full of its own self-importance. When found in isolation, F magnifies failure, rejection, and angst. But every so often, F puts on formal attire and appears as PH, radiating sophistication, status, and elevated rank via shared phonics.

Within the alphabet is an elite five-member club with a distinct purpose: vowels. A, E, I, O, and U can adjust the range and intensity of their individual sounds from long to short. But such vocal versatility doesn't diminish the stature of the quintet's consonant counterparts, whose forte is absolute consistency and deserves the utmost respect.

Each of the 26 alphabetical letters has its own unique look and sound. Some are quiet and unassuming while others are loud, even boisterous.

Together their individual geometric designs generate 44 separate and distinct sounds vocalized as diphthongs or monophthongs. Through the spoken and written word, these 26 letters translate our thoughts and ideas, creating a symphony for our ears, eyes, mind, and spirit.

However, one letter has absolute authority and power over the other 25, and it's one we often overlook: X. Striking an imposing form, this letter can stress exactness, stir curiosity, command attention, and even obliterate what's in its path (including other letters). The letter X is also a phonetic chameleon, expressing itself as "ks," "gz," "z," "kzh," or a hard "k" sound. But X can also remain coyly silent.

For some inexplicable reason, I've always been transfixed by the letter X, which rummages around the English language like an unwanted relative. Our first exposure to X comes when learning the ABCs (a lesson inextricably tied to xylophones). Reading about ancient history in the sixth grade, I was introduced to Xerxes the Great (deserving of the superlative if only because his name included two Xs). The fourth king of the Achaemenid dynasty of Persia is even mentioned in the biblical Book of Esther. Alas, Xerxes was assassinated by political rivals in 465 BC (or, phrased more succinctly, he was X'd out).

X does exact a certain loyalty from cruciverbalists, devoted souls who excel at crafting or solving crossword puzzles. Unexpected answers excite them, like xanthic (yellowish), xyster (a bone scraper, as in "Do you have a xyster for my sister?"), and the abbreviation XP (one of the earliest Christograms, formed by the first two letters of the Greek word for Christ).

The Romans gave X a value of ten. In the eighteenth century, X was used to symbolize the sawbuck since its construction resembled the Roman numeral. (Later on, "sawbuck" became slang for a $10 bill, on which an X formerly appeared.)

At one time, people unable to write their name on a contract or agreement would instead make their mark with an X. Questionnaires and surveys request that respondents put an X in the box by all items that apply, while tests and quizzes ask students to X-out incorrect items or statements.

In entertainment, science fiction writers, filmmakers, and comic book creators favor X. The letter denotes mystery, the unknown, or trepidation.

Some examples include *The Man from Planet X*, *X-15*, *The X-Files*, and *X-Men*. In the early 1950s, the radio program *Dimension X* tantalized listeners' imaginations with depictions of "Adventures in time and space... told in future tense."

Childhood promises were often accompanied by the saying "Cross my heart and hope to die," making an X over our heart to signify the solemnity of our oath. But conversely, X is also shorthand for adventurous, unrestrained risk (see: the X Games). X is often used today to warn the public of danger—road conditions, consumer products, hazardous materials, and other situations—that could potentially jeopardize our well-being and safety.

Returning to the historical use of X, pirates paired a skull with bones crossed in an X on a black flag (the "Jolly Roger"), a combination that symbolized the severity and brutality of their lawlessness. Treasure maps are marked with an X to show where riches are believed to be buried, while a placement of an X on other types of maps indicates the exact location of an event, destination, or some other stop or endpoint.

Fittingly, my favorite X is one on a framed map of Indiana Dunes State Park, marking the spot of an after-prom get-together with my high school classmates in May 1958. Let me just say that I had an "X-cellent" time!

(2018)

X-Rays for Fun and Profit

As a kid who grew up in the 1940s listening to the radio, the term "X-ray" has always awakened feelings of both excitement and fear. Broadcast three times a week, *The Adventures of Superman* captivated my imagination, and one of Superman's most mysterious and impressive crime-fighting weapons was his X-ray vision, used to thwart bad guys from doing bad things. The Man of Steel's intensive stare always meant that good would triumph over evil. So to a 9-year-old Superman fan, X-rays were cool!

Later, watching the Saturday matinee of black-and-white movie serials at the Capitol Theater in Whiting, Indiana, X-rays were used by nefarious criminals to blackmail society, threaten world domination, and commit unstoppable crimes. Such potentially destructive X-rays were the stock-in-trade of "mad scientist" instruments concealed in a hidden laboratory, where they flashed bolts of manmade lightning. Moviegoers' senses throbbed with the unnerving buzzing sound emitted onscreen from these strobing electrified coils. Adding to the intrigue were Bunsen burners and an array of beakers, test tubes, and flasks that boiled, bubbled, and created foggy emissions from their secret chemical formulas.

Each episodic chapter sustained the drama and tension toward the inevitable showdown. As the serial's climax approached, would good triumph over evil? Would the world be saved? Would the scientist conquer renegade X-rays, instead using such power to benefit society? After 14 consecutive Saturdays spent gulping cups of Coca-Cola and consuming copious boxes of Dots, Jujyfruits, and Good & Plenty candy, the crowd of sugar-loaded boys leapt from their seats in raucous cheers when the bad guys were captured and the powers of evil were finally vanquished!

X-rays were not all apprehension and anxiety though, nor left only to the big screen. Beginning when we were very young, Mom took my siblings and me to Chicago to shop for school clothes and shoes. Having worked in the city, she was familiar with department stores in the Loop and the economic savings offered by their high-volume sales. So a couple of times a year, we'd catch the bus in Whiting and be chauffeured to Chicago. The Shoreline limousines were dependable and economical.

By fifth grade, I was now wearing out shoes on two fronts—playground activity and pure growth—so Mom decided a trip to the Loop was again in order. Once inside Goldblatt's, we took the elevator to the floor for children's apparel. Adjacent to the clothing racks was the boys' shoe department. Chairs were provided for customers to try on selections after the shoe salesman had measured and discussed available styles and colors (even as Mom remained unpersuaded, partial to a standard brown oxford). Above all other skills, good salesmanship required Mom's approval!

As soon as new shoes were laced up and tied, we traipsed over to the shoe X-ray machine to check the fit. Resembling a floor model wooden console radio, we stepped up to the unit's platform, slid our feet into the opening at the bottom, and looked though an enclosed goggle-shaped eyepiece. The shoe-checker pressed the single control button and the machine immediately came to life.

A buzzing sound filled the ears and a ghostly green light filled the eyes. Peering into the eyepiece, we saw the bones of our feet encased inside the perimeter of a shoe. Moving our toes, we could watch the bones cooperate with muscles and nerves as they responded to the cognitive command to wiggle. Kids loved that machine—it was so cool!

Of course, back then we were unaware of the hazards of X-ray exposure. It all seemed so harmless and fun. Every time we visited a store with one of these shoe X-ray machines, we'd slide our feet inside and watch our bones do their thing, shrouded in that ghostly green light. Again and again, I zapped my feet with X-rays. I wonder how many kids' feet glowed in the dark back then!

A number of years later, without explanation or fanfare, shoe X-ray machines quietly disappeared from stores (so much for green glow-in the-dark feet). Thereafter, shoes were properly fitted based on questions from salespeople: "How do they feel?" "Is there enough room?" "Take a few steps. Do you find the shoes comfortable?"

Today, conventional medical X-rays are commonplace, having become a valuable tool in diagnostic health care. Even more advanced X-ray technologies like CT scans and MRIs help further clarify problematic anatomical issues, though at considerable financial expense. A physician's referral and robust health insurance is necessary to procure and defray the cost of such tests, but once upon a time X-rays were free. We just had to press the button and wiggle our toes!

(2018)

GUEST CHECK

TABLE	PERSONS	46394	SERVER
Y	3		S-9

Yearbook
Yesterday Once More
You Can Go Home Again

TAX

THANKS FOR VISITING THE MIND CAFETERIA

Yearbook

One treasured high school tradition is purchasing the yearbook. Toward the end of every school year, students—and faculty and administrators, too—await its publication and distribution, excited to review the past year's activities in words, pictures, and graphics. Then with yearbooks in hand, freshmen, sophomores, juniors, and seniors gather signatures and comments from the classmates and teachers who touched their lives over the past 180 days of scholastic instruction and extracurricular endeavors.

Whiting High School, in Whiting, Indiana, was founded in 1898. The first senior class graduated in 1900, a group of just five students. The school's first yearbook wasn't published until 1913, and while no formal record exists, its name, *Reflector*, was most likely chosen by a committee of students and faculty.

Early editions of the *Reflector* featured the history of the City of Whiting's founding, its prominent residents, and important businesses and industries. Along with such municipal information, the yearbook also included a history of the Whiting schools. Woodcuts, illustrations, and photographs added significance and value to the *Reflector*, and each edition heralded a new cover design selected by the yearbook staff.

Since the first edition in 1913, over 100 volumes of the *Reflector* have chronicled the life and times of Whiting High School students. Each serves as a time capsule for research, review, and remembrance of the four most important years of adolescence—important because high school is a time of transition: An entering freshman arrives as an old child, and four years later, graduates as a young adult.

Inserted between the pages of yearbooks are keepsakes: photos, receipts, event programs, pressed flowers, and handwritten notes that enriched and embellished the teenage years. Yearbooks serve as diaries and provide snapshots from our lives. Initially they're of the moment, reflecting both current events and the recent past. But here's the wonderful part: Yearbooks do not change with age. As the years go by, they become a personal inventory of frozen moments.

Yearbook owners, on the other hand, do change with age and serve as a living reference for once-upon-a-time. It's the retrospective contrast from yesterdays to today that generates melancholy memories of moments that sped by far faster than we could ever have appreciated. Like growth marks etched on a door frame, yearbooks measure the way we were, showing through pictures and words just how much we've changed. Poignantly, they convey how much "the way we were" is no more. Photographs of classmates and teachers who have passed give special pause, recalling the sweetness of carefree teenage moments shared in classrooms and hallways, on athletic fields, throughout neighborhoods, and at Whiting Park.

I became a full-fledged Whiting Oiler on September 7, 1954, and was awarded alumnus status on June 4, 1958. The 1955-1958 editions of the *Reflector* capture the essence of those four years in crisp black-and-white print and photography. But what enriches the personal value of this quartet of yearbooks are the signatures and notes from the classmates and teachers who touched my life.

Initially, there were difficult days when struggle, anxiety, failure, and embarrassment affected classroom efforts. Home dysfunction, limited resources, and hand-me-downs all added to personal discomfort, which I attempted to deflect with comic antics. Without question, I stumbled both personally and academically during my freshman year.

Luckily, my teachers and classmates never gave up on me, making the majority of my high school days positive and productive. In spite of problems and limitations of means and maturity, they always supported, counseled, and encouraged me to do better. Their individual and collective goodness, kindness, and friendship became my life's treasures.

Every time I look at photographs in the *Reflector* or read a classmate's words written so long ago, a sweet-sad feeling arrives and gently reminds the heart, "Another place, another time." Afterwards, with my yearbooks returned to their keeping place, "I'll Be Seeing You," the Class of 1958's song, plays in my mind.

A closing thought: They say living in the past is not a healthy thing to do. And I totally agree. But a visit to the past every now and then is wonderful!

(2016)

Yesterday Once More

Though familiar with the adages "You can't go home again," "What's past is past," and "Once upon a time never comes again," I decided to challenge the wisdom of sages and see if just a few moments from yesteryear could be recaptured.

When I was 19, I purchased a 1960 Oldsmobile 98 convertible. It was a time when drive-in restaurants and outdoor movie theaters beckoned cars and fun-loving youths—the original *American Graffiti*, live and in color. Countless times my convertible was filled with my best friends as we made the rounds to the Calumet Region's many drive-in restaurants: Art's, Kelly's, Son's, Sammy's, Serenade, Blue Top, Patio, Fat Boy, Hutsler's Frostop, A&W Drive-O-Matic, Dog & Suds, and Pow-Wow. At each stop, we'd enjoy a quick snack of a Coke and fries, as hot rods, customized street sleds, and Blue Coral-polished Fords, GMs, and Chryslers vied for attention under neon and incandescent lights.

Carhops were checked out, teased, and cajoled for dates. Drivers arrived in revving V8s, showing off glistening chrome details, high-performance carburetors, and purring mufflers. Parked in their favorite spot, cool guys role-played movie stars by wearing sunglasses long after sundown, their ducktail haircuts well-lubricated and cigarette packs rolled up in T-shirt sleeves. From speakers connected to a jukebox inside the drive-in, favorite songs played as long as patrons fed the Seeburg a steady diet of coins. Loud AM car radios countered with DJ chatter and Top 40 hits, adding to summer's symphony.

In concert with drive-in restaurants, outdoor movie theaters provided a way to see current films from the convenience and comfort of a car. Families, for instance, arrived by station wagon with pajama-clad kids in the back. But the majority of drive-in patrons were young romantic couples ready to enjoy an extended evening of unsupervised conversation and togetherness.

While the Region didn't lack in traditional movie theater options, the draw was outdoor venues like Griffith's Ridge Road Drive In, Merrillville's Y&W Drive-In, and my favorite, Hammond's 41 Outdoor Theater at the junction of Calumet and Sheffield Avenues. Together, the combination drive-in-restaurant-and-outdoor-movie date was the premier choice of youthful romantics.

Because the 41 Outdoor was located in close proximity to both a lake and a swamp-like habitat, mosquitos enjoyed a nightly feast at the movies. To prevent these unwanted donations of serum, I made custom-fitted window screens for my convertible. With the top up and the screens in place, movie watching and togetherness were uninterrupted by pesky insects. But as encapsulated in the Four Lads' song "Moments to Remember," watching the movie at the drive-in was never the priority.

On numerous occasions, there were also trips in the convertible to Chicago for an evening of dining, State Street window-shopping, and downtown entertainment. A highlight of the evening was a late-night, top-down ride home along Lake Shore Drive. Traveling under a summer night's sky awash in moonlight reflecting off Lake Michigan, while being entertained by east-of-midnight radio personalities and Top 40 music, these drives became Camelot moments.

A few times, the return journey began further north in Evanston, Illinois, affording passengers and driver a poetic panorama of architectural styles and natural scenery as the elegant Oldsmobile 98 followed the ribbon of asphalt homeward. "Lake Shore Drive," the 1971 regional hit by Aliotta Haynes Jeremiah, musically captures the emotional exhilaration of traveling Chicago's Outer Drive.

Those days have long since faded into time. Recently, however, at 71, I purchased a 2003 Chevrolet Corvette convertible, the 50th Anniversary Special Edition, to revisit those moments. Without question, times are different: Excursions are limited to daylight hours, bedtime arrives considerably earlier, and movies are now viewed comfortably at home on TV, rather than inside an automobile. Even so, an unmistakable youthfulness of spirit takes hold while driving top-down under blue skies drenched with summer sunshine. Cruising familiar streets and locations elicits memories of once-upon-a-time adolescent adventures and classmates and buddies whose gifts of friendship enriched my life.

In a wonderful, unexplainable way, the "film clips" of these memories that unspool in my mind leave a delicious taste. For a few brief moments, this retired white-haired geriatric fires up his vintage roadster, buckles in an aging anatomy, increases the volume on a CD of favorite oldies, and travels back to earlier days when the wind was green—remembering soft summer nights, a special girl with perfumed hair, music that became the soundtrack of my life, and a convertible filled with friendship and the celebration of youth.

All too quickly, those moments passed and life happened. But when those memories return for a visit—however briefly—it becomes yesterday once more and it's magic!

(2012)

You *Can* Go Home Again

Thomas Wolfe's posthumous 1940 novel *You Can't Go Home Again* is the story of writer George Weber and his journey back to his hometown. The title has since become ingrained in our culture, a phrase both poetic and prophetic to anyone who has ever left home and returned a number of years later, only to be affected by changes that occurred over the period of their absence.

In late September, members of the Whiting High School Class of 1958 came home to Whiting, Indiana, to celebrate their fiftieth anniversary of graduation. It was a weekend filled with remembrance, renewal, and melancholy reflection. Activities began on Friday with an informal get-together at this writer's home and continued at the Whiting Elks Club with dinner and more conversation. On Saturday evening, classmates enjoyed a banquet at Villa Cesare in Schererville, and culminated their celebration with a Sunday picnic at Whiting Park. Friends from the classes of 1956 and 1957 also joined in the camaraderie, exchanging war stories embellished by a half century of memories with the "youngsters" from the Class of 1958.

A number of classmates now living out of state, as well as those who had moved away from the Calumet Region, took advantage of the delicious autumn weather to tour their hometown. Many returned to neighborhoods where they'd lived as teenagers, visiting favorite places. I, too, traveled the community that shaped my life, remembering those who served as role models and helped me along the way. Although I lived the majority of my life in the Whiting-Robertsdale area—only recently moving south to Dyer—I still like to visit the places where so many moments and memories are part of my life.

In 1949, when I was in third grade, my family moved from my grandmother's house on Oliver Street to Cleveland Avenue. It was the house in which I grew up and where I lived until I married in 1965. One of the joys of youth was walking to school each day with neighborhood classmates and friends. First, we walked together to Sacred Heart School, and then as high school students, the two additional blocks to Whiting High School.

After a half century, I still vividly recall many of those journeys as we laughed, talked, and shared friendships, bonding us for a lifetime. Some days we used sidewalks, and on others we'd cut through neighbors' yards and use the alleys. Over the course of our four years at Whiting High, routes to and from school and home were modified to meet adolescent priorities. Each day, the camaraderie, friendship, and affection for each other increased.

Inside the covers of my Whiting High School *Reflector* yearbooks from 1955 to 1958, yellowing pages reveal moments captured from times long ago. Traveling through town, photos of yesteryear are compared with current observations. Several locations that once housed storefronts and familiar establishments are now either vacant or have been torn down to make way for new developments.

Landmarks like the Whiting Community Center appear subdued today, no longer pulsing and throbbing with the vibrancy of energetic youngsters. To teens of the 1950s, the Center was our mecca—ground zero for gathering, activities, and for some like me, employment. I still recall the bowling alley's aroma and the ambiance of the pits as I plied my pinboy skills on alleys 3 and 4. Images of Hardy Keilman (who managed the bowling alley) and Andy Yanas (who managed the Community Center and supervised the pinboys) are still vivid in my mind. Most of the graffiti we wrote on the ceiling and walls has since eroded, but the spirit of those days remains.

We used the corners along 119th Street for informal seminars, hung out at drugstores to quench our thirst, and stopped by Neal Price's Firestone Store to preview the latest 45 rpm records and dream about the many items that filled the shelves. We regularly feasted at Hot Dog Louie's, gulping down soft drinks and his famous chili. On other visits, we savored Louie's hamburgers and mustard-drenched hot dogs. Now suitably immunized from all known bacteria and viruses, we'd cross the street and head for Nick's Pool Room, where snooker tables and pinball machines beckoned our adolescent skills. A boys-only establishment, Nick's served as a sanctuary where teenage guys could smoke and carry on without disdain. Recalling the sights, sounds, and aromas of this marvelous parlor of pool balls and pinball, green felt tables, and neon lighting after 50 years still generates welcomed remembrances of youthful antics, creative language, bottomless appetites, cast-iron stomachs, and fun-filled hours of adolescence.

A restaurant has replaced Salmon's Barber Shop, where my greaser haircut was trimmed and prepped for the next application of Charles Antell's Formula No. 9. Walgreens now occupies the original location of Ande's Pizza. Sacred Heart School closed its doors to students long ago. And because of municipal upgrades to neighborhood streets, many of the mature trees that once canopied Oliver Street by Whiting High School have been replaced with saplings. But to this day, White Castle stands sentry to the entrance of my Mayberry. The perfume of steam-grilled sliders and onions activates my salivary glands, and I fight the urge to ingest a half-dozen geometric belly bombers. Passing by the places of my youth—Whiting High School, Whiting Public Library, and Whiting Park—saturates my mind with cherished memories of childhood and adolescent adventures.

Completing my personal tour of the town, I say a few words of thanksgiving for the people, places, and once-upon-a-time moments that gave me the opportunity to do better. Rarely has a finer gift been presented and appreciated. And if I could talk to Thomas Wolfe, I'd tell him without reservation that you can, indeed, go home again—especially if you're a member of the Class of 1958 and your hometown is Whiting, Indiana.

(2008)

GUEST CHECK

TABLE	PERSONS	46394	SERVER
2	1		S-9

Zzz: The Last Word

TAX

THANKS FOR VISITING THE MIND CAFETERIA

Zzz: The Last Word

There are certain words in the English language that immediately conjure specific feelings whenever they're pronounced. "Cozy," "caress," "soothe," "snuggle," and "dreamy" are a few that quickly come to mind, but the one that best captures the feeling of restful tranquility is "zzz." Defined as the sound used to suggest the state of sleep or snoring, "zzz" is typically illustrated by placing three successive Z's in a cartoon balloon directed toward a person—a peaceful symbol of relaxation.

Now some may argue that "zzz," which contains zero vowels, can't possibly be a word. But three English language dictionaries—the *Random House Dictionary*, *Macmillan Dictionary*, and *Cambridge Dictionary*— have given their endorsement as "zzz" is the last word in each. "Zzz" is also fully sanctioned in the *Official Scrabble Players Dictionary*. For this writer, if "zzz" is acceptable when playing Scrabble, it's definitely a word!

"Zzz" is not alone in eschewing vowels. Consider "nth," "brr," "hmm," "psst," and "tsk-tsk." The English language features a symphony of sounds spun into sight. Consider all the sound words used as interjections in daily communications: "ah," "achoo," "bam," "blah," "duh," "er," "ha," "tut," "uh," "uh-oh," and "yadda yadda yadda." Over time, the English language has evolved and been refined to not only include all proper and conventional arrangements of the alphabet's 26 letters, but also to allow abbreviations, euphemisms, and initials that fully capture and convey meanings found in no other language. No vowels? No problem!

Two other dictionaries wrap up their "Z" sections with words composed of vowels and consonants. *The New Oxford American Dictionary, Third Edition* closes with Zyrian, a language spoken by the people of the Komi Republic. *The American Heritage Dictionary* ends its "Z" entries with

Zyzzyva, a genus of tropical American weevils. Perhaps in future editions, the editors will complete their work with "zzz" and then catch some Z's.

The English language invites users to apply their individual imaginations and perspectives to create puns, turn phrases, employ double entendres, play on multiple meanings, and offer interpretations (and variations thereof) to communicate their thoughts. But why engage in such cognitive gymnastics when simpler, more direct words might suffice? Energizing the full inventory and scope of the English language is mind-healthy. It challenges us to increase our vocabulary, elevate the quality of our oral and written communication, and expand our language skills. Just as a rainbow of nutritious foods is necessary for physical health, a rainbow of words is essential for our intellectual health.

Consider how boring it would be to be limited in vocabulary and phraseology. Imagine if the only answer to the nighttime question of "Where are you going?" was "To sleep." Thanks to the versatility of the English language, we have a plethora of responses from which to choose: "To call it a night," "To take a catnap," "To crash," "To doze off," "To get 40 winks," "To hit the sack," "To sleep like a log," "To slumber," "To go beddy-bye," "It's pajama time," "To saw wood," "To enjoy some pillow time," "To get some shut eye," "Going to dreamland," "To grab a snooze," "To zonk out," "To turn in," "To retire," "To hit the hay," "To call it a day," "To go night-night," "To hit the feathers," "To hit the pillow," "To rest," "To bed down," "To call it a night," "To hit it the sheets," "To catch up on my beauty sleep," "To conk out," "To count sheep," "Off to see the sandman," "Going to sleepy town," and of course, the aforementioned "Catch some Z's."

Researchers classify sleep as four stages comprised of two types, REM (active sleep) and non-REM (quiet or dreamless sleep). Sleep studies have further identified three (formerly four) cycles of sleep in each stage. That's all very well and good if you're interested in the science of beddy-bye. But all I need is a comfy bed and I'm out like a light. Matter of fact, that sounds like a good idea. Visit with you later—it's time to hit the pillow and catch some Z's. Zzz, zzz, zzz, zzz.

(2018)

GUEST CHECK

TABLE	PERSONS	46394	SERVER
APPX.	4		S-9

Appendices

A: The Whiting High School Class of 1958

B: Whiting High School Honored Educators, 1954-1958

C: The "Faculty" of Inland Steel Plant 1 Machine Shop

D: Map of Whiting-Robertsdale, Indiana

TAX

THANKS FOR VISITING THE MIND CAFETERIA

Appendix A

They came from all parts of Whiting, Indiana, with a few from out of town. From public grade schools and parochial parishes, they arrived and registered at Whiting High School, the city's only high school. For some, this was merely a continuation, a transition from eighth grade to ninth. For others, it was a beginning, a fresh start, and a new adventure away from the rigid discipline of parochial education to the more relaxed structure of a public high school.

Nothing out of the ordinary marked these first days in September 1954, when a new freshman class crossed the threshold of Whiting High School. Though every new class of students projects optimism, this particular assemblage of teenagers seemed as ordinary as the 55 preceding freshman classes. There was no indication of the chemistry that would later manifest itself and become the hallmark of a truly remarkable class. Who were these kids? And where did they come from?

Like countless Whiting High School students before them, these newly registered freshmen were the sons and daughters of local refinery and factory workers. They were the children of the business people, sales associates, clerks, and professionals who made up the area's workforce. They were kids from down the block, across the street, and the other side of town. They attended church, went to the movies, played in the city's park and playgrounds, pursued activities at the Whiting Community Center, and as teenagers, kept things lively with their youthful energy and antics. In September 1954, they added one more occupation to their brief resume: high school student.

After four years of growing, sharing, and caring, the Whiting High School Class of 1958 had become like family. There were strong feelings of belonging and togetherness. It would be easier to explain this bond if some specific formula had made it possible for this group of classmates to capture the values and long-lasting friendships that have sustained it over the past 60 years. Rather, it's best understood as a gift given to an ordinary group of teenagers as they entered high school in the mid-1950s. Somehow the right ingredients came together in the right amounts in the right place at the right time, resulting in a vibrant human chemistry with a spirit that remains strong after six plus decades.

Below are the names of those who are forever proudly part of Whiting High School's finest class.

The Whiting High School Class of 1958

Arlene Abner, Michael Adzima, Barbara Anderson, **Margaret Arnold**, Otho Barton, Gale Beeler, Francis Bernard, **Dennis Blazewick, Richard Bonczyk**, Mildred Brown, **Benedict Bubala**, Donald Bubala**, Clyde Buckmaster, Gerald Burke, Mary Calfa, Norma Jean Carroll**, Donald Carter, **Gilberta Ciesar**, Helen Collier, Deonia Copeland, **Annette DeCarlo, Susanne Doman, Barbara Dunker, Judith Dvorshak, Donald Elledge, Denver Ferry, Elaine Foster, Patrick Gallivan, Thomas Gambini, Constance Geffert, Leroy Girman, Elizabeth Green**, Carolyn Gruba, **Virginia Gyure, Charlotte Hall**, Richard Harding, **Frank Harrison, John Hart**, Mary Hayes, Leonard Helpingstine, **Nancy Hill, William Hurt, Daniel Jacobs, Diana Jamrose, Janet Johnson**, Mary Anne Jurbala, **Thomas Justak, Judith Kamradt, Lawrence Kenda, Sharon Kinnane**, Michael Klym, **Irene Kobe, Albert Koch, Ernest Kochis, John Krivacic**, Katheline Kroslack, **Thomas Kujawa, Stephen Linko, Melton Litavec, Patricia Louis, Joseph Lovasko, Marion Lunde, Annette Lynch, Donald Maicher**, William Marlowe, **Marjean Maxwell, Marian Mayernik, Clifford Morden, Joyce Mowell,**

Diana Mrzlock, Elaine Muday, Linda Novotny, Mary Payton, Alberta Phelps, **Henry Plawecki, Dennis Plesha, John Pohl, Roberta Progar, Frank Pustek, Gayle Pustek, Jerry Reeves**, Arnold Reneer, **Donald Richardson**, Milton Riggs, **Janice Roe, Nancy Rosdil, June**

Rowe, **Karen Sabo**, Norma Satterlee, Leonard Scher, **Jack Scott, Jack Sims, Bernadette Skalka, Diane Skundrich**, Anna Smith, **Catholine Smith, Elaine Smoltz, Margaret Smriga**, Mary Carol Sorrells, **Phyllis Strabavy, Patrica Sullivan, Carolyn Thornton, Joan Tolley, Robert Turich, Judith Walsko, Marilyn Wandell, Wayne Westerfield, Sharen Williams, Ronald Wilson, Florence Wingert, Rudolph Wunder, David Yadron, Evelyn Yasvec**, Anita Young, and Dorothy Zencka.

Note: This list includes classmates who transferred to and from Whiting High School during the period from September 1954 through June 1958. Bold print denotes graduating seniors.

Appendix B

I present the names of my teachers at Whiting High School, in Whiting, Indiana, with appreciation and gratitude for their individual and collective contributions to my academic, social, and personal education. Some became lifelong friends, with our correspondence continuing long after the symphonic strains of "Pomp and Circumstance" had faded. Their pedagogical influence, expertise, and counsel enriched my journey from adolescence through adulthood.

Whiting High School Honored Educators, 1954-1958

Jesse Allen, James Buckley, William Buerkholtz, George Burman, Delma Byers, George Calder, Shirley Crutchfield, Edward Decker, Joseph DePeugh, Irene Dougherty, Ruth Espenlaub, Thomas Faulkner, Stephen Fowdy, Raymond Gallivan, Norman Hall, Donald Hogue, Wesley Humphrey, Alice Jenkins, Alexander Kompier, Henry Kosalko, Peter Kovachic, Charles Leckrone, Marie Lentvorsky, Adam Lesinsky, Elizabeth Matson, Joseph McAdam, George McClure, Michael Mihalo, Edward Pawlus, Ann Marie Petersen, Joseph Piatek, Bernard Qubeck, C. E. Riehl, Emmit Riordan, Von Stoffer, Jack Taylor, La Donna Thue, Arnold Turner, James Ulrich, Bernard Vesely, Marion Wagner, E. L. Watkins, and Mary Jeanne Wiesen.

Appendix C

Over the years, I've been blessed with success at many levels. But the footing and foundation of my success formally began at Inland Steel's Indiana Harbor Works in East Chicago, Indiana.

The six years I worked in the Plant 1 Machine Shop, 1958 to 1964, were the most insightful, meaningful, and beneficial to me—academically, socially, and personally. It really was as if I was attending the University of Inland Steel. I gained essential skills and learned life lessons regarding trust, honor, respect, responsibility, organization, work ethic, creative thinking, problem solving, and task analysis.

Although I "graduated" from Inland Steel more than 50 years ago, the images, sights, and sounds remain as vivid today as if it were yesterday. And the memories of the individuals at Plant 1 who touched my life are even more meaningful. In addition to the guidance of seasoned machinists, my peers and coworkers supported and helped me learn, grow, and live.

Not a day passes when I don't offer prayerful words of thanksgiving for their individual kindness, goodness, guidance, and support. In my mind, I visualize the machine shop and see the faces of those who taught me and generously shared their insights, talent, wisdom, laughter, and friendship. It was the best of times.

In the final analysis, we are all teachers. We learn from one another. So with profound appreciation and gratitude to the "faculty" of Inland Steel, who made invaluable contributions to my life, I offer this special recognition.

The "Faculty" of Inland Steel Plant 1 Machine Shop

Shine Anderko, John Anderson, Louis Appleford, Maryann Appleford, Joe Babas, James Balanoff, Don Barman, Ken Bart, Wendell Battersby, Dan Becerra, Martin Becerra, Rex Bennett, Steve Berkos, Cliff Blanchard, John Bobinski, Robert Bogus, Harold Borem, Adam Breisch, Stan Busch, Paul Canady, Joe Cap, Rich Cassidy, John Cengel, John Chizmar, Verne Clapp, Dave Clark, Bill Cochran, Larry Corona, Orie Creapeau, Carl Creekmore, Gene Curtis, Doug Dixon, Leonard Doell, Rich Donaldson, Charlie Downen, Fred Dupaw, Ed Early, Phil Einsley, Chuck Elman, Al Faskas, John Fazeakas, Don Fedorawicz, A. J. Floyd, Gene Foster, John Freer, John Gajewski, Tom Gambini, Ernie Gerds, Ben Grenecki, Eugene Haines, Fred Haney, Bill Harder, Doug Harper, Wilbur Hasse, Steve Hewitt, Don Hickok, George Hime, Jim Hodges, Tom Holmes, Bill Hoppe, Walter Hovey, John Ingram, Joe Jags, Stan Jankowski, Karl Jauck, Chet Johnson, Dave Johnson, Jerry Johnson, Aaron Jordan, Fritz Jutkus, Bob Kampeen, Tony Kaptonevic, Kevin Kehoe, Bill Kennedy, Shorty Kevetic, Frank Kinach, Hank Klein, John Klobachar, Hank Kolodziej, John Kramer, Jim Krull, Herb Kruzan, Warren Kuehl, Tom Kunstek, Joe Kurzeja, Bernie Kuzma, John Larson, Mike Lascoff, Harry Legler, Ed Lewandowski, Harold Limey, Hans Linder, Harry Londy, Bill Long, Jerry Luce, Ed MacQueary, Rudy Maicher, Jerry McCaig, Phil McCormick, Bill McGrath, John McTaggert, Bill "Sparrow" Markovich, Jerry Markovich, Bill Marks, Stash Marlik, John Marlin, Louis Martin, Gus Mathes, Bill Matthews, Joe Matusiak, Fred Mauer, John Mauer, Frank Mavis, Mike Mazak, Ray Mazur, Red Messura, Sr., Red Messura, Jr., Rollie Meyers, Bob Minder, Bill Minowski, Bob Miston, Tom Modrak, Ed Moskalik, Ray Munoz, John Munteen, Hank Nadi, John Nedeff, John Negovetich, Bob Neiman, Chris Newrith, Ted O'Boy, John Obremski, Luelle Obush, Elmer Olson, Gus Oresko, John Oresko, Frank Oroz, Andy Orto, Vic Ostrojewski, Harold Parkinson, Bob Pawloski, Ray Pawlowski, Jack Paxia, Earl "Sailor" Peters, Harold Pilotto, Frank Pinsak, John Pipta, Dale Plaskett, Bill "Cookie" Poezneac, Lester Porter, Casimir Pularski, Dale Quaiff, Bill Queer, George "Red" Queer, Art Radtke, Bob Ranta, Alice Reagan, Harry Richardson, J.D. Roberts, Felix Rodriguez, Buck

Rogers, Jack Rose, Joe Rybicki, Andy Sabo, Adrian Santos, Ron Scher, Ed Scherer, Norbert Schroeder, Charley Scott, Charlie Scott, Ron Sheets, Mike Sinkewicz, Bob Skarwicki, Paul Skertic, Joe Skopieac, Mike Stacek, Carl Stavistke, Paul Studt, John Such, Steve Suhan, Jim Sulich, George Suliman, Frank Surchik, Clarence "Chuck" Surrena, John Sustrich, Paul Terpstra, Joe Terras, John Thill, Andy Tinkley, Joe Tomaszewski, Bob Traversky, Mike Trombetta, Bob Trotman, Don Turner, Stash Valdimar, Steve Vanco, Sam Vasek, Earl Weaver, Max Webking, Wally Weiss, Tony Weslowski, Larry West, Ed Witkowski, Bob Wolanin, Yolanda Youngkrantz, Jerry Zaborowsky, Ken Zaborowsky, John Zajac, John Zelanik, and these three individuals whose full names escape me: Chet (the machine shop office clerk), Godfrey (in the rate office), and John "The Preacher" (helper on the big planer).

Appendix D

Located on the southern shores of Lake Michigan in Indiana, the neighboring communities of Whiting and Robertsdale have long been interconnected. While separate entities—Robertsdale is part of the much larger city of Hammond—their symbiotic relationship offers mutual benefits to residents, schools, businesses, houses of worship, and more.

During the atomic age, the combined population of Whiting-Robertsdale reached nearly 13,000. The area became an industrial Mayberry, ground zero for youthful free-range adventures under the watchful eyes of friendly neighbors who never forgot what it felt like to be young.

From railroad siding to town and town to city, Whiting has thrived and flourished for more than a hundred years. It's a full-service city for all seasons, one that celebrates a historic past, a vibrant present, and an exciting future.

Today, "The Little City by the Lake" is in the midst of a renaissance: new housing, businesses, and enterprises, like the internationally famous Pierogi Fest and the Mascot Hall of Fame, an interactive children's museum. An extensive makeover of Whiting Park has transformed a former diamond in the rough into the sparkling jewel of the city, and alongside an enhanced Lake Michigan shoreline, has elevated Whiting to a whole new level.

One final note: The welcome mat is always out in Whiting-Robertsdale, inviting visitors from near and far to enjoy the area's charm and amenities. Come experience this real-life Mayberry of the Midwest for yourself!

About the Author

ALBERT R. KOCH is a retired high school teacher and writer. His monthly column, "Koch's Choice," which chronicles his younger exploits, his experiences as an educator for more than 40 years, and his perspectives on a wide range of topics, has appeared in print since 1990. His first book of collected essays, *Help Mom with the Dishes: Lessons from Life's Classroom*, was published in 2006. Born and raised in Whiting, Indiana (which he affectionately calls an industrial Mayberry), Koch proudly continues to make his home in the state's Calumet Region with his favorite carhop, S-9.